DATE		
MAR 1 0 1993		MAR 1 9 1998
APR 1 0 1993 MAY 1 6 1994		
JUN 1 1993 OCT 2 3 1996		
		MAY 1 2 1998
JUN 8 1994 MAY 1 2 1997 JUL 2 5 1998		
AUG 5 1994		
NOV 0 3 1994 SEP - 4 1997 FEB 2 6 1999		
AUG 2 1995		
	OCT 1 3 1997	
JUL 0 3 1996 DEC 1 7 1998		
FEB 1 0 1999		

A Basic Guide to
HORSE CARE
and
MANAGEMENT

Bruce Mills

and

Barbara Carne

HOWELL
BOOK HOUSE INC.
230 Park Avenue
New York, N.Y. 10169

Illustrations by Mary Jane Haggard

Published by Howell Book House Inc.
230 Park Avenue, New York, N.Y. 10169

Horse Guide

Library of Congress Cataloging-in-Publication Data

Mills, Bruce.
   A basic guide to horse care and management.

   Includes index.
   1. Horses. 2. Horsemanship. I. Carne, Barbara.
II. Title.
SF285.M67   1988   636.1   88-2949
ISBN 0-87605-871-3

Printed in the United States of America

This book is dedicated to the memory of
RICHARD AND CURTIS CARNE

Acknowledgments

We wish to thank the following persons for their help, encouragement and advice in preparing this manuscript:

R.A. Battaglia, Purdue University; John Boho; Dr. Robert Ewbanks; Mary Jane Haggard; Pete and Lisa Peterson; Lucinda Roberts; Les and Alice Shoemaker, Jim Taasas, Danny and Jan Thomas, Dave and Robbye Tinnel; and especially Lorraine Woodall and family.

We also wish to acknowledge with special thanks the following persons for their help and encouragement in preparing the second edition.

Cynthia Roe; George Purvis; Serena Early; Sue Ann Robertson; Kristine Mike; and Dick and Barbara Barker of Teton Trakehners, Jackson Hole, Wyoming.

Cover Photo: Sebine Klapproth riding "Luneur," owned by Teton Trakehners of Jackson Hole, Wyoming.

Contents

Introduction

This book is for the person who is past the stage of saying "I'd love to own a horse" and has either already bought that first mount or is ready to make that all-important purchase. In this book we provide the most essential practical advice required to make your experience as enjoyable as possible. Caring for a horse involves far more than merely "saddling up and riding into the sunset" and we want you to know everything required to keep your horse fit and ready to ride. For those now considering the purchase of a horse, all the very important factors to look for and look out for are included in these pages. For more experienced horseowners, the most practical information possible on the equipment and procedures necessary for keeping your horse healthy and happy are also found herein. And finally, we've provided you with suggestions on some ways to enjoy riding and showing your horse to the greatest extent possible.

Above all, we have aimed to make the book as practical as possible. We want you to avoid all the mistakes made by other horseowners so you can enjoy your horse fully. We are confident that if you follow the advice in this book you will find that owning a horse can really be the wonderful experience you have long dreamed about.

This Second Edition is updated with the latest information on tack, medications, showing and other particulars changed since the book was first written. While most of the information remains as appropriate as ever, we want the reader to have the latest, most pertinent information currently available.

CHAPTER 1

Getting to Know the Horse

There's a special kind of magic that infects those of us who struggle through the chores of caring for a horse only to find a tremendous sense of elation in the animal's speed, strength and beauty.

A horse is a different kind of a pet. He requires a great deal of time and care as well as expensive facilities. While he may come running when he sees you, it's generally out of hunger rather than affection. A horse can't easily be kept in a backyard. He needs at least a few acres to roam around in as well as decent shelter to protect him from the weather. He requires a great deal of expensive feed. He must be trained. He must be groomed. He must be shod. He must be looked after by a veterinarian. To transport him requires a special vehicle.

No, he's not like the puppy that sleeps on the back porch, is house trained and subsists on table scraps and a little dog food. Horses require a great deal of special care. But somehow we put up with all of this. There's an old saying that rings very true: "The outside of a horse is good for the inside of man." To ride a horse is to control speed and strength that man on his own can only dream of. To see a mountain

1

"The outside of a horse is good for the inside of man."

from horseback is to be not a spectator but a part of the wonder of the panorama.

While most of us keep horses as pets, simply for the pleasure of owning and riding them, for many others horses are tools of their trade and not pets at all. As you well know, horseracing is a tremendous industry in this country. Horses are raced in harness and under saddle, from distances of a fast quarter mile to longer races, on the flat and over fences. To own a racehorse can be tremendously expensive, but for a lucky few it provides substantial rewards both in pleasure and in money.

Draft horses are still used for farming by various religious sects throughout the country who refuse to use modern machinery. In some places it's still quite common to see a horse and buggy clip-clopping down the roadway. Also, the breeding of draft horses for shows and pulling contests is growing rapidly. Again, the special magic between man and horse existed even in the drudgery of farm chores and just won't die away.

The cowboy astride a horse is today very much a part of the west.

Team ropers practice one of the fastest growing rodeo sports in the West. (Photo courtesy of C M Ranch, DuBois, Wyoming.)

There are still many places where the only way to gather cattle is by horseback. Thus the cowboy sees his horse quite differently than most of us. His horse must perform well or he gets nothing done.

THROUGHOUT HISTORY

Although the horse has been around for about fifty million years, his close association with man developed only relatively recently. The problem was that the earliest horse, known as Eohippus, was only about a foot tall! But the horse is an interesting example of how a species adapts to changing conditions. Not only were these early horses quite small, they had four toes on each foot and were browsers rather than grazers—which means the Eohippus ate leaves from low-hanging trees and shrubs rather than grass.

The early horse developed largely in North America, but eventually

3

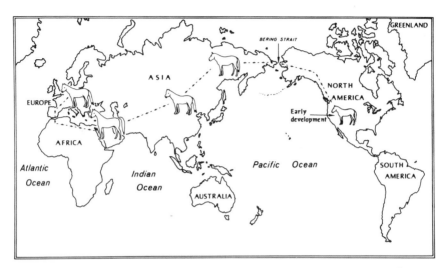

This map shows the early migration of the horse from America to Asia, the Near East, and Europe.

This early Egyptian painting depicts elegant, animated horses similar to those in use today.

migrated to Asia and later to Europe and North Africa. The horse then completely disappeared from North America, until it was brought back by the Spanish explorers.

The horses first domesticated by man were too small to be ridden, but they could pull carts and later chariots—vehicles specifically designed to be horse-drawn. This early meeting between man and horse probably took place in Egypt about 1600 B.C. Early cave drawings there show horses that are surprisingly elegant and agile.

The Near Eastern civilizations were the first to use selective breeding, which profoundly altered the later development of the horse. All of the characteristics which enabled a horse to survive in the wild, such as

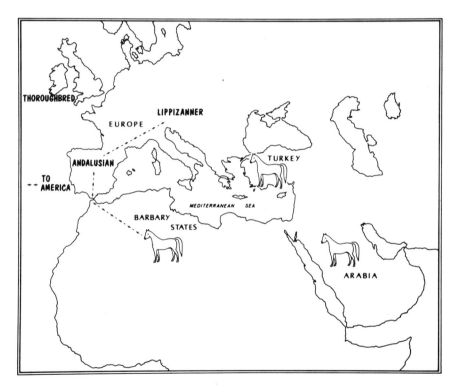

This map shows the development and spread of the foundation breeds from the Near East to Europe and then to America.

wariness and speed, were not necessarily the traits that best suited man. For example, prominent withers are of no use to a horse, but quite helpful to keep a saddle in place. Thus for the past 5,000 years man has interfered with the development of the horse, thereby creating something quite different from what would have survived in the wild.

The early Greeks and Romans made great use of horses in ruling their far flung empires. It's reasonable to assume it would have been nearly impossible for them to have ruled without fleet-footed horses to carry messages from one city to another.

Horses also had a great impact on the development of America right from the beginning. Mounted on horseback, the early explorers were a fearsome sight to the helpless Indians who had never before seen horses. Once settlement began it was the horse that carried the settlers farther and farther west.

As horses escaped from the settlers, they eventually were captured by the Indians and in many cases caused a drastic change in their lifestyle. The Indians could now roam farther, carry more and hunt with a skill they had never known before.

Finally, until only recently wars have been fought on horseback. The cavalry was the most important part of an army. In fact, it was only in the 1940s that the U.S. Cavalry was disbanded. An interesting offshoot of the cavalry, which did much to upgrade the quality of the horse in America, was known as the Remount Service. This service established quality stallions throughout the country. The local people bred their mares to these stallions, then the Remount Service came back in a few years to buy the offspring. In this way the cavalry was assured of an adequate supply of satisfactory mounts. As recently as the late 1940s, when the U.S. Cavalry was ended, there were 700 stallions in service throughout the country.

In America, the real heyday of the horse was the middle and late 19th century. During this period the horse was the most efficient means of travelling short distances. While railroads had become more popular, they were obviously limited as to where they could go. It was the coming of the automobile as well as mechanized farm machinery that foretold the decline of the horse.

From the beginning of this century until only quite recently, the number of horses was declining. But our love affair with the horse coupled with a great deal of new-found leisure time has caused a sudden upward spurt in the horse population in recent years. The horse industry as a means for a special kind of enjoyment is once again a rapidly growing part of American life.

Vision

When dealing with horses, it's difficult for most beginners to understand how a horse relates to the world, because it is so different from how we relate to it. A horse's eyes, for example, are very keen and he sees quite a different world from the one we see. One big easily noticeable difference is the fact that a horse's eyes are set quite far apart. This gives him a much wider range of vision than we have so that he can be more aware of any possible danger.

Another interesting fact is that horses have different mechanisms for focusing on objects than do humans. While the lens in our eyes changes shape for focus, the retina in a horse's eye is closer to the lens at the top than at the bottom. Thus, he focuses by raising or lowering his head. We've all seen horses startled by a fearsome object raise or lower their head in an effort to determine the extent of the danger.

Also, notice that the eyes of a horse are set on opposite sides of his head, as well as being quite far apart. While human eyes work together to see one scene clearly, a horse's eyes work separately so that he sees two distinct pictures. This ability to see to the side is very important to horses in the wild who must be continually on the alert. For our purposes, however, it's not an advantage to be riding a horse whose vision and attention strays to the side instead of keeping his mind on where he's going. This is why trainers sometimes use blinders on race horses to force them to pay attention to the business at hand.

Because of the way their eyes are placed, horses don't see very well directly in front of them, where the fringes of their side vision come together. It's well to keep this in mind when you approach horses. Don't walk towards them from directly in front. They'll see you much better and be less startled if you approach them from an angle which is well within their field of vision.

Because horses see a different picture with each eye, it's important that they are taught fundamentals such as leading and grooming from both sides. If you never work on the horse's right side, he will be very

7

confused when you do. This is simply because he has never seen these things with his right eye.

Also, it has been suggested that horses don't see colors as we do. But such theories are hard to prove or disprove, for obvious reasons.

Hearing

Horses have a much better sense of hearing than do humans. They are able to hear a greater range of sounds higher and lower in pitch as well as sounds that are too faint for us to hear. Their keen hearing is enhanced by their outer ears, which are perfectly designed receivers. The concave shape gathers in the sound while their mobility enables the horse to rotate the ear to pinpoint the source of the sound.

As anyone knows who has ridden a young horse in new surroundings, strange noises excite them as much as strange sights. On the other hand, horses seem to be soothed by soft, quiet sounds. This means that whenever you handle a horse, your tone of voice is undoubtedly as important as the words you use. In training a horse, for example, it's essential not only to repeat the same command words, but to use the same tone each time. Also, single words such as "walk," "trot" or "whoa" should be used, rather than a long sentence which is beyond the horse's ability to understand.

Of special importance to us is the fact that a horse's ears are an excellent indicator of his mood, and experienced horsemen use this to their advantage. When a horse is intent, his ears will be pricked toward the object of his attention. This will be confirmed by any rider who has had a horse shy.

A horse whose ears are intently forward is not paying any attention to his rider, but rather to his surroundings. Horses that are involved with their work will rotate one or both ears in the direction of their rider. But ears plastered back are a sure sign of trouble. They show that the horse is unhappy with something, so watch out!

Taste

In horses, as with most other animals, the sense of taste and smell are very much related. Quite often a horse will sniff a new kind of feed and then reject it based on what he considers an unacceptable odor. At other times he will sniff the feed, eagerly dive into it, only to reject it then because of its taste.

Occasionally, when horses taste something new they will shake their head up and down, apparently trying to decide if they like it. And, just like people, horses seem to enjoy sweet foods such as apples, sugar and molasses. Based on this, we've often used molasses to mask the flavor of deworming medicine or other medication in the feed. Here again, the strong, pleasant aroma of the molasses undoubtedly has a lot to do with the horse not noticing the medicine.

Basically, horses enjoy the taste of the natural grains and hays that make up the bulk of their diet. In the case of most wholesome mixed grain rations, the molasses is added because it keeps the mixture together. Horses aren't usually as enthusiastic about the protein meals, however. If you add these to your grain mixture, you'll probably have to add a little molasses to improve the flavor.

If you want to give your horse an occasional treat, we recommend apples or carrots. Not only are they more nutritious than sugar, a horse can get downright obnoxious looking for the little cubes every time you come around.

Smell

As with most other animals, the horse's sense of smell far exceeds that of humans. Stallions are especially good at detecting mares in heat by their odor, even when separated by some distance.

While horses don't sniff the air as do animals which are hunters, they certainly do give their surroundings a once over by smelling everything in sight. This smelling seems to put the horse at ease whenever he is confronted with new objects. Trainers take this into account by letting young horses smell any newly introduced equipment, from saddles to trailers. As a matter of fact, one of the first things horses do when becoming acquainted with each other is sniff into each other's nostrils.

Touch

Perhaps the horse's most acute sense is that of touch. It is largely through this sense that we can communicate with the horse. While dogs are trained to respond to hand or voice signals, horses are primarily taught to respond to different sensations of touch.

9

For example, a well trained horse will immediately respond by cantering on the correct lead when cued by a slight touch of the rider's leg. Saddlebreds are taught to "stretch" in response to a slight touch behind the elbow. Hot blooded horses such as Thoroughbreds are said to be thin skinned, which means they are very sensitive to touch. Some ponies, on the other hand, are quite tough skinned and fail to respond even to urgent kicking by their young rider.

INTELLIGENCE

It is argued by most scientists that horses are not among the most intelligent of animals. Although this might be true in regard to the specific tests used, it certainly is not easy to evaluate the relative intelligence of different animals. In any event, we do know that the horse has the intelligence to learn many tasks quite useful to man. When teaching the horse, therefore, we need to be concerned with what his capabilities as well as his limitations are.

Horses easily learn to respond to simple verbal and physical cues. Thus, the basic method used to teach horses is repetition. A horse must simply be asked to perform the task again and again until he understands what is expected of him. In the beginning, this works best if simple cues are used. For example, when teaching a horse to stop, it won't mean much if you say "O.K., I want you to stop, so whoa now." A simple "whoa" spoken in the same tone of voice each time will soon be understood.

In addition to words, horses can learn to respond to physical cues given from the ground or from the saddle. Raising or lowering the whip during longing, shifting your weight in the saddle, or using leg cues; all can easily be understood

In addition to the repeating of cues, horses understand best if they are taught only one thing at a time. This means that if you want a horse to be ridden under both English and Western tack, it's best to teach one style thoroughly first, then turn to the next. Otherwise, you'll spend much time simply confusing him.

DISCIPLINE

As much as you love your horse, sooner or later he will have to be disciplined. Just as with children, good behavior should be encouraged while bad behavior must be punished. For example, if an experienced horse refuses to move forward when you use leg pressure, he must be disciplined either with spurs or a whip. Otherwise the horse will soon learn that he doesn't have to respond to the rider's legs. And once a horse learns he can refuse without being punished, bad habits will surely develop. Horses that bite, rear, or kick must be forced to behave and this can only be done through discipline.

It should be noted here that the horse should only be punished when he refuses to do something that you know he knows how to do. Punishing a horse that doesn't understand what he's being asked to do only confuses him further. If you watch professional trainers work with horses, notice that they inflict punishment only when the horse willfully misbehaves.

Two horses put in the same area will soon establish who is boss. To confirm his supremacy, the dominant horse will threaten his companion by biting or kicking, but seldom go beyond this. Once the pecking order is worked out, the higher rank of the leader will seldom be challenged. When humans deal with horses, the same rules apply. At first you have to let the horse know who's in charge, but once this is done he's not likely to ever challenge his position in life. In the manner of the leader horse, we can often instill respect with one or two sharp reprimands with the whip. People who repeatedly beat their horses are only showing their own lack of control.

Also, to be effective the punishment must be administered immediately after the act. Otherwise the horse will not associate it with the misbehavior. Then the punishment will not teach the horse anything; you'll only be confusing him.

REWARDS

A popular way to teach a dog to speak or bark on command is to hold a bit of food slightly out of his reach. In his eagerness to eat the food, the dog will eventually bark. At this point, he is given the food and verbally praised. These rewards reinforce the dog's behavior so much that soon his continual "speaking" will drive you to distraction.

This response is said to be a sign that dogs are more intelligent than horses, whose behavior can't be modified in the same way. As we said before, we don't think the intelligence level of the horse is as important as knowing how to communicate with him. Although horses won't work for a specific reward, they nevertheless can be taught. And that's what really matters.

As an example, it's not a good idea to induce a horse into a trailer by using a slice of apple, but there is nothing wrong with feeding him once he's in the trailer so he will have good feelings about the experience.

If your horse performs well, a pat on the neck and a soothing word or two will let him know he's behaved properly. We've all seen people gush over horses, complete with baby talk and unrestrained petting. As you can tell by their wagging tails, dogs love this sort of attention. Horses, on the other hand, don't particularly crave this sort of attention, nor do they enjoy being petted on their heads as some people insist on doing. Most horses enjoy grooming and stroking, but they won't work or perform to get this attention as dogs will.

PROBLEM SOLVING

Because of his large size and the way he lives, the horse makes a very poor laboratory animal. In certain ways he is awkward and not inclined to manipulate objects used in experiments. For these reasons, we really know very little about his ability to solve problems.

For example, if a horse sees grain outside the door, he won't know all of the manipulations required to get it. If, however, he accidentally unlatches the door with his nose, he'll surely remember and try it again next time. In cases of horses escaping like this, it probably wasn't reasoning that got the latch open the first time, just blind luck.

Some horses are more proficient than others at manipulating with their lips. Ponies particularly seem to be good at this. A pony of ours is forever picking up our gloves, grooming supplies, tools or anything else within his reach. This is a distinct personality trait of his, perhaps motivated by curiosity or boredom or both. Along with this, he's quite good at untying knots, which makes him quite a nuisance, but a lovable one.

ATTENTION SPAN

Young horses, like young children, have a very limited attention span. With maturity and schooling, horses can concentrate for longer periods, but it's doubtful they learn much after an hour of intense work. Experienced trainers are aware of this and use their schooling time wisely. They warm up the horse slowly, so that his muscles and mind are relaxed. Only after this do they demand maximum attention or new routines. Probably the best time for a horse to learn a new lesson is between 20 to 50 minutes into the period. After this, the horse is likely to be tired, both mentally and physically.

EMOTIONS

It is so much easier to understand and work with horses if we think of them as herd animals. In the wild, except for an occasional rogue stallion, horses live in groups. Within each group, the individual horse has its own rank. Higher status horses get the choicest morsels of grass, drink first from the stream, decide when the herd will move and where it will go. All of the horses, including those of lower status, feel secure in their close knit herds. As long as those in the bottom of the pecking order defer to those at the top, the herd is one harmonious group.

People, for the most part, have unwrapped this security blanket from their horses. We stall them individually, turn them out in separate paddocks and ride them alone, all of which is quite contrary to their natural state.

NERVOUSNESS

Because in his natural state the horse is constantly on the alert for danger, he startles easily at strange sights and sounds. This is quite important in the wild as his primary defense mechanism is his ability to run away quickly. As anyone who has spent much time with horses knows, this kind of reflex is not very far from the surface. When startled, a horse may shy or jump sideways and his next inclination will be to bolt or run away at full speed.

Horses vary greatly in temperament. Draft horses are usually quiet and docile, as are ponies. Quarter horses also have a reputation for reliability. Thoroughbreds, on the other hand, are a little higher strung as are some Arabians and American Saddlebreds. Horses that are inclined to be nervous are best handled by calm, competent horsemen.

Nervous horses benefit from regular daily routines, while such dis-

The older, docile horse is often a favorite with youngsters.

tractions as waiting unduly for feeding will worry them. Being handled in the same way by the same people makes them much less anxious. This is why handlers of race horses maintain a strict routine. Winning horses often have their personal grooms attend them wherever they go. If time allows, the horses are often shipped well before a race. This gives them a few days to settle down before the race.

MEMORY

While, in the animal kingdom, elephants have the reputation for a good memory, it's likely that horses can't be far behind. A horse's remarkable memory enables him to learn by repetition. Once learned, a lesson is seldom forgotten even if a long period of time has passed since the horse was last asked to perform.

Our horses are friendly and usually come to greet visitors, showing no fear of them. Yet if the veterinarian pulls into the driveway and approaches the gate, they are all off and running. Obviously, they're not too eager for their routine inoculations. They remember the veterinarian, regardless of the time between his visits.

Because of a horse's memory, it is particularly important that he has as few bad experiences as possible during his training. If he hurts himself or is badly frightened, you'll have to work extra hard to overcome his bad memories. In fact, sometimes a horse never forgets a frightening experience, no matter how hard we try to overcome it.

PERSONALITY AND DISPOSITION

As we said earlier, the horse is a herd animal. Most horses would rather be at the bottom of the pecking order of a herd, than be left by themselves. We have seen lower status horses that had been removed from the herd because they were driven away from any feed, nicker and call pathetically because they wanted to rejoin their "friends."

Some horses become quite familiar with their handlers, developing a satisfying relationship for the horse. We have no indication, however, that horses grieve over the loss of a handler the way dogs have been known to do. Of course, in our culture, the horse doesn't share our lives as intimately as some dogs. In Middle-Eastern cultures, however, horses shared the Bedouins' tent, while children took charge of the foals. Some people believe the Arabian horses of today are a more people-loving breed because of this history.

Nevertheless, man and horse can have quite a pleasant association. If treated sensibly, the horse will work quite willingly and become most trustworthy.

As much as their desire for companionship, most horses readily accept authority. Here again, because the horse is used to the discipline of the herd, he seldom challenges the dominant role of his handler once it has been established.

As long as a horse isn't threatened, he isn't likely to be aggressive. Of course, this doesn't apply to stallions, but mares and geldings are seldom malicious.

While most horses are generally predictable, many do have distinct personality traits. Experienced handlers are particularly aware of this.

Also, some generalizations can be made about the different breeds. It seems that as certain physical traits were bred in, certain personality traits were also established.

HOW TO GET ALONG WITH A HORSE

One of the most frequent mistakes beginners make with horses is to treat them as people, or worse yet as children. No matter how much you may want a human friend, a horse is still a horse. Admire him for his own qualities, which are unique in the animal kingdom. You must learn to accept his motivations and appreciate him for what he can and will try to do.

Some riders are able to get much more from their horses because they seem to have some sort of special sense which enables them to understand their horse. One jockey is better than another, not just because of physical traits, but an ability to understand and communicate with his horse. Show jumpers are asked to perform tremendous tasks, jumping heights the horse would never attempt alone. Yet some riders, confident of the horse's ability, are able to communicate this to the horse, enabling them to perform outstanding feats.

Most of us will have to be happy with more modest accomplishments. But that doesn't mean we shouldn't try to tune into the horse so that we get along with him as best we can.

First, you must try to remain calm. Regardless of what happens, don't lose your temper. If a horse gets into a tight spot or throws a tantrum, between the two of you at least one must keep his wits about him. One reason that horses are so good for children is that the child learns to make decisions and how to think on his feet, or on his horse, whichever the case may be.

A rider or handler must always be confident. The horse will look to you for leadership and you are going to have to provide it. Otherwise he's liable to get it into his head that he's the boss. Then you'll surely have your hands full.

You've probably heard people say that horses know when people are afraid of them. We're reasonably certain that this is true, whether it's from actions or some sixth sense. Fear, or lack of confidence, confuses horses. If a rider gets on a horse and lets it amble around without firm direction, the horse won't know what to make of the situation. Very likely, he'll try to get back to the barn, which is a place of security for him.

We've heard it argued by some horsemen that if there is a fork in the path and the horse on his own takes the left path, he should be turned and made to go to the right, even if you wanted to go left. That's the kind of thing you can't let the horse decide for himself.

You must always be consistent with your horse. All of us have our good and bad days. On our best days, we are usually more tolerant. Whatever the case, we must put aside our ups and downs whenever we enter the stable. The horse knows only what he has been taught through repetition. If we let him get away with misbehavior one day and are overly strict the next, he'll have no idea how he should behave.

Always be considerate of your horse and keep in mind his limitations. He doesn't cry or whine when he's hurt, nor does he stop running when he's tired. In her last race, the great mare Ruffian continued to run despite a broken leg and her jockey had to slow her down. It is up to us not to ask more of the horse than he can deliver and to notice when he's hurting.

CHAPTER 2

The Horse Breeds

As you become more interested in horses, you're likely to be puzzled by the many different breeds you see and hear about—all proclaimed by their owners to be the best! It's not easy to sort out the differences and decide which breed is best for what purposes, but in this chapter we'll try to explain a bit about some of those you're likely to come across.

While there are many breeds of horses to choose from, each has certain advantages and disadvantages, depending upon what the horse is to be used for. It's impossible to say that one breed is better than all of the others, even though you'll find many owners willing to argue this point. Each breed does certain things well and it's up to you to decide which is best for the kind of riding you expect to do.

What exactly is a breed? Well, it's no great mystery. A breed is just a group of horses with similar ancestry as well as similar abilities and characteristics. Today, to be eligible for registry in a breed association, in most cases both sire and dam must have first been registered with that association. If you look far enough back in a purebred horse's pedigree, you'll find all horses in that breed trace back to a common select group of horses.

The various breeds each began when horseowners decided they would like horses with a certain ability and began to breed selected horses in an attempt to produce that ability in the offspring. For example, when a fast horse was needed, the fleetest horses were mated, eventually developing the Thoroughbred. The fastest trotters were bred and eventually developed the Standardbred. Tennessee Walkers resulted from the mating of horses that could perform the running walk. Along with these unique abilities, certain physical characteristics developed that set these horses apart as distinct breeds.

As horses developed with these common traits, their owners joined together in associations to identify their horses as a distinct breed and provide certain standards for registration. The most obvious example of this is the Standardbred. Initially, certain horsemen began to breed horses for speed at the trot. To identify their horses as having this ability, they formed a breed association and limited horses eligible for registry to those that could trot a mile in a "standard" time.

We should also mention that, in addition to breeders interested in developing certain abilities in their horses, there are those who breed specifically for color. These persons have also formed organizations known as color registries. A color registry is not the same as a breed association, because the horses registered in it have no distinct physical characteristics in common other than color. Essentially, all that's required for admission to a color registry is that the horse be a certain color.

Registered horses generally command higher prices than grade horses, so why buy a registered horse? As you grow more experienced as a rider, you'll find you enjoy doing certain kinds of riding more than others and certain breeds will do these things better than grade horses or other breeds.

For example, if you're interested in Western riding and rodeo events, you'll probably find a Quarter Horse would best suit your purposes. Quarter Horses are particularly good at these events with their bred-in ability to start, stop and turn quickly, as well as their smooth, easy jog and lope.

Arabian owners are often struck by the beauty and versatility of their horses. Arabians are smooth and sleek and aesthetically very pleasing.

The presence and showiness of the Saddlebred is frequently the deciding factor for their owners. Saddlebreds are especially suited for the show ring and if this area interests you, a horse of this breed would be an excellent choice.

If you prefer a certain color, you could select from the spots of the Pinto, the speckles of the Appaloosa or the gold and white of the Palomino.

Another reason for selecting a registered horse is that if you're at all interested in showing you'll find many shows sponsored by the various breed associations and limited exclusively to their particular breed.

And finally, you'll find in a breed association many people who enjoy talking about horses and what their horses can do. An important function of breed associations is to promote their breed and to do this they have clinics, shows and meetings where the members get together and spend many hours discussing horses and horsemanship. It's an excellent place to meet people with similar interests, and to gain much helpful information from others who have faced many of the same problems you're sure to have.

THE POPULAR BREEDS

QUARTER HORSE

In terms of sheer numbers, the Quarter Horse is easily the most popular breed in America. The American Quarter Horse Association is the largest and fastest-growing registry in the world. As of 1987, it had 150,000 members and had registered more than 2,550,000 horses. This is quite a feat considering the registry was formed as recently as 1941. What accounts for this spectacular rise in popularity? One reason is undoubtedly the ability of the Quarter Horse to excel in Western and rodeo events. This, along with the nostalgic lure of the Old West, has caused many horseowners to chose the horse most associated with the West, the Quarter Horse. Then too, the breed is well noted for its temperament and that is important to many horseowners.

It's easy to recognize a Quarter Horse because of his generally stocky build and extremely heavy muscling, particularly in the hindquarters. Quarter Horses are usually short (14 to 15.1 hands) but heavy, weighing from 1100 to 1300 pounds. This gives them the extremely low center of gravity necessary for the quick turns and sudden stops needed in Western events.

Two of the most important considerations for the beginner are the versatility and quiet disposition of Quarter Horses. You can use them equally as well in shows or simply for hacking around trails or your backyard.

Also, Quarter Horse racing is becoming increasingly popular, with more than one hundred tracks now featuring Quarter Horse races. The All American Futurity held in New Mexico at Ruidoso Downs is

Mr Impressive, sired by Impressive out of Joak Easter Girl, named 1976 Grand Champion Stallion by the All-American Quarter Horse Congress. (Photo courtesy of MBJ Quarter Horses, Wichita, Kansas.)

among the world's richest races. Whereas Thoroughbreds often race a mile or more, Quarter Horses run about a quarter of a mile. Because of this short distance, Quarter Horse racing is done on a straightaway rather than on a circular track. As you might have guessed, the name Quarter Horse is derived from the distance at which he runs his best race.

Quarter Horses are extremely popular among persons from all walks of life and are shown extensively in all parts of the country. In 1986, 2,590 shows were sanctioned by the American Quarter Horse Association. These shows have a wide variety of classes including the traditional rodeo events as well as Western Pleasure, Jumping, Trail Horse, Working Cowhorse, English Pleasure and many other classes.

ARABIAN

Many people find great pleasure in the elegant beauty and grace of the Arabian. This breed has a long and distinguished tradition that dates back to before the time of Christ. In fact, Arabians have been selectively bred for many centuries to produce a horse that is hardy, versatile, gentle and most of all, beautiful.

According to legend, sometime in the seventeenth century B.C., Saloman was leading a band of mares that had travelled many days without water. They came to a spring and the horses rushed toward the water. Suddenly Saloman summoned them to battle and the five mares (Al Kamseh) that resisted the water and heeded his call became the foundation mares for the Arabian of today.

Speaking practically, you'll find the Arabian to be an excellent all-round horse. They can do many things well, if not quite as well as the breeds that are bred specifically for certain events. Being compact in conformation, Arabians are famed for endurance; this has been demonstrated by their excellent record in endurance rides. In 1975, according to the North American Trail Horse Conference, twenty-three of the top twenty-five endurance horses were Arabians or part Arabians.

Arabians are generally small, ranging in height from 14.2 to 15.2 hands. Their coat is fine, soft and silky. The mane and tail are long and very fine in texture, with the tail set high on the body and carried in a graceful arch. Arabians are distinctive in their refined,

23

Serenity Sonbolah, an Arabian imported from Egypt and named the 1971 United States National Champion Mare. Notice her extreme quality, elegance, and femininity. (Photo courtesy of International Arabian Horse Association.)

highly finished type. Their head is wedge-shaped and slightly dished below the eyes with a relatively small muzzle. They have large, expressive eyes, an arched neck and sloping shoulders.

Arabians are rapidly growing in popularity in the United States. They were first brought here in the late nineteenth century and since then many more have been imported from Europe and the Near East. Today there are more registered Arabian horses in America than in Saudi Arabia.

With the recent increase in the popularity of the horse in America, there has been an even greater rise in the number of Arabians. Many Arabian owners are most interested in breeding to improve their stock. Often this is their major reason for owning horses. Others find joy in owning a horse of great natural beauty that is at home in English or Western tack, on the trail or in the show ring.

THOROUGHBRED

It can be said that the Thoroughbred horse is a direct result of man's competitive spirit. This breed is the culmination of many generations of careful breeding in an attempt to produce a faster horse. Thoroughbred is not another name for purebred. The Thoroughbred is a distinct breed, while a purebred is any horse with a pedigree acceptable for registration with a breed association.

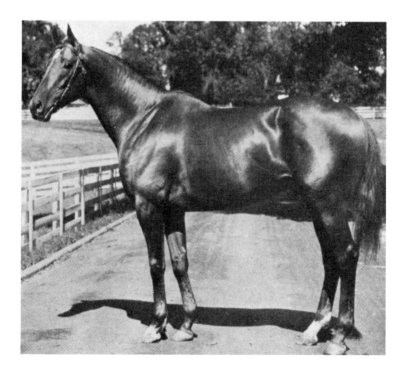

Swaps, winner of the 1955 Kentucky Derby. After his racing career ended, Swaps was syndicated and stood at stud at Spendthrift Farm in Lexington, Kentucky. (Photo by "Skeets" Meadors.)

25

The Thoroughbred is an animal built for speed from his slender nose to his flowing tail. He is generally a tall horse, ranging in height from 15 to 17 hands. In race condition, a Thoroughbred will weigh from 900 to 1100 pounds, but he will put on about 200 pounds when fitted for breeding. The breed is characterized by a long body, deep chest, rather long legs and a generally refined appearance. This slender appearance can be misleading because although the Thoroughbred may seem delicate in comparison with other breeds, he has hard, dense bones that make him able to withstand strenuous physical activity.

Though primarily found on the race track, Thoroughbreds are also used for other purposes. Horses that aren't quite fast enough to race often make excellent hunters, jumpers and polo ponies.

The versatile Thoroughbred, although bred for a career on the race track, is the preferred mount for many riders. Detractors of the breed argue that they lack hardiness and tend to be highly nervous. Undoubtedly, with his vitality and strong will, the Thoroughbred does require skillful handling and is probably not suited for beginners. However, when properly managed they can give a discriminating horseman many hours of pleasant riding.

American Saddle Horse

American Saddle Horses, or Saddlebreds as they are called, are the peacocks of the horse world. They have been bred for flash and style in the show ring and this makes them very exciting to watch. For these same reasons, on the other hand, they would also probably not be the best choice for the beginner who is looking for a quiet pleasure horse.

Saddlebreds are best known for their animation and brilliance. They are shown in a three- or five-gaited class or as a fine harness horse. Three-gaited horses, often called "walk-trots," are shown at the walk, trot and canter. The five-gaited horses perform these gaits plus the slow gait and the rack. The slow gait is a high stepping four-beat gait performed in a slow, restrained manner. Most demanding is the rack, a fast, flashy gait that is difficult for a horse to learn and strenuous to perform. The slow gait and rack are artificial gaits. By this,

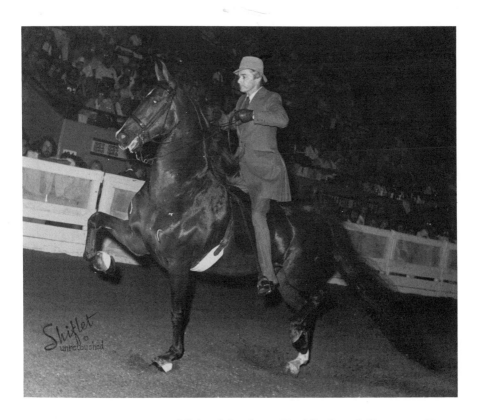

Imperator, an American Saddlebred, has been World's Grand Champion Five-Gaited Horse four times. He is shown here ridden by Don Harris. (Photo courtesy of Shiftlet.)

we mean that a horse doesn't do them naturally, but certain families of Saddlebred can learn them more easily than others. A great deal of training is necessary, however, before five-gaited horses are ready for the show ring.

You can tell three-gaited Saddle Horses by their roached or clipped, mane and tail. Five-gaited horses have a full mane and tail. Both classes have the depressor muscles in their tails cut in an effort to produce a high tail carriage. After this the tail is kept in a tail set while the horse is in his stall. An irritant, ginger, is inserted into the horse's rectum before he is shown to make sure he doesn't lower his tail.

Saddlebreds are most often found in the show ring handled by professional trainers or their skilled owners; however, they are sometimes seen on the bridlepath or ridden simply for pleasure. Because they are so highly sensitive and animated, Saddlebreds probably aren't a good idea for beginners but they do make enjoyable mounts for experienced riders.

MORGAN

While not as common as Quarter Horses or Arabians, Morgan horses have many of the same qualities of disposition and versatility that make these more popular breeds excellent pleasure horses.

Morgans are unique in that they are all descended from one sire, Justin Morgan, foaled in Vermont in 1793. This horse was a rare individual in that he was sturdy enough for farm work, gentle and supple enough for a pleasure horse and could trot well enough to pull the family buggy. Justin Morgan lived until he was nearly thirty and from him and his offspring developed the breed known today as the Morgan.

Morgans are usually small, standing about 15 hands. They are extremely compact and sturdy with a short back and legs, a thick barrel and massive shoulders. They are heavily muscled, with a short neck and heavily boned legs. The gaits of the Morgan are quick and "trappy" with brisk steps caused by their short, powerful leg muscles.

One of the most important traits of the Morgan is his temperament. He is gentle, but spirited and known particularly for his willingness and perseverance. Morgans generally live to be quite old. Justin Morgan's death, while in his late 20s, was due to an injury and until that time he was completely sound.

This breed was extremely popular as a trotter until the 1850s when the faster Standardbred began to be raced. After that, the Morgan breed nearly died out as they were mated with Standardbreds to make them faster and to Saddlebreds and Thoroughbreds to make them smoother-riding and more showy. Because of this, true Morgans are now rarely found.

The breed has survived, however, to today. This is largely due to a

Colonel Battle, who in 1907 donated a farm in Middlebury, Vermont, for the purpose of carrying on the Morgan breed. It is the only United States Government Agricultural Experimental Station devoted exclusively to one breed.

Fortunately, Morgans are becoming more popular today largely because of their versatility. They can perform many tasks adequately, from driving in harness and pleasure riding to hunting, jumping and working on cattle ranches.

TENNESSEE WALKING HORSE

Tennessee Walking Horses are a distinct breed because of a unique gait they are able to perform known as the running walk. This is a rapid, gliding gait covering up to nine miles per hour, during which the horse nods his head in an exaggerated manner in time with each step. The speed, which causes very little discomfort for the rider, results from an overstriding in which the horse steps with his hind foot in front of the print of his front foot. This overstriding is inherited by the Tennessee Walker, but it can be extended by special training and by using special shoes. Naturally, the overstride can measure up to eighteen inches, but with training it can reach up to fifty inches. This overstriding is referred to by Walking Horse people as the "big lick."

The Walking Horse averages 15.2 hands in height and weighs from 1000 to 1200 pounds. He has a plain head, set on a long graceful neck, with well muscled, sloping shoulders and substantial legs with hard, dense bones particularly in his knees and hocks. His mane and tail are often long and flowing, but show horses also have their manes and tails embellished with wigs.

Walking Horses have been controversial in recent years because of cruel training methods used to enhance their gaits. These methods include making the legs sore or using harsh mechanical devices. Recent action has been taken by the Tennessee Walking Horse Breeders Association and the American Horse Show Association to limit these practices. They now require the removal of the horses' boots at shows to inspect for signs of illegal training methods.

As a pleasure horse, Tennessee Walkers have an even temperament and are generally quite manageable. This characteristic, along with their easy gaits, makes them ideal for a child or beginner as well as

Shades of Carbon, the 1976 World Grand Champion Tennessee Walking Horse owned by Joe and Judy Martin Stables, Shelbyville, Tennessee. (Photo courtesy of Tennessee Walking Horse Breeders' Association.)

someone past the thrill-seeking stage. There is even a special show class for riders over fifty years of age.

The highlight of the Walking Horse show season is the annual show held in Shelbyville, Tennessee, at the end of the summer. Here, Walking Horses from all over the country vie for top honor at the Walking Horse Celebration, as the show is called. Although Walking Horses are shown extensively, particularly in the South, most are used as pleasure horses and for trail riding. Their comfortable gaits allow their riders to spend many long hours in the saddle. If you're interested in a quiet, ambling ride through the countryside, you should consider a Tennessee Walking Horse.

STANDARDBRED

Probably the first thing we should mention about Standardbreds is that they are *not* riding horses. They are bred exclusively for trotting and pacing on the race track. All of the horses you see at harness races are Standardbreds.

These horses are known as Standardbreds because, beginning in 1879, eligibility for registration depended on an ability to trot or pace a certain distance in a "standard" time. Today, this is no longer required. Any offspring of registered breeding stock is eligible, regardless of ability.

Harness races are run at two distinct gaits, the trot and the pace. A trot is a two-beat gait, in which the left front and right hind legs move forward together. In contrast, when pacing, both the left front and the left hind legs move together, then the right front and right rear. When urged to go faster, it is natural for a horse to run or gallop, but a Standardbred is trained either to trot or pace and not to break stride and gallop.

Although some families of Standardbred tend to be trotters and some tend to be pacers, the gait is largely determined by shoeing, training and special equipment. Some horses have shown ability and have raced at both gaits, with the horse Steamin Demon having both trotted and paced a mile in less than two minutes.

The Standardbred looks much like the Thoroughbred, from which he is descended. He is generally smaller, standing from 15.2 to 16 hands and weighing from 900 to 1250 pounds. Standardbreds typi-

A Standardbred, Norby Hanover, moving at a racing trot. (Photo courtesy of the United States Trotting Association.)

cally have more substance than the Thoroughbred and show less refinement in the head. Their speed at the trot is due to their ability to lengthen their strides and repeat them rapidly. They are able to do this because of their long forearms and their long narrow muscles.

Standardbreds were originally bred so their bodies would be longer than their height and many horses are built this way today. It was thought that a longer body would allow freer play of the legs, but now this has been found to be unnecessary. The Standardbred is very hardy with extremely sound legs and great endurance. This endurance is demonstrated in that Standardbreds warm up by trotting or pacing approximately six miles before each race. They warm up slowly moving clockwise, or the wrong direction, around the track. They are trained to work at speed whenever they go counter-clockwise, the correct way around the track.

Most Standardbreds are found at harness racing tracks around the country. In 1986, nearly 21 million people attended harness racing events in the United States. Many of the spectators are lured by pari-mutuel betting; however, the many races run in states which don't allow betting shows that other people come simply because of the sheer excitement of the races.

Harness racing in the United States is governed by the United States Trotting Association with headquarters in Columbus, Ohio. This association also acts as the official registry for the breed.

EUROPEAN BREEDS

The breeds we just discussed developed largely in the United States. In Europe, there are several other breeds commonly found. Following is a little about each of them simply for your information.

THE ANDALUSIAN

The breed is tall, generally 16 hands, and is distinctive because of his animation and lively way of traveling. These are the horses used in Spain for bullfighting, a sport which requires agility, maneuverability and dependability, as well as courage on the part of the horse, which is frequently in danger of being gored by the bull.

Andalusians have been important in the formation of many other breeds, particularly the Lipizzan, which we'll talk about next. The American Mustang and many South American breeds are the result of the Spanish Conquistadores bringing Andalusian stock to the New World.

LIPIZZANER

In 1562, Archduke Maximilian of Austria began importing and breeding horses from Spain, intending to develop a lighter and more agile cavalry horse. Eighteen years later his uncle, Archduke Karl, established a royal stud farm in Lipizza, a tiny village in the hills near Trieste, from which the horses get their name.

The Lipizzaner breed is composed of six family strains, each family being named after the sire which founded the strain. The six strains

33

are: Pluto, Conversano, Maestoso, Favor, Neopolitano and Siglavy. Each Lipizzaner is given two names; the first is his family name and the second is his given name.

The history of the breed is filled with suspense with the horses evacuated many times from the onslaught of various wars. The most famous rescue was carried out by U.S. General George Patton during World War II. When it appeared certain the horses would be destroyed in battle, Patton, a former Olympic Equestrian competitor, made the horses the ward of the United States Army and protected them until they could safely be returned to Vienna.

Lipizzaner horses are very gentle. They are predominantly grey, with an occasional bay or chestnut. They are medium in size, just over 15 hands, and are heavily muscled. The head is somewhat large and the eyes are large and expressive. They show quality in their mane, tail, ears and small feet.

Lipizzaners have become known through their association with the famous Spanish Riding School of Vienna which was established in 1858 in the village of Piber near Vienna. They have been bred to carry out the difficult maneuvers of Haute Ecole. Their initial training is on the ground, but those sufficiently talented are selected to learn the spectacular "airs above the ground" such as the Capriole, when the horse leaps into the air drawing his forelegs under his chest and at the height of the elevation kicks out violently with his hind legs.

Recently, Lipizzaners have been imported into the United States in limited numbers. Horses bred at the state stud in Austria are distinguishable by an L on their left cheek and the Austrian Imperial Crown on their left haunch.

COLOR REGISTRIES

A breed is a group of animals with a common beginning that gives them a similar appearance and temperament. All of the breeds discussed up to this point are recognized as such and additionally are registered in a breed registry. A color registry is an organization which keeps stud books and, for a fee, records accepted horses in them. In America, registries have been growing rapidly because of the great interest in breeding horses especially for color. Truly, these can't be considered breeds, because often the only similarity between the horses is the color of their coat. The prime reason for breeding two horses for a color registry is simply the possibility of achieving this color. Also, in many cases, even the color does not breed true from generation to generation.

Since machines have taken over much of the work horses used to do in the past, they are now largely kept for pleasure—and much of the pleasure in keeping a horse is his appearance. On the other hand, the color registries have been maturing rapidly. They are now much more concerned about conformation and perhaps can develop definite physical characteristics in their horses so that in the future they will be registering what will be considered separate breeds.

APPALOOSA

The Nez Perces Indians, located in the northwestern section of the United States, was the only Indian tribe to breed their horses selectively. They culled out the inferior stallions and castrated them instead of letting them breed mares indiscriminately. Choosing their animals for performance, the Nez Perces selected for breeding only those that could swiftly chase buffalo and fearlessly ride into battle.

Appaloosa horses are distinctive for unique color carefully bred into them by the Nez Perces. They usually have a solid body with colorful spots over the hip and loin. To be referred to as an Appaloosa, the horse should have vertically striped hoofs, mottled skin about the nose and white scelera around the eyes.

The Appaloosa Horse Club was formed in 1938, and in 1986 had registered over 500,000 horses. There are no conformation requirements for registry other than that the horse must be 14 hands or over and have no pony or draft characteristics. Horses showing obvious Pinto markings are not admitted.

According to registration rules, "Appaloosas foaled after 1970 must have both parents registered or identified with the Appaloosa Horse Club and/or a recognized breed association in order to be eligible for registration." However, also included as eligible for registration are geldings or spayed mares with easily recognizable Appaloosa characteristics. It is pretty obvious that it's impossible to establish breed type with an open registry such as this. In fact, for Appaloosas

The Appaloosa stallion, Dreamfinder, 1985 National Grand Champion. (Photo courtesy of Harold Compton.)

there are two different types of registration papers issued. Permanent registration is issued to horses exhibiting typical Appaloosa coat markings. Breeding stock registration is accorded horses which may be of a solid color but have the white scelera, mottled skin and striped hoofs of the Appaloosa.

Today, Appaloosas are used primarily in Western-type events. There is a growing number of Appaloosa shows. If you are interested in a horse with this coloring and if you can find one with good conformation, then an Appaloosa would be an excellent choice.

PINTO

The term Pinto or "paint" refers simply to a spotted horse. Other less accurate words used to describe this coloring are piebald, skewbald, and calico.

Naturally, the distinguishing characteristics of these horses are their color. There are two distinct color patterns, the overo and the tobiano. The tobiano horse has patches of white on various parts of his body and limbs. Usually his head is marked similarly to a solid colored horse. White markings on the legs below the knees and hocks are common. On the overo, the white markings extend upward from the belly and the face is frequently white.

Pintos may range in height from 14.1 to 16.2 hands and weigh up to 1300 pounds. For registration, they should be of saddle horse conformation. Glass eyes (blue eyes) are eligible for Pinto registration, although they are excluded from other registries. Horses showing draft or pony blood are ineligible.

Pintos are mostly used for pleasure riding and are especially eye-catching as a parade horse. The number of pinto shows is rapidly increasing, with many held along with Quarter Horse Shows.

PALOMINO

The breeding of golden Palominos dates back hundreds of years and first took place in Spain where they were reserved for use by nobility and high officials.

There are currently two Palomino registries, the Palomino Horse Association, founded in 1946, and the Palomino Horse Breeders of America, founded in 1941. To be eligible for registration, the Palomino must be golden in color. This color should be that of a newly minted coin or three shades lighter or darker. The mane and tail must be light. Ivory, silver or white is acceptable, with not more than 15 percent dark or chestnut hair in either.

Their eyes must be dark. Their usual height is from 14.2 to 16 hands and weight from 1000 to 1200 pounds. Another requirement for registration is that the sire or dam must be registered in one of the recognized light horse breed registries.

Some geneticists feel that the Palomino color cannot be fixed and it has been learned from observation that Palomino can be produced from several kinds of matings. When breeding Palomino mares to Palomino stallions, the color of the foals average one-half Palomino, one-quarter albino and one-quarter chestnut. Mating a chestnut and albino is the only way to produce Palomino foals every time.

Despite the uncertainty of breeding, Palominos remain popular as pleasure, show and parade horses because of their splendid color.

PONIES

Ponies stand under 14.2 hands, and weigh up to 900 pounds. Today most ponies are used as riding animals for children, although some are trained to drive and others are kept as show animals. There are many breeds of pony, however most are of mixed breeding and classified as ponies simply because of their size. Among the most popular breeds are the Shetland, the Welsh and the Hackney.

SHETLAND PONY

The Shetland pony gets its name from the Shetland Islands where they originated, located in the North Sea two hundred miles north of Scotland. The harsh climate and rugged terrain of these islands are largely responsible for the breed's small size, shaggy coat and thick mane.

The Shetlands bred in America are a definite improvement over those from Scotland, having longer legs, a more slender build and a better disposition. Interestingly enough, the American Shetland Pony Society will no longer register animals imported from the Shetland Islands.

Shetland ponies are unusually small, 10 to 11 hands, and weigh from 250 to 500 pounds. Often shown today in fine harness classes, they are more commonly used for small children to ride.

WELSH PONY

Welsh ponies are very striking in appearance, often resembling a miniature Arabian with its fine coat and limbs. In America, Welsh ponies are divided into two classes: the original mountain pony type under 12.2 hands and the riding pony up to 14 hands. Often gray in color, they are most frequently used as mounts for children and in a wide variety of roles from parades to hunting, to dressage and as a pleasure animal.

HACKNEY

Hackney ponies are found almost exclusively in light harness classes among society circles, as showing Hackney ponies is among the most expensive of equine sports.

Hackney ponies are high-spirited and are noted for their high knee-action and a generally refined appearance. They vary greatly in height, ranging from 12 to 16 hands; however, show ponies are limited to a maximum of 14.2 hands.

OTHER PONIES

Less widely distributed pony breeds include the CONNEMARA, a refined large pony averaging about 14 hands which originated in Ireland. This pony is an excellent saddle animal and is frequently used as a pony hunter.

The GALICENO pony originated in Spain, but was not officially introduced to America until 1958. This pony stands from 12 to 13 hands at maturity, and makes a fine child's riding pony.

The PONY OF THE AMERICAS is an intermediate-sized pony, ranging in height from 11.2 to 13.2 hands. As the name implies, this breed is native to America. To be eligible for registration, the animal must have Appaloosa-type markings. The Pony of the Americas makes a fine Western-type using pony.

Whenever a small child shows interest in horses, parents usually first decide to buy a pony. Because of their small size, this seems to be logical. Ponies, however, have both advantages and disadvantages.

Because most ponies are of mixed breeding, they frequently have little or no training. Most ponies by nature are "thick-skinned"—stubborn and difficult to manage. On the other hand, ponies are very quiet and will usually put up with rough treatment without reacting violently, although rough treatment usually makes them more stubborn. Ponies are easy to keep and can live on a minimum amount of hay if no pasture is available.

In selecting a pet and playmate for a child, a pony probably would be an excellent choice. Their quiet disposition and low initial cost and upkeep are quite attractive. However, if you're interested in a child devel-

A Pony of the Americas stallion, MP's Jim's Goldseeker is owned by Dan Hoffman. (Photo courtesy of Dan Hoffman.)

oping riding abilities, then a small horse with a tractable disposition might be the answer, unless a well-bred, well-trained pony can be found. Unfortunately, ponies like this are not often available, and when they are, they command very high prices.

DRAFT HORSES

The importance of the horse to man before the popularization of the automobile and other self-propelled machinery in the twentieth century cannot be overemphasized. The saddle horse made it possible for man to travel great distances in a shorter time than could otherwise be imagined.

Draft horses is a term used to describe any horse 16 hands and over, weighing 1600 pounds or more. These horses are bred to work and since most of the jobs they had to perform have been taken over by machines, they exist today only as a reminder of a bygone era.

The heyday of the horse came in the latter part of the nineteenth century, when stationary sources of power such as the steam engine were producing large quantities of merchandise and horses were the only practical way to transport this merchandise short distances. Improved farm machinery was also coming into use and draft horses provided the only mobile source of power to move these machines. Today, draft horses are found mostly in parades and at work for certain religious sects who avoid the use of modern inventions.

Draft horses, or "drafters" as they are often called, are as a group heavily muscled and have more bone and substance than saddle horses.

Bardrill Glenord, a Clydesdale stallion owned by Anheuser Busch, Inc. Notice his typical draft horse characteristics including heavy bone and extreme size. (Photo courtesy of Anheuser Busch.)

41

They are considered "cold-blooded," which means they are quiet and docile. Draft horses are bred to pull heavy loads at a relatively slow pace, as opposed to saddle horses that are lighter, faster and more agile.

The major breeds and a short description of each follow.

PERCHERON

This breed originated in France and later became very popular in America. Among the draft breeds, they are third largest in size and are usually gray in color, which resulted from early breeding with Arabians.

Generally, the Percheron has a distinctive, clean-cut head and neck. These horses are considered easy to keep as they are usually quiet, but sufficiently energetic in temperament to work willingly.

BELGIANS

Belgians take their name from Belgium, their place of origin. As a breed, they are considered very drafty. This means they show the characteristics generally found in draft horses. They are extremely stocky, low set and compact, lacking the refined appearance of the Percheron and Clydesdale. Belgians are quiet to the point of being sluggish.

SHIRE

Bred in England, the Shire is also commonly known as the English Carthorse. The Shire is the largest of the draft breeds and is very drafty and muscular. This breed is known for being unusually sluggish and sometimes coarse in the legs.

Like the Clydesdale, the Shire is referred to as feather-legged because of the long silky hair which grows on the back of the leg from the knee and hock to the hoof.

CLYDESDALE

The Clydesdale originated in Scotland and because of its stylish way of moving and snappy, showy trot is today a popular parade horse. Among the most famous parade horses today are the Budweiser Clydes-

This eight-horse hitch of Clydesdale horses is owned by Anheuser Busch, Inc., and shown extensively in parades throughout the United States. (Photo courtesy of Anheuser Busch.)

dales which pull a replica of a beer wagon and travel 40,000 miles each year appearing in parades and shows throughout the country.

The disposition of the Clydesdale is less phlegmatic than the other drafters. They are also less drafty in appearance, and without the coarse legs of the other breeds.

SUFFOLK

The Suffolk originated near Suffolk, England, and has since been extensively imported to America. This breed is characterized by very short legs and wide, deep bodies. They are usually chestnut, have little white on their faces and legs, but frequently have flaxen manes and tails.

43

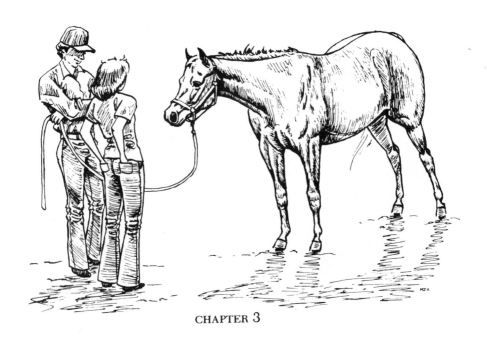

CHAPTER 3

What Makes a Good Horse?

If you plan to buy a horse, or even if you already own one, something you really need to know is what makes a good horse. The truth is that most people can't tell a good horse from a bad one. They are always asking whether this horse or that one is any good. Too often it's after they have bought a horse they can't begin to manage or one that has broken down. All of a sudden they need advice on what they should do, when their problems could have been avoided in the first place if they had simply known what makes a horse good or bad.

There's no mystery about what makes a good horse. Of course, it depends somewhat upon what he is to be used for, but there are some basics that every horse must have to be considered good. Remember that the harder a horse is to be used, the better he must be if he is to stay sound. A backyard horse can get by with some faults that would ruin a race horse.

44

A horse must first be put together correctly. Unlike a dog or cat that just has to lie around and be lovable, we ask our horses to work hard carrying us on their backs. Like anything else that is worked hard, if a horse is not put together right, it will sooner or later break down. We'll talk about structure a great deal in this chapter simply because the better your horse is put together, the longer he'll be usable; which is what having a horse is all about.

Only a few months ago, a friend of ours bought a gelding and paid a substantial amount of money for it. He was so impressed with the size and color of the horse that he failed to notice some bad leg faults. The horse is now lame and our friend is not sure when it will again be usable, if ever. He's now feeding a horse that's of no use to him, and it all could have been avoided if he had remembered that a horse *must* have correct conformation to be a good horse.

Next, to be a good riding horse, a horse must be able to move well. You're probably buying a horse to have fun with by riding him. If the horse you select can't move well, he'll be a lot less comfortable to ride. If the problem is serious enough, he'll break down and you won't be able to ride him at all. For this reason, we'll discuss later on in this chapter some things to look out for in the way a horse moves.

Perhaps the most important thing a pleasure horse must have is a good disposition. Just what is a good disposition depends on what you're going to use the horse for. A bad disposition can make keeping a horse anything but enjoyable.

Finally, there are some special needs that you as an individual have that you need to think about when buying a horse. The ability to fulfill these needs won't make a horse good or bad, but they will make him *right* for you and that's certainly the most important thing.

When you're ready to begin looking for a horse of your own, keep in mind these few hints on how to find that right horse. Remember, there is no such thing as a perfect horse, but you do want to get the best you can for the money you have. Learning to judge horses is the art of compromise. It means deciding what faults you can live with and what you can't. Beware of any glaring faults or unsoundnesses that should disqualify a horse immediately. You should look at as many horses as you can before making a final decision. The more horses you look at, the better judge you will become and the better decision you'll be able to make. Always remember that it costs just as much to feed a bad horse as

45

it does a good horse! Buying a horse involves not only money, but a big investment in time and concern. You want your time spent with your horse to be as enjoyable as possible, and this comes with buying a good horse.

PUT TOGETHER CORRECTLY

You wouldn't buy a car that has a wheel on crooked or a tire a different size from all of the others. That car would soon have problems unless the wheel or tire is promptly replaced. The same principle applies to a horse. If a part isn't "on" right or correct to begin with, it will soon cause problems. Unfortunately, the "bad" parts of a horse can't be replaced. If something breaks down, the horse is simply no longer usable.

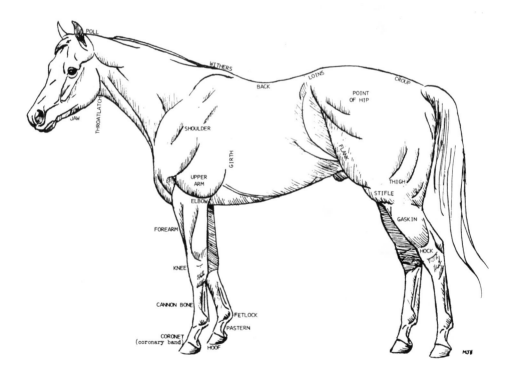

The best way to avoid this is by making sure that the horse is put together correctly to begin with!

The first thing to look for is how well-balanced the horse is. To begin, stand back and take an overall look at how the horse is put together. He shouldn't look like he's made of spare parts. Everything must look as if it fits together properly. If a part is out of balance, something must absorb extra stress and could eventually break down. You can judge balance by dividing a horse's body into thirds; from the point of his shoulder to his withers, from his withers to his hip, and from the point of his hip to the point of his buttocks. Each part should be equal in length and fit together so that the thirds look balanced. The ability to judge balance is acquired by looking at a lot of horses, especially good ones. You'll soon find out what a good horse is supposed to look like and sort out those that might have problems.

While you're looking at the overall horse, something else to consider is substance. A horse with substance has adequate muscle and bone for what he is expected to do. Muscling generally falls into three categories: (1) light muscles with little power; (2) sufficient, long muscles with adequate power, suppleness and length of stride; (3) bunchy muscles with plenty of power, but a loss of fluid movement. For a pleasure horse, look for adequate, but not bulging, muscles, particularly in the forearm stifle and gaskin. Bulging muscles in these areas tend to hinder the stride and for a riding horse suppleness is more important than power.

THE LEGS

We can't emphasize enough how important the legs of a horse are. Legs cause more problems than anything else. This is one place where you must be very careful in compromising. If your horse goes lame, obviously you can't ride him and if this is what you're keeping him for, he's absolutely no good.

Each leg is a column supporting nearly 300 pounds. When a horse moves, this force increases tremendously. Thus, it's easy to see that if one of these columns has a serious crook or bend or other defect in it, it's going to eventually wear out and break down. If a horse has any serious problems with a leg, whether it be crooked, or enlarged or whatever, this will immediately disqualify him as a good choice for a riding horse.

Most problems occur in the front legs of a horse, so you need to judge very carefully whether they are good enough to hold up under what you expect the horse to do. It's often said that if the front legs will go, the back will follow; but, first, the front legs have to be sound.

The front legs support nearly two-thirds of the horse's weight and to do this, and support your weight too, they must be as sound as possible. When looking at the horse from the front, notice if his feet are as far apart as the legs are at the chest. If they're not, the horse is base narrow and his legs will tend to interfere with each other when he moves.

The most important factor in the forearm is length. A long forearm produces a long, fluid stride. On the inside of each forearm you'll find a small, semi-horny growth known as a chestnut. These are found on all horses and are the remnants of what was once a toe.

The knees should be flat, wide and as nearly square as possible. Knee placement faults are common and often cause horses to break down.

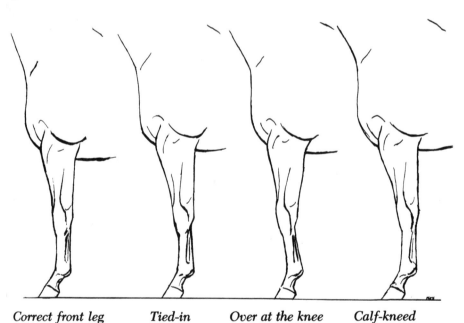

Correct front leg   Tied-in   Over at the knee   Calf-kneed
                                            or buck knee

We've listed several of the most common to look out for in the accompanying drawings. Keep in mind the tremendous weight each of these legs must support. If there's any kind of bend at the knee, extra stress is put on the joint and it's much more likely to break down.

The cannons are made up largely of bone and tendon and contain no muscle. They should be short, appear narrow from the front and broad from the side and have what horsemen refer to as flat, dry bone. This means that the skin is stretched tightly over the bone and tendons and there are no bulges or signs of puffiness.

Common cannon faults to look out for include signs of puffiness or a constriction of the tendon below the knee which is called being tied-in. A horse that's tied-in is less able to stride out properly and puts additional strain on the tendon. This problem is inherited. A bowed tendon is one which curves outward. It's caused by severe strain and the horse will never really be sound again.

There's an old saying among horsemen "no pastern, no horse." This is true because the pasterns serve as the primary shock absorbing mechanism. If they aren't working correctly, the tremendous force of each stride must be absorbed by the other, less elastic parts. Under hard use, a horse with incorrect pasterns is sure to break down.

The pasterns are able to absorb this force because they contain an elastic formation of bone and tendon. There's a long tendon that runs down the back of the pastern to the hoof. If you watch when your horse moves, you can see the pastern recede toward the ground while the tendon stretches and absorbs much of the force.

To work best, the pasterns should be long and at about a 45° angle

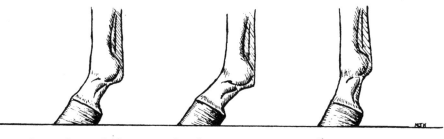

Correctly angled　　　*Angle of pastern*　　　*Straight pastern*
pastern　　　　　　*is too great*

49

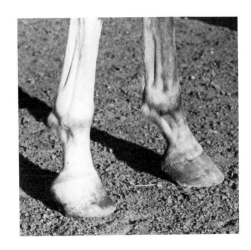

An example of straight pasterns. Note the steepness, particularly in the left foot. This would cause the pastern to have little flexibility and shock-absorbing properties.

from the ground. If the pastern slopes more than this, the ride will be smooth, but the pastern will be weaker. If it is short and doesn't slope to at least 45°, it won't absorb much force and this shock will damage other ligaments and tendons while the rider is treated to a choppy, jarring stride. Another problem with straight pasterns is that the weight is

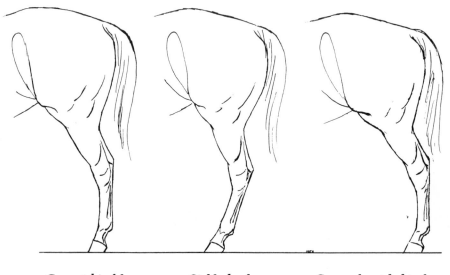

| *Correct hind leg* | *Sickle hock* | *Camped out behind* |

distributed over the navicular bone, which is where most hoof problems occur among horses.

The hindquarters furnish the force that propels the horse forward and therefore should be somewhat heavily muscled, particularly in the stifle, thigh and gaskin. The thigh should be heavily muscled on the inside as well as the outside and this muscling should extend well down into the gaskin. Horses that lack muscling in the gaskin are said to be cat-hammed.

The hocks should be somewhat large with well defined, sharply sculptured bones. Hocks are of primary importance in moving the horse forward and lessening the force of the hooves striking the ground. Hocks are subject to many unsoundnesses any of which can make a horse not a good choice for riding.

When viewed from the back, the hock should point straight ahead or deviate slightly inward. This is acceptable only if the cannons remain parallel. If the hindlegs of the horse spread outward at the bottom, the

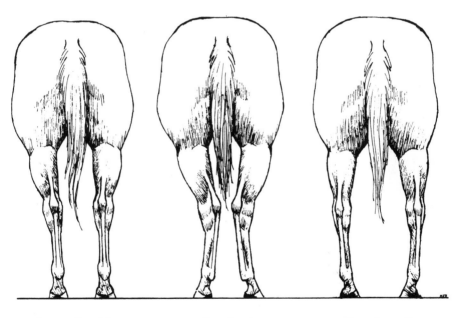

*Correct hind leg
placement*　　　　　*Cow hocks*　　　　　*Bow-legged*

horse is said to be cow-hocked. If the hocks deviate outward, the horse is said to be bow-legged or bandy-legged. This is a serious defect as it puts extra stress on the hocks and causes them to rotate when the horse moves.

The feet should be of a size that appear to fit the horse. Too large a foot will tend to make the horse clumsy, while feet that are too small are prone to unsoundness.

The forefeet should be round, while the hind feet are elliptical or somewhat more oval than the front. When viewed from the front, the forefeet should point straight ahead.

The hoof should extend from the pastern at about a 45° angle. A

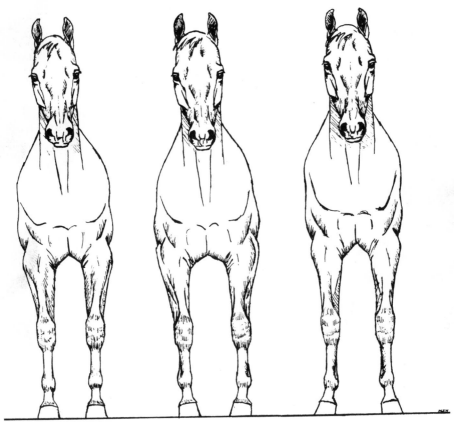

Correct front leg
placement

Toeing-in

Toeing-out

good hoof will be full and wide with no sign of contraction at the heel. The outer horn of the hoof should be smooth and hard without ridges, cracks or excessive dryness. Although it has not been proven conclusively, many horsemen believe black hooves to be more durable than white.

Many people have the mistaken idea that the hoof is a hard solid structure all the way through. Actually, the outer horn that you see covers a highly complex inner structure that helps absorb the shock of each step and pumps blood back up the leg through a maze of tiny blood vessels.

The hoof is made up of bone, horn, and sensitive and elastic tissue. The three bones in the hoof are the short pastern bone, the coffin bone and the navicular bone. The coffin bone is wedge-shaped and is the bottom-most bone in the hoof. It is here that the many nerves and blood vessels are contained and the sensitive laminae and cartilage are attached. The underside is smooth, but it's rough where the flexor tendon attaches. The navicular bone is the smallest in the hoof, but it is associated with a very common disabling lameness found in horses. It lies behind the point where the short pastern bone and the coffin bone meet. Its primary function is as a pulley over which the flexor tendon glides. The short pastern bone lies between the long pastern bone and the coffin bone.

In contrast to these bones, the rest of the hoof is flexible and gives under pressure to help absorb the shock of the footfalls. The two parts of the hoof that are particularly flexible are the lateral cartilage and the plantar cushion. These are referred to as the elastic tissues. The lateral cartilage encloses the plantar cushion and attaches to the upper end of each side of the coffin bone. The plantar cushion serves as a cushion in the hoof. It's a springy pad located behind the bones and above the frog. When the horse is standing still, the plantar cushion is rather large, but under pressure it flattens and expands outward, increasing the width of the heel slightly. This is why the fit of the shoes at the heel is very important, as we'll discuss later.

The third type of tissue is called the sensitive tissue and includes the coronary band, the perioplic ring, the sensitive laminae, the sensitive sole and the sensitive frog. The inside of the outer wall is made up of sensitive laminae. The visible, horny sole and frog grows from the sensitive sole and frog which lies just below the plantar cushion.

The four types of horny tissue are the wall, bars, sole and frog. Their function is to protect the more sensitive inner parts. The wall or horn is what you see on the outside and extends from the hairline to the ground. The horn grows from the coronary band or coronet which encircles the top of the hoof. Just above the coronary band lies the perioplic ring that secretes a varnish-like covering over the hoof wall to keep the hoof moist. The bars are on the bottom of the hoof and turn inward at the point of the heel. They are weight-bearing surfaces and keep the hoof wall expanded.

The horny sole covers most of the bottom of the hoof. It looks white and concave and is rather tough, although it is not meant to bear weight. The frog is the rubbery V-shaped structure found between the bars on the bottom of the hoof. It should extend down and must be in contact with the ground. It grips the ground to help prevent slipping, acts as a shock absorber and, by expanding and contracting, helps blood circulation.

HEAD AND NECK

The first thing most people see when they're looking at a horse is the head and neck. While these areas don't cause problems as often as legs, you do need to look them over carefully and make sure there aren't any serious faults that could make the horse less than enjoyable to ride.

As we discussed earlier, balance is very important in a horse. Because of this, the head should fit the rest of the body and most importantly not be too large.

You may not think it's necessary that we remind you to make sure the horse you're looking at is able to see well. The problem isn't so much with vision as it is with the kind of disposition that results from poor vision. Horses that can't see well are nervous and tend to shy a lot, because they can't decide whether or not the things around them are harmful. A friend of ours had a blue-eyed mare with eyes that were very sensitive to light, so she wouldn't open her eyes completely in direct sunlight. This mare was always scraping and cutting her head simply because she squinted when she was in the sun and couldn't see where she was going. Obviously, this made her less than a safe and pleasant riding horse.

A horse's eyes should be large, set far apart and show that he's interested in what's going on around him. Dark eyes are supposed to be best since it's thought horses with a lot of white around their eyes are nervous. Eyes that have a white, pearly iris are called glass eyes or wall eyes. They are just as good as dark eyes, but some people don't like their appearance. Blue eyes as well as small eyes are weak and should be avoided. Eyes that are too small are called pig eyes, while those that are too large are called pop-eyes.

The only way a horse can breathe is through his nostrils, so it's best if they are wide and he is able to flare them. All horses have a slight, clear discharge running from their nose, so this is nothing to get alarmed about. Only if this discharge is cloudy or colored should you become concerned. The color of the membrane around the nostrils is a good sign of a horse's health. If he's healthy it will be pink when he's at rest and change to a deep red when he exerts himself.

Horses have excellent hearing and you can tell a lot about their mood by watching their ears. Ears that are laid back usually mean a horse is in a sour humor, so watch out! If his ears are constantly pricked forward, the horse is nervous. A calm, assured horse will use his ears by rotating them toward a sound and generally show that he's interested in what's going on about him.

Most people prefer short ears rather than those that look too long for the head, but this is something you'll have to decide for yourself, because it obviously doesn't affect the usefulness of the horse. When a horse's ears droop to the side, he is called lop-eared, which you'll have to admit looks a little funny.

A horse uses his neck as a balance beam. Just as a tightrope walker carries a long pole for balance, if a horse's neck is long he'll also have better balance. Watch a top jumper clear an obstacle and notice the way he stretches his neck out at the point of the jump for perfect balance and resumes a normal position as he canters on around the course. Riding horses should use their necks in much the same way.

Because of this, horses with short, heavy necks should be avoided. As we just mentioned, this affects the balance and makes them less handy by hindering suppleness and length of stride. A horse having a neck that dips on the top where it should be arched is said to have a ewe neck. Because it also bulges on the underside, it's sometimes called an upside-down neck.

Horses that are coarse in the throatlatch or throttle are not desirable

Notice this pony's thick, cresty neck. Obviously, a horse or pony with such conformation would be unhandy to ride.

Horse with a ewe neck.

A horse's teeth change gradually as he grows older. These drawings show what to look for in attempting to ascertain the age of a horse. In a young horse of about five (left), the teeth are nearly vertical. During the middle years (center), a horse's teeth begin slanting toward the front and taking on a more triangular shape. In old age (right), the horse's teeth have slanted forward sharply. They appear longer and more triangular.

as riding horses. This is the area where the head joins the neck and the windpipe passes through. When a horse with this condition tries to flex his neck, the fatty tissue cuts off the air through the windpipe so the horse will carry his head out rather than tucked in as is sometimes necessary.

Even though there has been a great deal written about how you should try to tell a horse's age by his teeth, after he's five it's pretty tough to do and not always reliable. If you think that someone is lying about a horse's age, there's probably something else more serious that's wrong, so you wouldn't want the horse anyway.

You *do* want to look in a horse's mouth to make sure the teeth meet evenly. If they don't, he won't be able to chew his food thoroughly and this could upset his digestive system. A horse with receding lower teeth is said to have a parrot mouth, while one with protruding lower teeth is said to have a monkey mouth.

THE BODY

The shoulder of a riding horse is very important for several reasons. A sloping shoulder helps absorb the shock and enables him to make long,

57

smooth strides. Horses with straight shoulders have a short, choppy stride and must take more steps to the mile.

Ideally, the shoulder should be long and set at about a 45° angle. You need to look for the outline of the shoulder blade and then decide whether you think it has enough length and angle.

The point where the shoulder muscles attach to the spine is called the withers. While withers don't mean too much to a horse, they mean a lot to the rider by helping to keep the saddle on. They'll seem more important once you've had a horse without withers and have to keep tightening the girth to keep the saddle from slipping. A horse that is low and round over the shoulders is said to have mutton withers, which tends to make him heavier on the bit and more likely to be short striding.

When viewed from the front, the horse should appear moderately broad in comparison to his height, be well muscled and have sufficient

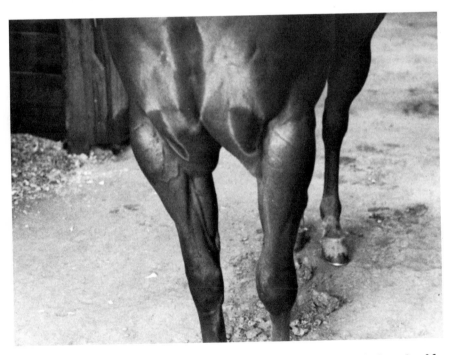

This horse displays the extremely well-defined muscling particularly valued by Quarter Horse breeders.

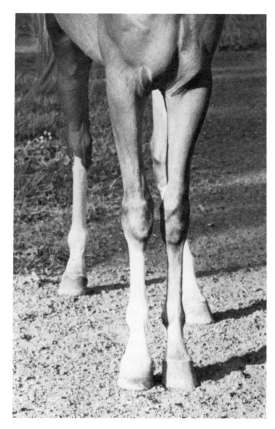

This is a very narrow-fronted horse. Note the closeness of the knees, the lack of width in his chest and the narrow placement of his feet. It is easy to see how a horse with this conformation fault could have difficulty in moving well.

distance between his legs. Too narrow a chest is associated with a lack of stamina and power. Draft horses are required to be wider in the front than saddle horses. In saddle horses, it is felt that excessive width decreases handyness.

When viewed from the side, the horse should have considerable depth at the girth and flank and have a long underline between the front and rear legs. The heart and lungs are located in the area enclosed by the girth and a deep girth indicates these organs are well developed. Horses lacking depth at this area almost always lack stamina. The girth should measure at least as much in circumference as the horse measures in height. An excess of ten inches is considered excellent. It should be deep and oval in shape rather than round, as is found in some horses lacking withers.

59

A low-backed young horse.

Saddle horses should have a long underline and a short back. This is achieved by a long, sloping shoulder and a long hip. The topline of the horse varies from breed to breed. Saddlebreds and Arabians should have a level topline, with the tail set high on the body, while in other breeds more slope in the hindquarters is preferred. In all saddle horses, however, the withers should always be higher than the hindquarters, or the rider will feel he is constantly riding downhill.

The back of the horse should be neither higher nor lower than the rear quarters. If the back is low, the horse is said to be sway-backed. This is not considered as strong nor as attractive as a straight back and is often associated with old age. A convex, or arched, back is called a roach back. While not commonly found, a roach back is very undesirable as it reduces proper extension and flexion of the horse's legs.

In well-muscled horses, the backbone sits in a slight depression formed by heavy muscling on both sides. A horse having a prominent backbone is said to be razor-backed and this trait is caused by the muscles falling away too sharply on each side. Additional weight, or the lack of it, is an important factor in this condition.

The rib cage should be moderately well sprung and curved outward. Long, flat or slab-sided ribs are associated with lack of stamina and with horses that are poor keepers. In a saddle horse, if the outward curve of the ribs is too great, it will be difficult for the rider to grip properly

60

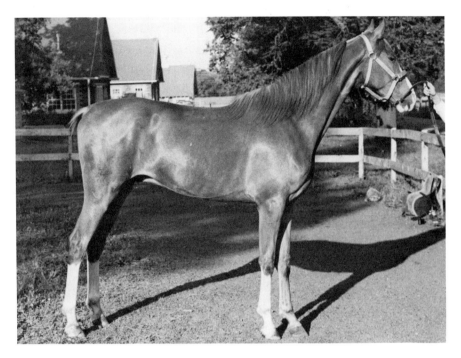

This horse shows lack of substance by his weak hindquarters and slight muscle definition.

with his legs. The ribs should also project slightly backward, as a long chest also contributes to a short, strong back.

The loin region of the horse begins with the last rib and extends back to the hip. Horses should be broad and heavily muscled in the loin. Also, maximum strength is found with a short loin. Those that are narrow and long in this area are said to be "slack" in their coupling. Strong loins contribute to weight-carrying ability.

The flank, or area below the loin, should be deep. This is the case if the last ribs are long. If the horse is shallow in the flank, he is said to be tucked-up or wasp-waisted.

The croup is the area from the hips to the buttocks. There is great variation of preference among the breeds concerning the proper topline from the hips to the tail. If the croup slopes sharply downward, it is called a steep croup. This conformation places the hind legs too far under the body and affects his ability to extend. If a horse has too sharp an angle in the croup, he is said to be "goose-rumped." The most desirable croup is characterized by length, breadth and adequate muscling. The croup should very definitely be long as this increases the power and length of stride. Power in a horse comes from behind. Smooth, round hips are preferred in saddle horses, while draft horses often have square, prominent hips.

MOVES WELL

In all likelihood, the main reason that you want to own a horse is to be able to ride. This means that for your horse to be a good horse, he must be able to move well. By this we mean that he moves truly and freely with even, elastic strides. A horse is said to move true when his legs step forward in a straight line with no deviation to either side. If a horse doesn't move well, he'll be a lot less fun to ride and if the problem is serious enough, it could cause him to break down.

It's easy to spot faulty action. Just stand ahead of or behind the horse and notice whether or not the legs move forward in a straight line. A horse that doesn't move correctly usually has poor conformation in the first place. If a leg isn't straight, then it's not likely the movement of the leg will be true and this extra stress could eventually cause it to break down.

GAITS

The different ways that horses have of going are called gaits. Each gait has its own distinctive movement of the feet and legs. Entire breeds have been developed for horses that perform a gait well, such as the Standardbred and the Saddlebred at the trot, or the Thoroughbred at the gallop.

Horses have three natural gaits, the walk, trot and gallop, as well as man-made gaits such as the canter, rack and pace. While the gaits may be the same, there are wide variations on how they are performed by the different breeds. Notice the high, flashy trot of the Saddlebred, the fast ground-covering trot of the Standardbred, the delicate, floating trot of the Arabian and the slow, comfortable trot of the Quarter Horse.

While the gait may be the same, each breed performs it differently and for each it has a different purpose.

Walk: The walk is a slow, diagonal four-beat gait. Each foot is lifted and strikes the ground separately. The beat of a gait refers to the rhythm of each foot as it strikes the ground. Thus, with a four-beat gait such as the walk, you'll hear a separate beat as each foot hits the ground.

Trot: The trot is a diagonal, two-beat gait. This means that a front foot on one side and hind foot on the other side are lifted and then hit the ground together.

Canter: The canter is a slow, collected gait where the horse shifts his weight to the rear and moves his hind legs under his body. You'll hear three distinct beats as the horse pushes off one hind leg and shifts his support to the hind leg on the other side and the front leg on the same side. He then extends the other front leg, which lifts the horse back to the original leg.

With a good canter, the horse will lift himself up more than push forward and this gives the gait the desired slow, collected manner. In the show ring, the inside front leg should be the one extended or leading.

Gallop: The gallop isn't at all an extended canter. It's a four-beat gait with the hind legs much farther behind the body to push the horse forward, while the front legs extend forward to collect the motion and get ready for another push from the rear. Speed at the gallop comes from long, fluid strides with a lot of extension. This requires long, sloping shoulders and powerful hindquarters.

Pace: The pace is a fast, two-beat, lateral gait in which the legs on each side move forward together. Just like the trot, there's a period of suspension between the beats when the horse floats through the air. It's a little faster than the trot, but slower than the gallop. An awkward, rolling motion makes it very uncomfortable to ride. The pace is characterized by extremely low action as the feet barely get off the ground. Because of this it's used only by harness racers at the track where the ground is smooth and level.

Stepping or Slow Pace: This is the slow gait used by most five-gaited show horses. It's slightly different from the regular pace, in that the legs on each side don't move forward exactly together. This gets rid of most of the rolling motion that makes the regular pace so uncomfortable to

This photo shows a Standardbred moving at the pace. Notice how the legs on each side move together. (Photo courtesy of the United States Trotting Association.)

ride. Each of the feet strike the ground separately, making it a four-beat gait.

Fox Trot: This is sometimes used as a slow gait by five-gaited show horses, but not nearly as often as the slow pace. It's a slow, broken trot with the hind foot hitting the ground a little before the diagonal front with the horse nodding his head in time with the beat.

Running Walk: This is a slow, four-beat gait done a little faster than the walk. It is easy on the horse and very comfortable for the rider. In performing this gait, the hind foot oversteps the front foot, producing a gliding effect. Often the horse will nod his head in time with the beat.

The Rack: This is a flashy, fast, unnatural, four-beat gait that should be performed brilliantly. It's quite easy to ride, but very hard on the horse. Saddlebreds "racking on" is one of the most exciting show ring spectacles.

DISPOSITION

For just about every horse-owner, the most important thing a horse must have is a good disposition! Just like people, horses have all kinds of temperaments such as the fiery stallion, the quiet draft horse or what most of us are interested in, the willing pleasure horse that has spirit when that's what you want, and is quiet when calm is more appreciated.

A horse with a good disposition must first be willing to work for you. You want a horse that's energetic, but still manageable. It's no fun to have to beat your horse to get him to trot, and it can be a real headache if he tries to run off every chance he gets. A willing horse has a good attitude about people and the work he's asked to do. You can tell about this pretty early by the way a young horse learns to accept being led and groomed. Those that learn these lessons easily usually turn out to be more intelligent, well-adjusted and pleasant to handle.

As well as being willing to do what you ask, a horse should be bold and confident. A confident horse isn't likely to shy or bolt and adjusts a lot better to new situations. Of course a horse that's too daring and doesn't pay attention to his rider is certainly not a good prospect for a pleasure horse.

The only way to find out the disposition of a horse is by handling him and noticing how he reacts to your handling. Notice whether he's quiet and sleepy or nervous and excitable. You have to decide whether this kind of disposition will be right for the kind of riding you expect to do. Keep in mind that a calm, quiet horse may be fine on the trail, but totally out of place in the show ring; while a flashy, energetic horse is fine in the show ring, but no good on the trail.

SELECTING THE RIGHT HORSE FOR YOU

The horse that's right for you must be more than just a good horse. He must be all of the things that will give you the greatest amount of enjoyment. Of course he must first be a good horse and have correct conformation, action and the right disposition, but after these requirements have been met, there are some other things that will make him just the horse for you.

Purebred or Grade?

In the first chapter we talked about the major breeds of horses and their common uses. If you have in mind buying a horse for a specialized task, maybe one of these breeds would suit you best. If a jumper is your goal, you would probably choose a Thoroughbred or Thoroughbred cross. If you have gaming events such as barrel racing in mind, then a Quarter Horse would be a good choice. Gaited show horses are selected from American Saddlebreds. If you want a versatile horse that you can use either on the trail or in the show ring, perhaps an Arabian or Morgan would do.

The best horses for each of these events are members of specific breeds, but if you are simply interested in a backyard horse that can be quietly ridden on trails along with your friends, a grade horse could be a very good choice.

The majority of the horses in the United States don't belong to any one particular breed, but are of mixed ancestry and known as "grade" horses. Grade is another term for horses with mixed breeding. A grade horse is often as usable a horse as one that is registered, but it will probably be priced considerably lower.

Registered horses are simply horses whose dam and sire are both registered with a particular breed and whose ancestors had certain unique characteristics or traits. Because of these characteristics, people who liked this particular kind of horse joined together and bred their horses, eventually excluding all others. These horses were bred for special purposes and can perform these skills especially well. This certainly doesn't mean that the grade horse for sale at a lower price won't serve your simpler, unique needs as well as a registered horse would.

A grade horse, however, would be a poor choice if you are looking for a show horse, because of the lack of any organizations that sponsor shows. Also, breeding grade horses is usually not profitable because their foals don't bring the high prices that registered horses command. If you want to breed horses, certainly a registered horse should be your choice. Breeding can be very frustrating, because of the poor conception rate and long gestation period. It would become an even more frustrating experience if there isn't any market for the resulting foal.

Another disadvantage of grade horses is that they are often bred and trained by amateurs and subsequently the quality of the horses and their performance suffers. Too often, a grade mare is bred to a stallion simply because it is convenient, without the owner thinking about the quality of the resulting foal. The training of grade horses is often neglected entirely or not properly carried out. Too often, amateurs will consider a horse trained if he simply allows a person on his back and turns or starts and stops with enough urging from his rider. Unless a grade horse has exceptional athletic ability, further training is usually not economically justified and the horse remains only partially trained.

If price is an important consideration in selecting a horse, a grade horse adequately trained can be as good a mount as a better bred horse. Grade horses are often a sensible choice for a first horse because of their reasonable price. This would give you time to decide what kind of riding and what breed of horse, if any, you would like for the future.

Mare, Stallion or Gelding?

One of the first considerations is whether you want a mare, stallion or gelding. Each has certain advantages and disadvantages that depend on why you want a horse to begin with. For a simple riding horse, either a mare or a gelding is probably best. Their disposition is often better and they are definitely easier to keep and take care of than stallions. Geldings are castrated stallions and by and large make the best pleasure horses, as this is their only reason for existing. They aren't as moody as mares or as difficult to handle as stallions. On the other hand, there is the chance that a serious injury could make them useless as a riding horse, while an injured mare or stallion might still be used for breeding. Unlike stallions, geldings will usually get along together in a pasture, although if a mare or two is added, one of them might try to herd the mares. If you are buying your first horse, a well-trained experienced gelding is probably your best buy.

Mares are somewhat between stallions and geldings as far as ease of handling goes. They have heat periods every twenty-one days and are likely to be irritable during this time. Once a mare is bred, her heat periods stop, but she still might be irritable while she's pregnant. Because of this, mares just aren't as steady and consistent as geldings.

Mares are usually worth more, however, because they can be used for breeding. This is especially true if the mare is a good horse and has a good pedigree. If you have a good mare, it is possible to have a foal or two you can sell to help pay for keeping her.

Stallions are, or at least should be, primarily breeding animals, except in the case of a top show horse or race horse where they often give greater effort. There's no reason for not gelding all but the very best stallions. These should be reserved for breeding and have no business in the hands of amateurs who don't intend to stand them at stud.

Stallions of some breeds are handled more easily than others, but there are still some things that should be said about their disposition. Stallions generally need more discipline, are more difficult to manage and are more cunning than mares or geldings. Stable arrangements for stallions can be difficult, as can pasturing. The lure of a mare in season is quite strong and only the strongest stall and the sturdiest of fences will keep most stallions confined.

Among registered horses, geldings usually sell for less than mares or stallions simply because they can't produce foals. The price of a gelding will vary depending on the amount of training he's had, his ability to perform and his age. Registered mares and stallions are the most expensive, simply because they are able to produce foals. Mares are worth more, of course, because they can produce foals. Unlike stallions that are sometimes not suitable as a pleasure horse, mares can be used for riding most of the year, with the added virtue of their capability of producing a foal. An exception to this would be an outstanding performance horse whose price is determined solely by its ability.

AGE

The age of a horse is an important factor to consider when you're looking for the horse that's right for you. The right age depends on how much training and experience you've had yourself, as well as what you expect your horse to do.

The age of a horse is measured from January first of the year in which it's born. Thus, if a foal is born in June, his age will be measured from January 1st of that year and the next January, even though chronologically he'll be only six months old, to the horse world he'll be a year old. For this reason, breeders of race horses and show horses will breed their mares to foal in the early spring, so the foals will be as mature as possible for their age group.

Pleasure horses usually begin training when they're between two and three. They shouldn't be asked to carry much weight on their back until they are three, or until the trainer is sure that the knees and other joints are fully developed. Race horses are usually ridden much sooner because their owners want to find out if they have any potential before too much time and money are invested.

By the time he's four, a horse might be considered trained, but he still won't have the experience of an older, more settled horse and wouldn't be a good horse for a beginner. At the other extreme, many horses are used until they are well into their twenties. Those that are, are sound to begin with and have been treated intelligently during their working years.

It is best to buy a horse between the ages of four and fourteen. After a horse is fourteen, he can still be sound and very usable, but you have to assume his useful years are limited. Most livestock insurance companies won't insure horses after their mid-teens. If you buy a horse that's under four, you must consider the cost of keeping him until he's usable and also the considerable cost of having him trained. Of course, if you want to do the training yourself, a young horse is the only logical choice.

Generally a good rule to follow is "the younger the rider, the older the horse." The idea of a child and a horse growing up together may sound nice, but it's seldom practical. Young riders generally need the patience, experience and miles under saddle of an older horse.

Following are some terms used to describe the various stages in the life of a horse.

FOAL A young horse under one year of age.
SUCKLING A foal which is still nursing.
WEANLING A foal from the time it is weaned until it is one year old.
YEARLING A young horse from one year of age until it is two.
COLT A male horse three years of age and under.
FILLY A female horse four years of age and under.
STALLION A male horse four years of age and older.
MARE A female horse five years of age and older.
GELDING A castrated male horse at any age.

AGED A horse considered to have a smooth mouth, usually twelve and over. Aged does not mean the horse is past his prime. It merely means you can no longer accurately judge his age by looking at his teeth.

SIZE

Just like anything else, horses come in many different sizes and this is something else you need to consider in finding the horse that's right for you. A horse of the right size will be much more enjoyable to ride and will stay sound longer.

Horses are measured from the ground to the top of their withers. The term used in measuring horses is a "hand," which is equal to four inches. This means a horse that is 15 hands tall will be sixty inches from the ground to the top of his withers. If you're going to measure a horse, make sure he's on level ground and his head is in a normal position, since these things can cause differences in measurements from time to time. Saddle horses range in size from 14.2 to 17 hands. A horse less than 14.2 is considered a pony, and can be easily ridden by people of smaller stature.

Be sure to bear in mind your own size in relation to the size of the horse. Consider his breadth and width, as well as making sure he's tall enough. Just because a horse is tall doesn't mean he has a lot of weight-carrying ability. There's some indication that when a horse measures over 16 hands, weight-carrying ability decreases. If you're concerned about a horse being able to carry your weight, consider such things as width, heavy muscling and bone density, as well as height. Large people should be careful to select a horse with plenty of substance. While a fine-boned, delicate horse may look pretty, he won't be worth much if he breaks down because he wasn't strong enough to carry your weight. At the other extreme, a short, fat pony can be just as broad as a large horse, making it difficult for a child to use his legs properly.

Usually a small person is more comfortable riding, and is better able to take care of, a small horse. It's pretty exasperating for a short person to try to bridle a horse that's holding his head out of reach, while nothing looks sillier than a tall person mounted on a horse so small that his legs dangle nearly to the ground.

Size is the big reason people get ponies rather than full-sized horses for children. Because ponies are small, children can groom, saddle and bridle them without any help. Don't get a pony for a child, however, simply because he's small and forget the other, important things to consider—especially disposition. Ponies are often stubborn and difficult to handle and the frustration of a child trying to ride such an animal may more than offset the advantage of size. For this reason, horse-pony crosses are often an excellent choice. They have the advantage of smaller size, without many of the problems of ponies such as a poor disposition and a choppy stride.

TRAINING

Having a horse that's well-trained and responsive certainly makes riding a lot more enjoyable. The only problem is that training by a competent professional is expensive, so you can expect to pay more for the training, although it's usually worth it.

Because training is so important, if you're buying a young horse, you should consider the expense of having him trained as well as what it will cost you to keep him until he's grown to a usable age. Unless you plan to train the horse yourself, it could be that a more expensive, trained horse is a better buy, particularly since the actual ability of the young horse is still unknown.

You're going to find horses in several different stages of training. A horse with just a minimum of training is called green or green broke. This means that he has learned to walk, trot and canter under saddle and has probably been ridden mostly in a ring. At this stage a horse is still very impressionable and will need careful guidance in the hands of a skilled rider before he can be considered finished. Because he still needs more training, a green horse isn't a good choice for an inexperienced rider who could easily undo all of the horse's earlier training. As well as knowing his gaits, a finished horse can collect himself, canter on the correct lead and should be safe for the average horseman. A finished horse will be more dependable because of his having more miles under the saddle.

Horses that advance past this stage usually specialize in a particular event such as dressage, jumping, stock work, etc. Horses that do these things well command a high price and are not suited for the average horseman, since they need a skilled rider to perform at their best. Also, a horse that's very good at one event usually isn't versatile enough to do the different things most of us expect of a horse. It would be unlikely that you could ever change a brilliant gaited show horse into a calm trail horse, or for that matter, would want to.

You're also going to find many horses that have had haphazard, inferior training, as well as those that have been spoiled by bad training. A horse that rears, tosses his head, bucks or misbehaves in any way has definite bad habits. These are very hard to correct and certainly beyond the ability of most amateurs. Retraining a spoiled horse involves much more time than correct training to begin with and it requires skilled professional help, which makes it quite expensive.

In selecting the horse that's right for you, be sure that he has the training to do the things you expect of him. It's much better to pay a little more for proper training than to suffer the disappointment of keeping a horse that is unable to do what you want him to do.

COLOR

All too often a prospective horse owner is dazzled by a flashy color and forgets the other more important things that really make for a good horse. The color of a horse has nothing to do with his usefulness. On the other hand, since you want a horse for your own pleasure and enjoyment, if you really want a particular color, by all means get it! Just remember to consider all the other factors involved in selecting a good horse.

Regarding color, however, keep in mind that dark shaded horses such as bay or chestnut are easier to keep clean. A disadvantage is that dark horses don't stand out as much in the show ring and aren't as likely to be noticed by a judge. Just remember one thing: beware of buying a bad horse simply because of his color. Novice horse owners are too often blinded by a flashy color and miss seeing a very serious fault. By all means get a color you like, but first make sure you're choosing a good horse.

The colors used by horsemen are a little out of the ordinary, so we've listed the most important below.

BLACK The coat color as well as the muzzle and flank must be jet black.
    If a question arises concerning the color of a black horse, the color

of the hair around the flank and muzzle determines the color of the horse.

BROWN The coat color can be either black or brown; however, the hair around the muzzle or flank must be brown.

CHESTNUT The coat color varies from light red (which some registries call "sorrel") to copper, to deep liver in color. Some chestnuts have their mane and tail the same color as their coat, while others have a light mane and tail.

GREY Grey horses are born black, bay or chestnut, but gradually fade until they are white. They change through various colors during this fading process, and sometimes achieve a striking dappling effect. Grey horses can be distinguished at birth by a sprinkling of grey hair around the eyes.

BAY The coat color varies from golden tan to deep mahogany. The mane, tail and lower legs must be black.

PALOMINO The coat color is golden and the mane and tail is white or silver.

ROAN The coat can be any of the darker colors, but it is mixed with white throughout. Chestnut mixed with white is referred to as a strawberry roan. Black mixed with white is referred to as a blue roan.

BUCKSKIN The coat color is a dull, light brown with a black dorsal (back) stripe and a black mane, tail and lower legs.

DUN The coat color is yellow-grey with a black dorsal stripe, a black mane, tail and lower legs.

PINTO Pinto horses have large spots and are classified in two ways. Overo pintos have a colored coat with large white spots. Tobiano pintos have a white coat with large dark spots.

ALBINO The coat is white or cream while the eyes may be blue.

MARKINGS

The markings on a horse refer to various white markings other than the main coat color and are usually found on the face and legs. Horses are identified for registration by their coat color and other markings, so if you're buying a registered horse, be sure the markings on the registration papers are the same as those on the horse.

| *Star* | *Stripe* | *Star and snip* | *Blaze* | *Bald face* |

Facial Markings

BLAZE A blaze is white covering the face, extending from the forehead on down the face to cover the nasal bone.

STRIP A strip is a narrow white marking down the face.

STAR A star is a white marking on the forehead.

SNIP A snip is a separate white marking between the nostrils. A snip may be in conjunction with either a star or a strip.

Leg Markings

A horse may have only minimal white markings on a leg in which case the marking takes its name from the point at which it terminates, e.g., coronet, heel, pastern, fetlock.

SOCK White above the fetlock, but extending not further than halfway up the cannon bone is referred to as a sock.

STOCKING White extending farther than halfway up the cannon bone is referred to as a stocking.

LOOKING AT HORSES

By now, you should have some idea what the horse that's right for you is like. The next problem involves finding this horse.

74

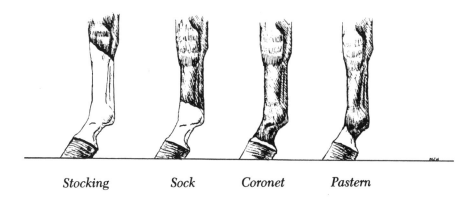

Stocking   *Sock*   *Coronet*   *Pastern*

WHERE TO LOOK

There are many places to look, any of which could have the right horse. If there are any public boarding stables in your area, you can begin by telephoning the manager and asking him if he knows of any horses that are for sale. He'll usually get a percentage of the selling price, but you can expect him to be pretty honest in describing the horse, since news of any shady dealings would soon get around and damage his reputation.

If you've decided on a particular breed, you should visit some of the local breeding farms. All major breeds have magazines that contain advertisements for these farms. Also, most breed associations will send you a directory of breeders on request. These farms often have older, mature stock for sale as well as some young horses. They should represent their horses fairly and honestly and if they have nothing suitable for you, will send you to another who may.

Professional trainers often have horses for sale. They sometimes buy young, untrained horses, train them and resell them for a profit. An owner who has left horses with a trainer might have something for sale the trainer would know about.

Finally, there's no reason why a perfectly suitable horse can't be found in the classified ads of one of the horse magazines or even your local newspaper. Just remember to use caution and good judgment. Always try to find out why the owner is selling the horse, so that you don't inherit someone else's problems.

The horse trader and the auction are probably the least likely possibilities for the beginner and should be approached with a great deal of caution. A horse trader is different from any of the sellers we just mentioned because he only buys horses to resell them as soon as possible for a big profit. The horses he buys are often those the owner can't sell to anyone else because of some unsoundness, vice or old age. The horse could be a cull that a breeder wants to get rid of because it's a poor example of his breeding. A horse trader can't have a very good history of the horse and too often they make up a story, so you simply have to judge what you see.

Another easy place to find a horse you'll be disappointed with is the auction ring. This doesn't refer to the many excellent breed sales where horses are selected for consignment, but rather to the local sales where any horse able to walk into the ring is sold. At an auction it's impossible to know anything about a horse, other than what he looks like at a distance. Horses are usually sold at an auction because they can't be sold privately. Although it's certainly not a common practice, faults can be disguised by such tactics as drugging the horses to quiet those that are unmanageable.

In order to find the horse that is just right for you, be prepared for a lengthy search. Regardless of your frustration, it is much better to be selective rather than lower your standards and buy a horse that is less than suitable. Having a horse that's fun to ride and easy to keep is certainly worth a little extra effort in the finding.

CHOOSING A HORSE

Now that you've decided to go look for a horse, we'd better give you some advice on how to deal with that terrible fellow, the horse trader. We should begin by mentioning that everyone selling a horse is not a crook. In fact, there are some very nice people selling horses. On the other hand, however, we'd be less than candid if we didn't warn you to be careful. In the horse business, the rule "buyer beware" is the accepted practice. It's up to you to decide whether the horse will fit your needs. Because of this we're going to give you some pointers on how to go about choosing your horse.

First, don't be timid in approaching the seller. You can't expect him to tell you about all the horse's faults. Only by observing and by asking questions will you ever find these things out. If you want a trail horse and don't ask whether the horse has ever been ridden on a trail, you can't complain when you're disappointed.

By all means, call the seller first and make an appointment. This gives him a chance to groom the horse and show him to best advantage. It's only common courtesy and will definitely be appreciated. The seller will then be able to allow enough time to show you his horse properly. Having an uninvited guest in the middle of stall cleaning or while another horse is being shown is very annoying and certainly won't put anyone in a mood to bargain over price.

All of the time you're being shown a horse, watch his behavior very closely. If the horse is in a pasture, notice how easy he is to catch and how he reacts to people. A horse shouldn't resent people and one that's nervous and shies away may be either poorly trained or mistreated. Look for signs of poor manners such as laid back ears, attempts to bite or kick or efforts to avoid being handled such as backing away or tossing his head. Any of these things can mean the horse has a bad disposition, which must be avoided in a pleasure horse.

Once you've watched how the horse behaves either in a stall or pasture, have him brought out so you can look at him. Too many people are afraid to ask a seller to have a horse stand for inspection, yet this is the only way you can judge any horse's conformation. The horse should be stood in a well-lighted area with enough room to look at him from all sides. If the owner doesn't want you to look at the horse carefully, be suspicious of a serious fault. Believe it or not, we know of a man who bought a horse after looking at only one side. The problem was that when he got the horse home, he found a huge hernia on the other side that at any time could strangulate and kill the horse!

Look carefully for any unsoundnesses. If you find a serious problem, there's no need to keep looking at this horse. Judge his conformation just as we discussed earlier in the chapter. Keep in mind that you have to weigh his good points against his faults and decide whether the horse will be able to do what you want him to.

It's a good idea to pick up the horse's hoofs. Look for any cracks and make sure the frog is well-defined and relatively soft. How well the horse reacts to this will give you a good idea of the amount of handling he's had.

Once you've decided the horse doesn't have any serious conformation faults, have him walked away from you and trotted back so you can look at his action. Notice the correctness of his movement and be sure to watch out for any serious problems such as extreme dishing or paddling, i.e. swinging the forefeet out sidewise when trotting. Also, watch how willingly he does these things. A horse that doesn't want to be led isn't likely to want to be ridden either.

If the horse is supposed to be trained, have the owner ride him first so you can stand aside and watch him perform. Then ride him yourself so you can judge the amount of training he's had from the saddle. It's a good idea to saddle and bridle him yourself. Any horse should accept this willingly and with a minimum of fuss. There are many levels of training, so don't simply take the owner's word for it that the training is of championship quality.

By this time you should have a pretty good idea about whether the horse would be right for you. Regardless of how perfect the horse might seem at the moment, it's usually a good idea to put off making a final decision until you've thought it over for a few days. This will give you some time to weigh the advantages against the disadvantages away from the sales pitch of the owner and the lovable presence of the horse. You might find that the horse that seemed so right at the time just wouldn't do, now that you've thought about it.

Also, before you make a final decision, have a competent veterinarian examine the horse. He will be better able to find any unsoundnesses or illnesses that could effect the usefulness of the horse. If you have a friend who knows a lot about horses, you might ask him to look at the horse. Beware of imposing on people in this way, however. Giving advice on buying a horse can be tough to do, and no one wants the burden of having approved a bad horse.

If the horse is supposed to be registered, check the registration papers carefully to make sure the horse you're buying matches the one described on the papers. Under no condition should you buy a horse as registered unless the papers are in hand. If the seller says the horse can be registered but isn't, it's likely he couldn't be registered in the first place. Unscrupulous dealers sometimes use this ploy to increase the value of their unregistered stock, so don't be tricked into paying registered prices for grade horses.

If everything else is in order and the veterinarian pronounces the horse sound, the next step is to arrange for payment and other matters such as who will transport your horse to his new home. The payment should be verified by a bill of sale stating the terms of the purchase. Sometimes a seller will accept payment over a period of time, but you'll have to arrange this with him. Usually the seller requires you to insure the horse at least for the unpaid balance. Finally, you're ready to take your horse home. If the distance isn't too far, most sellers will transport the horse for you. If it's very far, however, you should be prepared to arrange for the transportation yourself.

In some cases, the seller will let you try the horse for a trial period and return him if he isn't satisfactory, but this is ordinarily done only if the seller has been previously acquainted with the buyer.

Perhaps the best way to go about buying a horse is to shop around and compare both quality and price. Be prepared to get just what you're willing to pay for. Be wary of any bargain horses; they often turn out to have something wrong with them that makes them worth even less, if anything.

Don't allow yourself to be pressured by the seller. There are a lot of horses for sale and many will meet your needs. The more horses you look at, the better judge you'll become and the better decision you'll be able to make.

CHAPTER 4

Where to Keep Your Horse

So you've decided to buy a horse! Before you bring him home, however, you're going to need somewhere to keep him. Unless you have a very large backyard (at least an acre or more), you'll first have to find a place to board him. Although your horse may be just a pet, he is rather large and will need shelter from the weather and enough room in which to exercise.

BOARDING

Prospective horseowners quite often already live in rural areas on several acres of land. If you're in this position, fine. On the other hand, even if you live in a city, you can still own a horse—but you'll need to board him either at a public stable or with a farmer or other horseowner who's willing to keep an extra horse. To be honest, it's usually pretty difficult to find someone willing to bother with another horse, so your best bet is probably a public boarding stable, although they are usually the most expensive.

Boarding stables often will advertise in the newspaper or the yellow pages of your telephone book, but if you don't have any luck finding one in these places, ask other horseowners in your area or the people in local tack shops or feed stores.

Once you've located a boarding stable, there are some things to check into before you leave your horse there. First, make sure it's not so far away that you hate to go there because of the distance. The finest stable in the world won't be much good unless it's close enough so you can see your horse as often as you like.

The next thing you're going to be interested in is the cost. This will vary considerably and depends upon the services provided, such as frequency of stall cleaning and exercise as well as the quality and quantity of feed. Many stables have a basic rate that includes a stall and feed with exercise or grooming optional, if available at all. Probably the best way to evaluate the cost is to compare fees at several stables, keeping in mind, however, what each is providing. It's no bargain to save a few dollars a month only to find that your horse is losing weight because of poor quality or insufficient feed.

A large, well-kept boarding stable.

Once you've decided the cost is within your budget, inquire about the physical characteristics of the stable. The stalls should at least be ten feet by twelve feet, although a pony might get by in a slightly smaller space and a large Saddlebred might need a bigger one. While you're checking the size of the stall, make sure there are no holes where a horse could get one of his feet caught, or any sharp objects sticking out where a horse might hurt itself. Look to see if the feeder and water bucket are clean. Is the water bucket empty? Have the stalls been cleaned recently? All of these are signs of the quality of management, and if they look bad enough, it might be better to keep your horse elsewhere, even though it may cost a bit more.

Assuming you are satisfied so far, ask what and when the horses are being fed. They should be fed grain and hay twice each day. This is an easy place to cut costs, but it also could cause serious problems for your horse, so don't compromise. If the horses aren't getting nutritious feed at least twice a day, *don't* leave your horse at that stable.

Something else to notice is the attitude of the people at the stable who work around the horses. Are they pleasant and calm? Do they treat the horses like you want yours to be treated? Remember to find out where the tack room is located and how secure they keep it. You certainly don't want to haul your tack back and forth because you're afraid of its being stolen. A locked tack room is best, with only boarders and stable personnel having keys. A saddle rack should be provided for you along with enough room for a tack trunk.

Most large boarding stables have an indoor riding ring. While it might raise the monthly board bill slightly, an indoor ring is a real advantage for week-end riders, especially since it often waits until Saturday or Sunday to rain! If you work from 9 to 5, make sure the riding ring is lighted, for evening use. It's nice if the stable has bridle paths or trails available. When you board a horse away from home, there will be times when you're not able to ride as often as you'd like. If the stable has a paddock or pasture where your horse can be turned out for exercise, this is a real advantage.

Large boarding stables often require you to sign a boarding contract. While these contracts vary slightly, mostly they absolve the management of responsibility in case of accident or theft. Read the contract over carefully for any extra costs or termination stipulations. If you have any questions, take it to your lawyer before you sign.

In this barn the stalls are clustered together in the center so that the wide outer aisleway can be used as a riding ring.

Should the rates at boarding stables be more than you can afford, you might be able to find a farmer or another horseowner with stall space or a pasture to rent. Usually the cost is reduced, but make sure your horse will get enough feed and have available reasonably clean, comfortable shelter.

STABLING

Using an Old Barn or Other Building

If you live on the outskirts of town or in a rural area, and have sufficient land available, you might want to stable your own horse. It might be necessary for you to build a stable, but sometimes old farm buildings and garages can be satisfactorily converted to stall horses. Horses have been kept in converted garages, chicken houses and cow barns, but first some changes have to be made before these places are safe.

83

If you have a building available, the first thing to check is the ceiling height. The ceiling should be at least eight feet high and it's better if it is even higher. Horses are excitable and have been known to rear regardless of the consequences. We know of several horses that injured their heads because the stable ceiling was not high enough.

Next, see what kind of floor the building has. Clay is best for the stall area. Cement is not good for horse's feet and legs because it is hard, and slippery when wet or damp. If you must stall your horse on cement, be sure the floor is deeply covered with bedding. An excellent way to cover cement floors is to use rubber mats similar to those used in horse trailers. They have a cushioning effect and reduce dampness, too. On any building, notice the width of the doorways. For horses they should be at least four feet wide; but, of course, floors and doors can be changed much more easily than the ceiling height.

Finally, before you decide to remodel an old building for use as a stable, compare the cost of remodelling against the cost of a new building. It often makes sense to spend a little more for a new building than to put up with the inconvenience of something you've tried to convert.

BUILDING A STABLE

A suitable stable can be anything from a one-stall backyard building to a palatial heated establishment with an indoor riding ring and all of the comforts money can buy. For the horseowner of modest means, your stable will probably resemble the former more than the latter, but even a modest stable can be convenient for you and comfortable for your horse.

Basically, a stable needs to provide shelter for your horse, a place out of the weather where you can care for him and a storage room for feed and tack. First, to provide shelter for your horse you'll need adequate stall space. Then, the building should be dry, draft-free and have good ventilation. For your convenience it should be well-lighted and have an aisleway or overhanging roof where you can care for your horse in relative comfort despite the weather. Lastly, you should have a dry, convenient space to store a quantity of feed and your tack.

General Construction

In planning a stable, one of the most important decisions you're going to make is where to locate it. It should be at least 200 feet from your house because even the best-managed stables attract rodents and insects and have some unpleasant odors. On the other hand, try to locate it within easy walking distance from the house.

Another important factor in selecting a location for your stable is proper drainage. The site should be higher than the surrounding ground so the water drains away from the stable. Then water won't collect in the middle of the stalls every time it rains. As simple as this may sound, we know of several stables, including one large boarding stable, which were built in low areas with poor drainage. You can imagine the problems they have when it rains heavily and all of the horses are standing in water up to their fetlocks!

A small, safe, backyard stable.

This modern design backyard stable is attractive as well as efficient.

The exact dimensions of your stable will depend on the number of horses you intend to keep as well as your finances. Even if you have only one horse, you'll probably want at least two stalls to have room for a guest and have a stall handy in case you buy another horse. It's much more economical to plan ahead rather than try to add a stall later. The following illustration shows a well-designed, convenient stable with feed and tack rooms and an overhanging roof for protection from the weather. If you're interested in other plans for stables, contact your local agricultural extension service.

The exterior walls of a stable are usually built of wood, sheet metal or masonry. Which you choose will depend on the climate in your area as well as the cost. Attractive stables are often built to match the owner's home. An experienced contractor should be able to answer your questions about these alternatives. Something definitely to consider are the many prefabricated barns now offered by several different companies. These barns are well-designed and in most cases one can be found to meet your needs.

Because your horse will spend a great deal of time standing in his stall, the material you use for flooring in the stalls is important in preventing leg strain. Clay makes the best stall floors. It is more resilient than concrete, it packs down fairly well and it provides good drainage. Other alternatives include wood and concrete; however, concrete must be covered or your horse could develop leg problems.

The floors in the feed and tack rooms should be of concrete. This will enable you to keep them cleaner and will help keep down the number of rodents. Remember that wherever you use concrete floors, be sure to install drains and slope the floor slightly so you won't have any standing water.

Roofs can be constructed of most any material found on other buildings. The least costly is sheet metal, which has no insulating qualities and is cold in winter and hot during the summer. Skylights in the form of vinyl or plastic sheets are nice, particularly above the aisleways. They allow light to enter and help reduce electric bills. Panels such as these must be carefully installed or they will leak.

Stalls vary in size with 10' × 12' or 12' × 12' being fine for most riding horses. Stall walls may be built of either wood or concrete blocks. Blocks are more durable and easier to maintain. On the other hand, concrete can be damp and because of its rigidity might not make the best home for a confirmed stall-kicker.

Wooden boards, two inches thick, make an excellent stall lining. The back and sides of the stalls should be solid from the floor up to four and a half feet. Above this, vertical metal rails or metal grating can be used for added ventilation and light. The front of the stall should definitely be constructed in this way. Your horse will then be able to see out, but won't be able to bite at whatever annoys him in the aisleway. It's nice if all of the stall walls can be made this way. The only problem arises when a horse develops a dislike for his neighbor, in which case they are better separated by a solid wall.

One kind of metal grating that is economical and easy to use is known as hog panelling. It comes in 4' × 15' sheets which is a convenient size to use on the upper section of stall walls. A note of caution must be added, however, and that is never to use grating on the bottom four feet of the stall walls where a horse could kick and get entangled in it.

Each stall should have a ceiling at least eight feet high. A light bulb enclosed in a metal cage should hang from the ceiling in each stall. If there is only one doorway in the stall, the opposite wall should have a window for ventilation and light. It doesn't need to have glass and can be simply an opening in the wall that can be closed in bad weather by a hinged wooden door. If glass is used in the window, it will of course have to be protected by metal grating.

Each stall should have facilities for water and feed. Automatic waterers are a big time saver for busy horseowners. If you are going to use buckets, invest in the sturdiest you can find. Buy a four gallon flat back bucket or one designed to fit in a corner so your horse won't be inclined to play with it.

A good way to attach a water bucket to the wall is to first attach a strong ring to the wall. Then, snap one end of a two-ended snap to the ring and one end to the bucket. This way it's easy to lift the buckets on and off. Rather than carrying full buckets of water around the barn, we've found it much more convenient to have a hose long enough to reach all of the stalls so we can take the water to the bucket.

You'll need two separate feeders; one for grain and one for hay. Hay racks look like one-sided baskets with slats so the horse can get to the hay. Hay racks used to be made of wood, but many horses ate the wood instead of the hay, so now they are mostly made of steel. Grain feeders are usually tubs of some sort that should be attached to the wall at a height of three and a half feet. You can make them yourself, but if you use wood, cover the edges with metal strips so your horse can't eat it. There are many commercial feeders on the market and these are used by most horseowners.

Everyone has a problem with their horses spilling their grain while they eat. There are some commercial devices such as rings that you can buy and insert on top of the feeder. These alleviate the problem somewhat, while some people think simply putting large stones in the bucket helps. Just make sure the stones are too large for the horse to swallow.

When you install the hay rack, locate it above the grain tub so any loose hay will fall into the grain feeder where your horse can continue eating it. And when building a stable, consider leaving a small opening in the wall just large enough for a scoop over the grain tub so you can feed without even entering the stall.

Any stall doors should be at least four feet wide or you'll find your horse crashing against one side or the other as you lead him in and out. Sliding doors are best for the side leading into the aisleway, even though they may be more expensive. With sliding doors you won't have to worry about blocking the aisleway with open doors as you do with conventionally hinged doors. If you must use hinged doors, have a hook on the outside so you can leave the door all the way open against the wall. Install a secure stable latch on the stall door. These are specially designed for horses and can be purchased at your local saddlery. Although these latches cost a dollar or two more, a horse isn't likely to get it open and let himself out.

For stall doors that lead to the outside, it's nice to have dutch doors, which are the kind that are cut in half so you can open and close the top and bottom separately. In good weather the top half can be opened for ventilation and so your horse can see out.

A final word about stalls is a warning to cover all exposed wood edges with metal strips. Horses that spend long hours in a stall become bored and often relieve their condition by chewing on wood. Not only is this habit destructive to the stable, it isn't very healthy for your horse either! After you have protected the edges in this way, creosote all the wood to preserve it and to discourage wood chewing.

Aisleways need to be at least ten to twelve feet wide, so you can lead your horse through comfortably. Then too, wide aisleways give you enough room to drive a truck or tractor through, which you might want to do when stall cleaning or delivering grain and hay. Anything you can do to relieve the drudgery makes keeping a horse much more fun!

Be certain to put several electrical outlets in the aisle so it's well-lighted and so you can plug in electrical appliances such as clippers, foggers and small water heaters. The floor of the aisleway can be either cement or clay, each having its advantages and disadvantages. Cement is easily cleaned and permanent. Clay is better for horses' feet and legs, is less slippery and less costly.

Wherever your aisle has the least traffic, install crossties so you can securely tie your horse when you need to care for him. Crossties are best made of sturdy chain or heavy rope. Securely anchor them to the wall so they won't give way if a horse pulls back on them. The snaps which are used to attach the crossties to each side of the halter must be strong, too. Remember, this equipment is expected to hold over 1,-000 pounds. Horses sometimes forget their good manners, so it pays

Crossties may be needed when grooming a horse.

to install proper equipment right at the beginning. Set the crossties at a height of about five feet. Without a horse in them, they should just about meet in the center. Then they won't be so slack that a horse can dance around in them or so tight the horse can't move his head. If you have a cement floor, put down rubber mats where you have crossties so your horse won't slip and fall down. Make sure you have enough light and an electrical outlet near your crossties, since you'll groom, saddle and have the horse shod there.

Each end of the aisleway should have a sliding door as wide as the aisle itself. Then you can open these doors for ventilation and light, and trucks and tractors will be able to drive right through.

Next, plan an area or small room where you can store your tack. If you plan to build a small stable, your tack and feed rooms can be combined. Your tack will probably get a little more dusty that way, but if you need to save money combining the two is a good idea. Your tack room should have a concrete floor and doors that lock. You'll need saddle racks along one wall and these should be at least

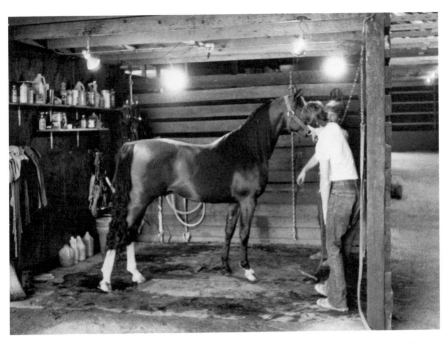

This wash rack is complete with running water, a drain, and needed supplies. Notice that rubber mats are used on the floor.

twenty-four inches apart. To save room, you can build another row above the first, but it can be a problem lifting heavy Western saddles up to this top row. It's a good idea to have pegs of some sort to hang bridles from. If you have a Western saddle, the horn is useful for this purpose. An old medicine cabinet or kitchen cabinet can be handy in a tack room for storing the many odds and ends you're sure to collect. Like most of us, you'll always have more equipment than you have storage space. Another invaluable piece of equipment in a tack room is the tack trunk. They are an ideal place to store blankets, sheets, leg wraps and the like. If you can't afford a tack trunk, maybe you can make one of plywood or substitute an old suitcase.

If the feed room has a cement floor, it will help keep out rats and mice. The room should be large enough to store at least a four-month supply of hay as well as three to four weeks' supply of grain. Barns and stables used to have hay lofts, but most modern barns do not,

A modest tack room with saddle and bridle racks.

probably because they are expensive to build. If you build a loft, have
a slot in the floor above the hay rack in each stall so the hay can simply be dropped down.

The feed room should have a secure container for storing grain or
feed concentrates. This container must have a tightly fitting lid to
keep out rodents and moisture. You might want to keep the feed
scoop in the grain bin, so you'll always know where it is.

A fundamental rule about feed rooms is that they must be kept
locked. Horses that accidentally get out of their stalls will head right
for the feed where they will eat until they are foundered or get colic.
Horses are most ingenious at getting the most secure lids off grain
bins, so if you can't afford a separate feed room, lock your feed containers. Never leave grain where a horse can possibly get to it!

And finally, when planning a barn consider locating a regular, peo-
ple-sized door leading from the outside to the tack room. It's frustrating to struggle with huge sliding doors in terrible weather when all
you want is to get yourself inside for a few moments.

Pastured horses have the opportunity for exercise as well as grazing.

OUTDOORS

PASTURES

Having a pasture to turn your horse out in is a great advantage both in keeping him fit and saving you expense in feeding him. In most parts of the country, a pasture with a small shelter is all that's needed to keep a horse. While a horse won't get in top condition if he lives entirely in a pasture, he will keep fit enough for most of our not-so-demanding needs; especially if he is fed a little grain to supplement his grazing.

A pasture of two to three acres is large enough to feed one horse in the summer if he's given supplemental grain. Of course, this won't keep a horse through the winter if you live in a cold climate where the grass stops growing after a frost. It should suffice for at least four to six months if the grass is lush and there is plenty of rainfall to keep the grass growing.

In the spring, horses should be kept in stalls or in a dry lot until the new grass is firmly established. Soft spring pastures can quickly be torn up by playful horses. When the ground firms and the horses are ready to be put out to pasture, introduce them to it slowly over a period of a few days. In this way, they won't be as likely to overeat the sweet tender new grass, which can cause founder.

Before turning your horse out in a strange pasture, carefully walk over it to be sure the fence is sturdy and there's no debris lying around on which your horse could injure himself. If a horse is being put in a pasture with other horses for the first time, we like to let them first get acquainted over a fence. Notice the reaction of the occupants to the newcomer. If they are noticeably hostile, try acclimating the newcomer slowly. For example, you could put them together for the first few days only when someone is around to intervene in case of trouble. We've seen unwelcome horses actually run through fences by jealous herd bosses, so be on the lookout for problems. Usually, time takes care of these hierarchy struggles, so don't be discouraged if your horse is not immediately accepted into a herd. Horses do love company and undoubtedly prefer companionship once they get their initial differences agreed upon.

FENCES

There are several kinds of fencing suitable for horses. These include wooden posts and rails, metal pipes or woven wire. Barbed wire fences should be avoided if it is at all possible. Cattle and other animals can be contained by barbed wire but horses, being somewhat more nervous, too often try to run through barbed wire and end up cut, if not permanently injured. If you must use barbed wire, tie strips of cloth on the strands to make sure the horses see it in case they suddenly panic and take off running.

Wooden or metal pipes are acceptable for fence posts, but the metal rods used for barbed wire fences are not sturdy enough for horses. If you are building a wooden fence, use eight foot long posts that are 4″ × 4″ square. These posts should be set three feet in the ground after being creosoted to prevent insect damage and rotting. This will leave five feet above the ground, which is a sufficient height for horses, although some smaller breeds can be kept in a four and a half foot high fence. Set the posts six feet apart. Nail twelve foot long rails to the inside of the posts, staggering them as shown in the illustration to increase the strength of the fence. The rails used should be

Split-rail wooden fences separate these small pastures.

2″ × 6″, although with rising lumber costs, you may get by with thinner boards. The minimum number of rails is three, with four or five better. The corner posts should be larger than the line posts and should be braced as should the posts on which gates are hung.

Wire mesh fences are also satisfactory for horses. In the Midwest, mesh field fencing is very common. Field fencing comes in a roll three hundred and thirty feet long. It can easily be anchored to round wooden posts, 4″ × 4″ square posts or split locust posts. The height of field fencing varies, but for horses it needs to be forty-seven inches high. The problem with this fencing is that horses try to eat over it, which eventually causes it to mash down. To help overcome this problem, we recommend a wooden rail or one strand of electric wire along the top.

Metal pipe fencing has the advantage of sturdiness, resistance to insects and decay and the inability of horses to chew on it. Additionally, it is safe, attractive and nearly maintenance-free. Although metal pipe fencing is rather expensive, it is ideal in warm, humid climates where wood tends to decay and is subject to nearly year-round insect attacks.

Made of metal, this wide pasture gate is very sturdy.

Gates can be constructed of any of the above materials. Wooden gates are often heavy, so when a gate needs to be longer than about ten feet, aluminum and steel are preferable. You'll need one gate per pasture, at least ten feet wide to accomodate a truck, tractor or manure speader. Remember to locate some smaller gates conveniently for people. If you make the smaller gate at least four feet wide, you can easily get your horse out without having to open a larger, more awkward gate. Another good idea is to put a couple of fence posts twelve to eighteen inches apart and leave this opening for people to slip in and out. Just remember to make the opening large enough for people to slip through, but not so large your horse can get through.

Many horses try to eat over a fence or lean over it when they become excited by something outside the pasture. One way to save a lot of wear and tear on your fence is to stretch a strand of electric wire along the top. Electric wire alone is never a recommended fence for horses. When panicked they can easily run over or through it, which leaves you with an injured or loose horse, or both.

Although we said earlier a fence four and a half to five feet high is adequate, stallions are an exception to this. Stallion paddocks should be higher and stronger, ideally high enough so they can't get their heads over the top. Then, too, a "hot" wire along the top might be helpful.

SHELTER

A horse needs to have some shelter from the sun and wind. If you have trees in your pasture, fine. You'll notice your horse lounging under them during the heat of a summer's day or using them to escape from a harsh wind.

If your pasture is treeless, or if you want to add a shelter, a three-sided shed may be the answer. These sheds should be built with the open side to the south and a sloping roof which drains away from the open side. A wide overhang will keep the sun from shining in, making it cool in summer. Sheds can be built just large enough for a horse or two or big enough for ten or more. Hay racks can be installed on the inside of the long wall to make it easier to feed those horses that aren't brought in to be fed.

You are fortunate if your pasture has a running stream. Then, as long as it doesn't run dry or freeze during the winter, your horse will have a constant supply of fresh water to drink. Ponds aren't nearly as good as streams because they can become stagnant and contaminated or covered with algae. Generally speaking, they don't provide as clean and safe a water supply as running, fresh water.

If you have no natural water supply, you'll need to provide another source such as tubs. Galvanized stock troughs as well as smaller tubs can be bought at most farm supply stores. Buckets are not recommended because horses tend to play with them and knock them over. Then too, they need to be filled so frequently that they aren't practical for more than one horse. Something that many people have used quite effectively has been old bath tubs. They hold many gallons of water and can easily be emptied and rinsed simply by pulling the plug. Automatic waterers are available for pastures, but they must be the kind that do not freeze. Because only one or two horses can drink from them at a time, they aren't practical for large herds of horses.

GRASSES

While we have given you some general guidelines on the size of pasture necessary to support a horse, this largely depends on the quality of the grass. Fields as small as an acre or two can be used as pasture as long as they are not overgrazed and allowed to rest when the grass gets short. On the other hand, if a pasture contains largely coarse weeds and little grass or if it is overgrazed and turned to mud, several acres may be necessary to support a horse.

There are many grasses on which horses thrive. Blue grass, timothy, brome and orchard grass all make excellent pasturage. To one of these, you might add a legume such as clover or alfalfa because of its higher protein level. Too much of these legumes could be harmful to horses. Being greedy, horses overeat legumes and can get colic or founder themselves. If you have questions about what grass grows best in your area, talk to the people at your state agricultural college or at a local farm supply store.

We don't feel that chemical weed killers should be used in horse pastures. The weeds must be kept down, but this is best done by mowing the field to a height of about eight inches. This won't affect the grass but will cut off many weeds before they go to seed.

THE DAILY SCHEDULE

Although you probably bought your horse to ride, if you decide to feed and care for him yourself you'll also discover there is a great deal of personal satisfaction in keeping a horse healthy and happy. On the other hand, as with most things we find rewarding, caring for a horse involves a lot of responsibility and hard work. Stabled horses need care every morning and evening. They get hungry and thirsty whatever the weather and regardless of how you feel about the chores at that moment. While caring for a horse is relatively easy work in nice weather, no one likes to leave a comfortable home on a cold, blustery day to feed and water his horse.

Assuming that you've made the decision to care for a horse yourself, your first reaction is probably, "Alright, I'm willing to do the work, but exactly what is it I will have to do?"

First, all horses need to be fed at least twice daily, at as evenly spaced intervals as possible. Unlike dogs or cats that can eat a lot of food at once, most horses are used to eating small amounts all day while they graze. They have small stomachs for their size, and because of this do better with frequent small feedings. Stalled horses, or those not able to graze, should be fed at least twice daily—once in the morning and once in the evening. A third ration at noon is a good idea if you can work it into your schedule. Many horseowners divide the grain rations evenly between the feedings, but reserve most of the hay for the evening meal. Two recommended schedules are listed below.

Schedule 1

7 a.m.   ½ grain, ⅓ hay
6 p.m.   ½ grain, ⅔ hay

Schedule 2

7 a.m.   ⅓ grain, ⅓ hay
12 noon ⅓ grain
6 p.m.   ⅓ grain, ⅔ hay

If your horse has good lush pasture available, he won't need hay and his grain ration can be reduced or eliminated depending on his condition and the work he's expected to do. Mature idle horses get along on grass alone, but those being worked under saddle a couple of hours a week should be given grain at least once a day.

Horses thrive on routine. They quickly learn the sound of familiar footsteps or the motor of their owner's car. We even know of horses that nicker as their owner's car passes by on an adjacent road. Horses learn to appreciate the opening of the grain bin and show their excitement with whinnies of anticipation. Because of this, it's less disturbing to feed in the same sequence each time, beginning and ending with the same horse.

The feeding itself should take only a few minutes per horse. Convenient facilities can do much to make this chore easy and safe. These conveniences include such things as openings in the stall for hay and grain as well as other helps that we mentioned earlier in this chapter about building a stable.

Horses drink about twelve gallons of water each day. Automatic waterers will ensure that your horse has available a fresh and constant supply. Naturally, automatic waterers cost more than buckets, but if you have a busy schedule like most of us, they may well be worth the extra expense. If you use water buckets, be sure to water your horse at least twice a day and more often in hot, dry weather if you can. Water is essential for horses to aid digestion and to maintain body temperature. If you use buckets or tubs to water, they should be rinsed and wiped out daily. Any water left over from the previous day should be poured out and fresh water added. When a horse has not drunk his water, don't just pass him by. Horses have been known to manure in their water bucket. Of course, they then don't drink the water so you'll have to empty the bucket, and disinfect and refill it with fresh water.

Another not-so-pleasant chore that goes with keeping a horse is stall cleaning. Luckily, most backyard horses are turned out in a pasture or paddock thus reducing the litter in the stall. In this case, the stall would need to be cleaned less frequently. Stalled horses, however, need their stalls cleaned every day with fresh bedding added each time. In fact, some well-supervised stables have the manure picked out of the stalls at least twice a day.

In addition to the daily removal of fresh manure, stalls should be thoroughly cleaned down to the flooring at least once a week. Remove all of the bedding and sprinkle lime liberally over the entire floor. The lime will neutralize the acid from the horse's urine and at the same time reduce stable odor considerably. Fresh bedding should be added until it is adequately deep. A bale of straw for a 12′ x 12′ stall or at least four inches of sawdust should do nicely.

BEDDING

The purpose of bedding is to absorb urine, to provide a comfortably soft place for your horse to lie down and to insulate him from the damp, cold ground. There are several popular beddings on the market. We don't especially recommend one over the other, but feel you can base your choice on availability, cost and storage facilities.

Wheat straw makes a fine bedding in that it is absorbent, economical and a good insulator. Straw is sold in bales which makes it convenient to store. The best straw is bright yellow, long-stemmed and free from dust. In some parts of the country or at certain times of the year, straw can be more expensive so this is something you'll have to check into. Then, too, some greedy horses eat straw bedding. Since little can be done to discourage these horses, other than muzzling them, they should be bedded down on a less palatable material.

Sawdust is another popular bedding. It can often be obtained free of charge from a sawmill. This material is loose which means you'll need a covered bin to store it in. An empty stall makes a nice storage space for loose bedding. Sawdust is economical and absorbent, but is not as good an insulator as straw. It can be drying to a horse's feet, too, if he is stalled on it all of the time.

Wood shavings have qualities similar to sawdust. They are economical and in fact are sometimes given away at sawmills. If this is not the case in your area, you might be able to buy them already baled. Shavings are absorbent, clean-smelling and make a fine bedding. They are not palatable and are recommended, as is sawdust, for greedy straw-eaters.

Once sufficient bedding is in the stall, you can pick out manure and soiled bedding as necessary. If you bed with straw, you'll need a five- to ten-tine manure fork for stall cleaning. An ordinary shovel works well when sawdust is used. The urine seeps through to the bottom of the bedding, so as you clean the stalls each day, check under the top layer of bedding to be sure to remove the soiled under-layer. Each day, replace the same amount of bedding you remove, so your horse will always have a comfortable, clean bed.

Some stables use a wheelbarrow to remove the manure from the barn, while others use a large wicker basket. You might even want to use both by dropping the soiled litter into a basket in the stall, then emptying it into a wheelbarrow which you can use to carry the debris to the manure pile. Try to coordinate the stall cleaning with the frequent grooming that stalled horses need, so that when you put your freshly groomed horse away he is returned to a clean stall.

EXERCISE

If your horse has a paddock or pasture he can get to from his stall, not only will he benefit from the exercise, but you'll save a lot of stall cleaning. Show horses that are being brought to peak condition need to be kept stalled all of the time, but most horses thrive on the fresh air and exercise of a pasture. On the other hand, simply running in a pasture won't get a horse in top condition. This requires a regular routine under saddle, in harness or on the lunge line.

All horses need exercise so they can keep both mentally and physically fit. Stalled horses that are not ridden or lunged should be turned out in a pasture or paddock for at least an hour every day. It is very sad indeed to see an otherwise healthy, active horse penned up in a stall day after day! Some large stables customarily turn out their horses in the daytime during the winter, while stalling them at night. During the summer months, this schedule can be reversed so the horses are stalled during the heat of the day and turned out at night. If you don't have time to ride every day and don't have access to a pasture or paddock, twenty to thirty minutes of lunging will refresh your horse and maintain his muscle tone.

PEST CONTROL

Although you may have designed and constructed a storybook stable and keep it perfectly clean, you're bound to be troubled at one time or another by unwelcome rodents and insects. The lure of warmth and spoiled hay and grain is inviting to mice and rats, neither of which is very desirable.

The first thing you must do is to try to keep them out in the first place. Keeping the aisleways, tack and feed rooms swept clean of debris will reduce a number of hiding and breeding places. Grain stored in tightly closed containers will reduce their food supply. Remember, rodents can and do chew through paper feed sacks, so this is not a good way to store grain.

After you've followed these methods to keep rodents out, we next recommend a good barn cat. Horses and cats usually get along well together. One of our confident mother cats even had her litter of kittens in an occupied stall. Surprisingly enough, none of the kittens was stepped on although we really don't think a stall is the best feline maternity ward! Ecologically speaking, cats are a safe and effective way of controlling rodents. We prefer cats to poison which can be harmful to other animals and whose careless use recently caused the death of several race horses.

Other than rodents, which are certainly a year-round problem, you'll also have to control insects during the summer. Again, prevention is of utmost importance. Manure piles and dirty bedding attract insects, so frequent stall cleaning and manure disposal is recommended. If your stable is relatively airtight, a good way to eliminate flying insects is the use of new devices that are attached to the wall and spray a fine mist of

This handy device is an electric insect exterminator.

insecticide at frequent intervals. An added advantage of these devices is that the insecticide can be replaced with air freshener once in a while.

There are also portable insecticide sprayers that can be used as they are needed. Be sure to follow the manufacturers' directions and be especially careful not to contaminate your feed and water supplies.

If you use good fly control measures in your barn, you won't need to use other products directly on your horse. When you take him out to ride, however, he might need to be sprayed or wiped with repellent. Ear nets worn by horses may look a bit silly, but they are effective if you're riding in an area where insects are a problem.

KEEPING YOUR STABLE SAFE

While it's nearly impossible to prevent all accidents around a barn, there are a few precautions you should take to minimize their occurrence.

General good housekeeping, or "stablekeeping" if you prefer, will reduce accident-causing situations. Putting rakes, buckets and pitch forks away immediately after use will keep people and horses from falling over them. Also, find a receptacle for the baling wire or twine you remove from the hay and straw. Then you'll never have to worry about tripping over it or having loose wire swept into your horse's stall for him to get tangled up in.

It's a good idea to have a fire extinguisher in your barn in case of emergency. Cigarette smoking is always hazardous wherever there is dried hay and straw. If you don't smoke and worry about others smoking in your barn, no smoking signs should be posted and highly visible to alert smokers to the danger and help discourage them.

MANURE DISPOSAL

Once you've carefully cleaned all of your stalls, the next problem to face is what to do with all of the manure you've collected. First, be sure to locate the manure pile where it's convenient to get to from the barn and with a truck. Then, if possible, locate it out of sight and smell.

Because manure has an unpleasant odor, is unsightly and attracts insects, have it hauled away as often as possible. Because manure is an excellent fertilizer, you should find people interested in getting rid of it for you. If you have a garden, you might want to use it yourself. You can check with farmers or greenhouse owners who might want to use it. You can charge for the manure, pricing it by the truckload, but we've been satisfied simply to give it away to anyone willing to come and get it.

HORSE TRAILERS

One major investment most horseowners make is a horse trailer. As more and more people are acquiring backyard horses, the two-car family is rapidly becoming the one-car, one truck and trailer family. This way, hay can be hauled, mounds of manure can be disposed of and horses can be transported about.

Today there are many new trailer manufacturers who are trying to capitalize on the horseowner's desire for mobility. Up until 1970, few trailers were built thus making few old trailers available. Combined with the high cost of new trailers, this has caused the price of used trailers to rise, sometimes higher than their original purchase price.

If you think you'd like a used trailer, remember that for each one available there are several potential buyers. If you find one, act fast because good used trailers are not for sale very long.

If money is a factor, and it usually is, we still urge you to avoid the home-made trailers that are sometimes available. We've seen wobbly one-axle contraptions as well as some with no springs at all. We'd never put one of our horses in one, and recommend you don't either. In other words, safety has to be your first consideration. A bit of flaking paint is no problem at all when compared with a rotted floor your horse could stick his foot through.

KINDS OF TRAILERS

Trailers range from luxurious, smooth riding, 12-horse vans to quite adequate and usable one-horse models. Some come equipped with living quarters in front and others with a dressing room. Most trailers hitch to the rear of your car or truck, while others attach to the bed of a truck. These are called goose-necks or 5th wheelers. If you want a four-horse trailer or one larger, this kind of hitch is preferable since the weight of the trailer is centered on the bed of the truck rather than on the bumper.

The most common trailer is a two-horse model with a tack compartment under the manger section. The trailer is constructed with two axles and four wheels that are attached to springs to help cushion the ride. Two-inch-thick hardwood provides the flooring. In less costly models, the trailer walls are made only of metal; however, better made trailers are lined with wood paneling. Deluxe models will also have an inner metal lining.

Dividers should be three-feet high and can be solid or only one-board wide. For mares and foals we prefer partial dividers so a foal can nurse and touch his mother. This divider also prevents a horse from scram-

A two-horse trailer.

bling since he has no inside wall to climb. Of course, horses that are inclined to kick are best hauled with solid dividers.

While standard models have rear doors five feet high, deluxe models also have upper doors which completely enclose the back. Such trailers usually have windows on the side rather than a simple opening. Although these features do cost more, when you have to haul in cold or wet weather, you'll be glad to have them.

Some trailers have a back ramp which is lowered for the horse to load and unload. Both kinds of rear doors have their good and bad points, so it's just a matter of taste. Sometimes horses load or unload better with a ramp so they don't have to jump into or step out of the trailer. On the other hand, an excited horse might scrape himself if he steps off the side of the ramp.

Most newer trailers have another small door called an escape door which opens into the right stall. This gives the handler a way out if he leads his horse into the trailer.

This four-horse goose-neck trailer includes living quarters and has a side unloading ramp.

Trailers should have electric lights and in some states must have electric brakes which are wired into the towing vehicle or hydraulic brakes which operate from the hitch. Regulations vary from state to state regarding lights and brakes, so check to see what's required in your state. We've used trailers without brakes, but never on curvy mountain roads or at high speeds.

If you have a limited budget, you might look for a used trailer. Most factory models have a metal plate which gives the brand, model number and year. As with horses, owners sometimes conveniently forget how old their trailer is, so check the plate. While an older trailer can still be sound and safe, the age does give you some clue as to its condition. Even though tires may not have much use, they do dry rot in time.

In inspecting a used trailer, lift up the floor mats—which you should never haul without—and very carefully inspect the floor. If it has rotted at all, you'll probably have to replace it. Make sure the electrical wiring works and that the doors close tightly. Heavy butterfly latches are much safer than the older, smaller latches. While new trailers are at least 6'6" tall, some older models are only 6' or 6'2" in height. Check this out because if you have a very tall horse, he won't ride too comfortably in a short trailer.

Make sure the trailer has butt bars or chains so the horse can't lean back against the trailer door and push it out. We've even heard of horses pushing out the back door of a trailer while it was traveling down the road!

Before buying a trailer, finally check the understructure and make sure neither axle is bent. Inspect the hitch for any signs of damage.

As with just about anything else, you usually get what you pay for so beware of any real bargains.

CHAPTER 5

Feeding

Most new horseowners are overwhelmed with well intended advice on what and how much to feed their horses. Feed stores carry an endless variety of feeds, all of which are highly advertised in glowing terms, which further confuses the issue. In this chapter we hope to show you just how simple feeding can be, although now you might think it is a highly complex subject.

First of all, the feed you give your horse is simply the fuel by which he grows and maintains his physical wellbeing. In addition to this, it provides the energy which is essential for him to function. Feed cannot grow a poorly bred colt into a champion, nor can it make a barren mare settle or turn an average runner into a stakes winner. But, on the other hand, good nutrition allows a horse to grow and function at his full potential.

Just as there are many roads to Rome, so too are there many ways to feed a horse. Although feed manufacturers would have you think otherwise, there is no magic formula to follow. The feed ration necessary for your horse depends upon his age, condition, level of activity and what feeds are easily obtainable in your area.

NUTRITION

Before we discuss the various kinds of feed, let's take a brief look at the horse's digestive system. Then you'll have a better idea of why you have to be so careful about what you put in there. The first thing to remember is that the horse, in his natural state, is a grazing animal. He is best equipped to consume food continually, rather than to gorge himself at one time as hunting animals do.

THE DIGESTIVE SYSTEM OF THE HORSE

Our traditional household pets, the dog and cat, have little trouble with their digestive systems. If they eat something that doesn't agree with them, up it comes in the form of vomit. We once had an Irish setter that ate a whole ham at one time with no ill effects. But the poor horse is not so lucky! If he sneaks into the grain bin, the result is likely to be colic or founder, both very serious illnesses.

Once a horse decides to eat, he first grasps the food with his lips and his incisors, or front teeth. If he is grazing, the incisors bite off the grass. The tongue then sends the food to the molars, which are located further back in the mouth. The function of the molars is to grind the food until it is of digestible sized particles.

As the horse chews, moisture providing saliva is produced along with an enzyme which begins the process of breaking down the food. Once the food has been chewed thoroughly, it is then passed through a longer tube called the esophagus to the stomach. The food is passed down the esophagus by a series of muscular contractions. At this point, it is important to note that these contractions are only able to pass food *down* the esophagus. If a horse somehow swallows something that doesn't agree with him, unlike humans and most other animals he has no way to bring it back up the way it went down. The only way out is through the rest of the digestive system. This is a major reason why digestive problems are so serious for horses.

The digestive process actually begins in the stomach. A horse's stomach has a capacity of about two to four gallons, which isn't really very large considering his overall size. As a matter of fact, it seems quite small when compared with other animals such as the cow, which has a ten gallon capacity.

The main purpose of the stomach is to break down protein and fats. Once a horse has eaten, the food passes through the stomach very quickly. So quickly, in fact, that the first part of a meal passes to the intestine before the last of a meal is consumed.

A horse's stomach operates best when it's about two-thirds full. Because he has such a small stomach, if a horse is fed too much roughage he may tire more easily. This is one reason race horses are not fed hay on the morning they are to race.

The contents of the stomach then pass through to the small intestine, which is a small tube only three to four inches in diameter when distended with food. It is about seven feet long and has a twelve gallon capacity. The small intestine also breaks down protein, fats and sugar. It does this with the help of bile from the liver and pancreatic juice.

Once this process is completed, the contents then pass on to the large intestine which is designed to break down the fiber in the horse's diet. The large intestine is composed of the cecum, great colon, small colon and rectum.

The cecum is about four feet long, one foot in diameter and is designed to break down fiber and cellulose which the stomach and small intestine are poorly equipped to do. Fiber is the main component of roughage such as grass and hay. As we mentioned, in the horse the cecum is located after the stomach and small intestine. In the cow, it's located ahead of the small intestine. Also, the horse's cecum breaks down fiber by bacterial action rather than more efficient enzymes as do cow's. This means that horses absorb protein and starch efficiently, but don't do as well with fiber. This is why horses need leafy hay with a minimum of fibrous stems. Because of this action in the cecum, hay serves not only as bulk for horses, but also provides other nutrients.

The next stage in the digestive process of the horse involves the twelve foot long, one foot wide great colon. In the great colon, which is almost always full of food, digestion by bacterial action is continued.

Most of the remaining nutrients are absorbed as the contents begin to solidify.

In the small colon, which is almost as long as the great colon but only about four inches in diameter, the contents become solid. As the remaining moisture is absorbed into the walls of the colon, the balls of manure form. Finally, from the small colon, the waste enters the rectum and is eliminated.

PURPOSE OF FEED

As we mentioned at the beginning of this chapter, feed is basically a fuel which provides a source of energy for your horse. Although there are many excellent feeds on the market, our problem as a horseowner is to find the formula which best fills our horse's needs. Just as an economy car doesn't have the same fuel requirements as a race car, a family pleasure horse shouldn't be fed the same feed as a race horse.

Another very basic purpose of feed is to maintain the horse's bodily functions. A mature horse at pasture still needs to eat enough to supply his body with the basic nutrients to keep his heart beating, maintain his body temperature, his digestive process and his limited muscular activity. If he eats more than is necessary for his limited activity, he gets fat. If he doesn't get enough feed, he loses weight.

Young horses require additional nutrients for growth. This growth period is limited, which means that after a certain period the growth stops. However, if a young horse gets an insufficient quantity of feed he might have enough to sustain life, but not enough left for growth. Unless corrected quite early, this leaves the horse permanently stunted. If a mature horse falls upon hard times for a couple of years, it's reasonable to assume that once he's fed properly again he will become fit and able to perform. This is not so with young horses. A poorly fed foal with an excessive number of worms simply cannot become as big physically as if he had been fed well. The capacity of his heart and lungs will not be the same, nor will his bones be as dense as they might have been.

Horses that work hard require more feed than those that are idle. Work, especially at fast paces, requires a great deal of energy which can only be provided by nutritious feed. Two or three year old horses in race training have particularly high feed requirements, because not

111

only must they have sufficient food intake to maintain themselves but to grow and work as well.

Pregnant mares also have special feed requirements. Although we may be careful about feeding a foal once he's born, he also has very definite nutritional requirements while he's still inside his mother. From the time of conception his growth begins, making it particularly important that the mare is fed properly. During the time the foal is nursing, the mare's food intake should also increase. Not only does she need to maintain herself, she must produce up to eighteen quarts of milk each day.

FEED FOR ENERGY

In order for a horse to be able to work as well as maintain himself, he'll have to eat enough feed to provide energy. These energy requirements are met through the intake of carbohydrates and fats. For horses, carbohydrates are more commonly supplied than fats. Carbohydrates are found in most of the common feeds, are economical and easily digestible. Fats, on the other hand, are not as easily digested by horses.

Horses which receive an insufficient amount of high energy feed lose weight and show lack of vigor. Generally, to increase the energy level for horses, the hay consumption is lowered and the quantity of grain is increased. This is why performance horses are fed more grain than lightly used pleasure horses.

PROTEIN

While energy is obviously needed in order for the body to function properly, protein is used for more specific purposes. It is required for the physical development of young horses, for the growth of an unborn foal, for the production of milk and to maintain vital organs and muscle tissue.

Providing the required amount of protein for a horse is not as simple as it is for most other animals that eat meat, a prime source of protein. Also, there are more than twenty kinds of amino acids that make up the protein requirement and some grains do not contain all twenty. Generally used plant proteins which are fed to horses include legume hay, linseed meal, cottonseed meal and soybean meal.

MINERALS

As with all living things, horses require certain minerals to maintain their well-being and, in particular, for their skeletal development. The skeleton of a horse weighs more than one hundred pounds, fifty of which is minerals and most of this is calcium and phosphorous. These minerals must come from somewhere and therefore are an obvious requirement in your horse's diet.

Since the bones in a young horse are constantly developing, it's very important that foals receive adequate amounts of minerals. The bluegrass of Kentucky is grown on calcium rich limestone soil, so it's no accident that Kentucky has a tradition of raising superior horses.

Recent studies suggest that a horse receive one and one half to two parts calcium to one part phosphorous. If an excessive amount of phosphorous is fed, a condition called osteomalicia can develop. It, in turn, can be corrected by adding calcium to the horse's ration.

If it's felt that a pasture might contain inadequate amounts of calcium or phosphorous, steamed bonemeal or decalcium phosphate should be offered to the horses' free choice.

Salt, or sodium chloride, is an important part of a horse's diet and should always be available. On the average, a horse needs an ounce of salt daily; however, this depends on the temperature and how hard the horse has to work. You've all seen the white stain left on a horse once his sweat has dried. This is salt that has been removed from the body and if it isn't replaced the horse will become tired and weak.

Generally, horses are simply allowed free access to a salt block, which is probably the best and easiest way to provide salt. Some horsemen add a given amount of salt to the feed ration to be sure the horse receives enough. This, however, is done primarily by trainers whose horses work at a fast pace and sweat a lot. A salt block usually does quite well for pleasure horses.

Trace mineralized block salt is the kind most often used. These blocks are usually brick red in color and, while they cost more than salt alone, are definitely worth the difference.

Other trace minerals required by horses include iodine, cobalt, manganese, copper, iron and zinc. While these minerals are usually found in sufficient quantity in the feed, by using a mineral salt block you can be reasonably certain no deficiencies will occur.

VITAMINS

Under normal conditions, a horse's vitamin requirements will be met by a well-balanced ration. Vitamin supplements might be indicated for growing foals, broodmares, breeding stallions, horses confined indoors for long periods of time, or for those having had a poor quality diet.

Presently, we know that horses need vitamins A, B, D and E. Vitamin A is not found in plants, but carotene, which converts to vitamin A in the animal's body, is. Leafy green hay is rich in carotene. As a matter of fact, the green color is said to be an indication of the amount of carotene it contains. As hay is stored it rapidly loses its carotene, with year-old hay being quite deficient.

Fortunately, horses are able to store vitamin A in their bodies. This means that horses grazing on low carotene winter pasture will replenish their vitamin A supply on the lush, green spring grass.

B complex vitamins include thiamine, riboflavin, niacin, choline, panthothenic acid and B_{12}. Again, mature idle horses being fed on good rations should take in adequate levels of the vitamin B complex. High levels of vitamin D are not found in most commonly used feeds, although sun cured hays are one source. Most vitamin D is produced in the horse through his exposure to sunlight. That is why it is important for horses that are kept indoors to receive supplemental vitamin D.

While sufficient vitamin E is probably contained in an adequate diet, supplementation might be recommended for horses under stress. Some breeders believe vitamin E increases the breeding performance of mares and stallions, though it has not been proven conclusively.

WHAT TO FEED YOUR HORSE

Now that we've discussed the nutritional requirements of your horse, we still haven't told you what you need to feed him. As we mentioned earlier, different levels of nutrients are required depending on a horse's age, condition and how he is being used. This means that there is no magic formula that can tell you what to feed your horse. Basically, it is up to you to evaluate the different kinds of feeds available and decide what your horse requires.

The two basic kinds of feed for horses are roughage and concentrates. Roughage includes hay and grass, while the different cereal grains and most pellets are considered concentrates.

Although they might not agree, mature, generally idle horses, can get along quite well entirely on roughage. Of course this assumes that the hay is of good quality, not merely sticks and stems, and the grass isn't grazed down to the roots.

The eating of roughage is nature's way of providing nutrition for horses. Also, it occupies the horse's time and keeps his stomach full. However, if you have a mare in late pregnancy, a nursing mare, a growing foal, breeding stallion or a horse working hard, you'll need to provide it with additional nutrients in the form of concentrates.

Concentrates include oats, corn, bran and barley, whether it is pelleted or whole, cracked, flaked or steamed. As the name implies, concentrates provide a lot of nutrients in each pound. They provide a horse with the extra nutrition he needs for growth or work.

A third type of feed which has been highly promoted is an all-in-one pellet mixture. Some animal nutritionists argued that these formulated feeds would revolutionize horse feeding practices. The basic concept was that by pelleting hay and grain, only one ration would need to be fed. Nutritionally, the concentrate was well-balanced, so it appeared that modern science had made a real breakthrough. But no one had bothered to ask the horse about this new feeding arrangement. It seems that since a horse could eat his ration in ten to fifteen minutes, he would spend the rest of his time eating his fence or barn or whatever else he could get his teeth into. Nutritionally he was satisfied, but psychologically he was bored to death. He had been in the habit of spending a lot of time eating and now had to find something to do with his time.

And yet another problem arose with the feeding of pellets. During the process of pelleting, the ingredients are tightly packed and most of the moisture is extracted to reduce molding. But if pellets are fed and the horse doesn't drink enough water to aid digestion, there is a real danger of impaction. So in the end, except in very special cases, we still rely on a hay and grain ration and suggest you do the same.

For thousands of years, horses were able to do quite well by grazing in a pasture. Of course, they spent most of their time eating, seldom having to exercise except occasionally to outdistance an enemy.

Pastures can still be a major source of nutrients for a horse. A mature, generally idle horse can subsist quite well on pasture alone. Growing horses, those required to work hard, pregnant mares or those nursing a foal will need a supplemental ration.

The grasses found in most pastures include bluegrass, brome, timothy, prairie grass and fescue. Clover, alfalfa and lespedeza are sometimes found in pastures but they are classified as legumes and not a grass. Grass is usually as nutritious as legumes, but not as high in protein. Also, grass has shallower roots than legumes, which means that when rainfall is short, grass dries up and turns brown. On the other hand, legumes have long roots to extract water and tend to grow and stay green even during hot, dry weather. Unfortunately, pastures made up entirely of legumes might be too rich for horses. Thus a blend of grass and legumes is considered best, with a ratio of 75 percent grass to 25 percent legumes ideal.

If you rely on pasture alone to feed your horses, you'll need at least one acre per horse and a good stand of grass. Of course, much more than this will be needed if the soil is poor and the grass sparse. You'll have to keep your horses off of a pasture during early spring, when their hoofs can tear up the tender, young grass in wet soil.

In spring when the grass is lush, a horse should be gradually re-introduced to prevent intestinal problems. For the first few days let him out for only a couple of hours so he won't overeat. We even feed our horses before turning them out, to help prevent overeating. Gorging on grass can cause founder or colic, which are two pretty good reasons to be cautious.

If you do have a good pasture for your horse, consider yourself lucky. Watch it during the hottest, driest months to be sure it doesn't get too short. After a frost, the grass will turn brown and stop growing. At this point, you'll have to start feeding hay, if you haven't already.

It's a good idea to have your pasture analyzed periodically. Talk to the people at your local Extension Service. They can give you the details on what is required. Also, we are convinced of the value of pasture rotation. By this we mean that the available pasture is divided into parts and one area is allowed to rest while the horses graze on the other. Not only does this allow the grass to grow, it reduces worm infestation.

HAY

Hay, along with the grass in pastures, is the most commonly found roughage. Because it is the mainstay of most horse's diets, it is important that good hay be fed. Hay varies greatly in quality, with the best being weed-free, cut before or at maturity and not rained on once it is cut. Good hay smells fresh rather than moldy and is crisp, green and leafy.

Hay is usually divided into two different groups, grass hay and legume hay. Grass hay includes timothy, prairie grass, orchard grass and brome grass. When properly cured, grass hay is very safe for horses, although it doesn't contain as much protein as legumes.

Legume hay includes clover, lespedeza and alfalfa. Although in the past horsemen usually considered timothy hay the best, alfalfa is today becoming more and more popular. It is particularly good for horses which need a lot of protein. The only problem with alfalfa is that if too much of it is fed, some digestive problems can occur, including soft stools or colic. Eight to ten pounds of alfalfa per day will meet most of a horse's energy needs as well as most of his protein needs. A good compromise, if you can find it, is to buy a good mixed hay which contains both legume and grass.

Buying Hay

Hay is ordinarily purchased either by the bale or by the ton. The price you have to pay depends on many things, but basically the amount of hay available in any given year determines the cost. In dry years and during the winter, when hay is scarce, the price will go up. We have found the most economical way to buy hay is right out of the field. Thus it goes directly to your barn, so that the farmer doesn't have to pick it up and store it himself. Besides, the best way to evaluate the quality of hay is when it's freshly cut and still in the field.

The usual procedure is for hay to be cut, allowed to cure or dry thoroughly and then baled. If it rains after the hay is cut and before it's baled, it will have to lay in the field longer to dry. This extra drying time causes the hay to lose nutrients as they tend to leach out.

Hay has the most nutrients if it is cut when it is in early bloom. After this, the food value begins to lessen as the plant begins to go to seed. Not only that, but the stems turn to cellulose, a main component of wood. Obviously, such coarse stemmed hay is harder for a horse to digest.

As we said before, alfalfa has very deep roots, which allow the plant to grow even during dry, hot weather. This means that several cuttings per year can be obtained from a good stand of alfalfa. The first cutting is usually coarse and contains more weeds. The second and third cuttings are better as they are finer stemmed and more weed free than the first cutting. Because of this, they are usually higher priced than the first cutting, too.

Bales are tied with either wire or twine. Wire is stronger than twine, so wire bales are usually heavier. Twine bales weigh from forty to fifty pounds, while wire bales weigh up to seventy-five pounds. Remember that as bales are stored they lose their moisture, so six months after they are baled they won't weigh as much.

Based on what we've told you, it should be pretty obvious that the cheapest hay is not often the best value. Small bales of over-mature, yellow hay is worth little nutritionally, nor are bales filled with weeds that are sometimes sold as "mixed" hay.

Something else to consider is that hay which is baled too wet has a tendency to mold. All hay sweats a bit once it's baled; however, hay that is too wet will trap the moisture inside. We must also provide a word of caution about feeding green hay, especially alfalfa! Before feeding, make sure the bales have no heat left in them. During the sweating period and for a few weeks after baling, alfalfa tends to heat up. Check for this heat by shoving your hand down in the bale and don't feed it until all of the heat is gone.

Finally, when you are trying to judge the quality of hay, look for fine stems with a high percentage of leaves. Most of the protein is in the leaves. Hay which has lost some leaves may not be as nutritious, but at least it is safe. The kind of hay to avoid at all costs is wet or moldy hay, which can be downright dangerous. To be perfectly honest, in dry years we've been forced to feed hay that wasn't very nutritious; however, we took this into consideration by supplementing in other ways. Just be sure you don't pay a high price for small bales or poor quality hay.

Hay is most expensive when purchased in small quantities from your feed store. Another middleman has been added who hopes to make a profit. It's much more economical to find a farmer who will sell to you. If you don't have much storage, he might be willing to let you take some as you need it as long as you contract to buy a larger amount.

When trying to figure out how much to buy, keep in mind that a horse eats one to one and a half pounds of hay per day per each one hundred pounds of his weight. The average riding horse thus will need ten to fifteen pounds of hay each day or about two *tons* per year. Nevertheless, good hay still represents a good value for the horseman.

CONCENTRATES

Concentrates are usually fed to very active horses or those with special nutritional requirements such as growing horses, broodmares or breeding stallions. Concentrates aren't necessary for idle, mature horses that have access to good pasture or hay. Ponies get fat from ordinary rations, so obviously they don't need concentrates. Concentrates, thus, are a feed supplement which increase the nutritional level of the diet.

As we noted earlier, concentrate feeds include the cereal grains, soybeans, linseed and cottonseed meals. While hay is not sold under brand names, many concentrates are. Basically, commercial feeds are mixtures in which the ingredients are the same, but different ratios are used.

OATS

The grain which has traditionally been fed to horses is oats. They are a very safe feed, and horses love them. If they are purchased just after being combined, they might undergo a heating period, so any new oats should be checked carefully before being fed.

The best oats are plump and free of any dust or mold. They are fed either whole or crimped. Crimped oats are mashed so the hull is opened slightly, making them more easily digested. Crimping is especially good for older horses whose teeth aren't as good as they used to be.

CORN

Corn is another grain which is often fed to horses. It is fed on the cob, shelled, flaked or cracked. It is also highly nutritious and horses love it.

Of all these various forms, corn is probably best digested when it is flaked. This flattens the kernel so it resembles a flaky breakfast cereal. When whole corn is fed, some of it goes right through the horse, as you'll notice in the manure. This is especially true if a horse bolts his food rather than chews it thoroughly. Feeding corn on the cob can be somewhat dangerous, especially if the horse bolts it, as he can eat part of the cob and choke on it.

Cracked corn is also often fed to horses. Cracking also improves digestibility; however, in this process some mills remove the part that contains the protein and use it for other high protein rations.

WHEAT BRAN

Wheat bran adds bulk to the diet. It has a slightly laxative effect, however, so it shouldn't make up much of the total concentrate ration.

Wheat bran is especially good for mares at the time of foaling, but the total daily intake shouldn't exceed about two pounds.

PROTEIN SUPPLEMENTS

Soybean meal and cottonseed meal are the most commonly used protein supplements. They are not intended to be used as the whole concentrate ration, but to be added to boost the protein level of the feed. Of these meals, soybean meal is often preferred because it has the most protein readily available to the horse. Until recently, linseed meal, which is made from flax, was the most preferred; now soybean meal has become more popular. Cottonseed meal is another source of protein which is readily available in most southern states.

All of these meals are heavy feeds which, if overfed, can cause digestive problems. Because of this, no more than one pound per day should be fed. Also, horses don't find these meals as tasty as the cereal grains. For this reason, they are often pelleted or used in a sweet feed which has molasses added.

120

Molasses is sometimes added to a feed to make it more tasty as well as to bind the other ingredients together. Since molasses contains little nutritionally, it should merely be a small portion of the concentrate ration.

CORN- AND OAT-BASE GRAIN MIXTURES

Corn and oat mixtures can be adjusted to supply various amounts of protein. Here is a chart of balanced mixtures supplying ten, twelve, fourteen and sixteen percent protein.

Ingredient	10% protein Corn base	10% protein Oat base	12% protein Corn base	12% protein Oat base	14% protein Corn base	14% protein Oat base	16% protein Oat base
			percent of total ration				
Corn	50.0	33.0	54.0	28.0	50.0	25.0	22.0
Oats	38.0	55.0	26.0	54.0	25.0	51.0	46.0
Dehydrated alfalfa meal	5.0	5.0	5.0	5.0	5.0	5.0	5.0
Soybean meal	—	—	8.0	6.0	13.0	12.0	20.0
Molasses	4.5	4.5	4.5	4.5	4.0	4.0	4.0
Limestone	1.0	1.0	1.0	1.0	1.0	1.0	1.0
Dicalcium phosphate	.5	.5	.5	.5	1.0	1.0	1.0
Trace-mineralized salt	1.0	1.0	1.0	1.0	1.0	1.0	1.0

Chart courtesy of R. Battaglia, Purdue University, West Lafayette, Indiana.

WHEN TO FEED YOUR HORSE

Because of their small stomach, horses need to be fed at least twice a day. For example, you might feed ⅓ of the hay and ½ of the grain ration early in the morning and ⅔ of the hay and ½ of the grain in the evening. Because the time from the evening feeding until morning is longer, the extra hay will help keep the horse satisfied during the night. Also, horses are usually worked during the day and shouldn't be fed too much just before they exercise. Finally, it takes a horse about fifteen minutes to chew and swallow a pound of hay. Feeding a larger portion in the evening will give him plenty of time to enjoy his meal.

Because horses are creatures of habit, they should be fed on a regular schedule as much as you find it possible. If they're fed at odd times, they'll tend to be more nervous and irritable. Not only should you keep a regular schedule, if you feed more than one horse, always feed them in the same order each time. In this way, they'll get used to the routine and be more content.

HOW MUCH TO FEED YOUR HORSE

Following are some suggested feed rations. Of course, the exact amount you feed your horse depends on many different factors. Some horses, called "easy keepers," require very little feed to stay in fine condition. Every good horseman watches his horses carefully and adjusts the feed ration as required.

BROODMARES

The feed ration for a broodmare should not be greatly increased until she is in her last three months of pregnancy. As a matter of fact, it's not good for a broodmare to get too fat.

During the first ⅔ of the pregnancy, feed a 10 percent grain ration at the rate of ½ pound per one hundred pounds of body weight. Along with the grain, feed good quality hay at the rate of one pound per hundred pounds of body weight per day.

As a mare nears the last three months of pregnancy, gradually increase the grain ration to about ¾ pounds of grain per hundred pounds of body weight. As the foaling day approaches, if she shows signs of constipation, add a handful of bran to each grain ration.

Because of the needs of the developing foal, a mare's ration must be well-balanced. Sufficient minerals and vitamins are quite essential.

Also, during the time a mare has a nursing foal, she's going to need large quantities of good feed. Thus, you need to gradually increase the protein level and quantity of grain. At the time of peak milk production, which occurs when the foal is two to three months old, the mare should be fed about one pound per day per hundred pounds of body weight of a 15 percent protein ration. Pasture or hay should be offered free choice.

At peak milk production, a mare will produce about thirty-five pounds of milk per day. In order to do this and stay in top condition,

A mare with a nursing foal must receive nourishing feed to keep her and the foal in top condition.

she must be well nourished. Also, she'll need fresh water available at all times. Iodized salt should be available, as should dicalcium sulfate or steamed bonemeal. The latter are mixed in most commercial feeds, so check the label. There is no point in adding them again.

GROWING HORSES

As soon as a foal begins to nibble food, he should be allowed free access to a 16 percent protein ration. Because foals have such small stomachs, it's important to provide them with as much nutrition as possible in each mouthful of food. For this reason, special foal rations have been developed which meet all of the known requirements foals need to grow. If you don't feed a special foal ration, at least add a high protein supplement to a normal 10 percent ration. Also, foals should be fed a nutritious hay, preferably a legume.

These pictures show the effect of proper feeding (and routine health care) on a growing horse. Notice the pot-belly and rough hair coat in the photo on the top, and the sleek, greatly improved condition of the same horse in the lower photo, taken four months later.

As a foal reaches his first birthday, he should be fed each day from one to two pounds of 13 to 15 percent per hundred pounds of body weight, plus all of the hay he will eat.

There has been a great deal of discussion over how much a young horse should be fed. One argument is that too much feed produces excessive fat, which is unhealthy. Another school argues that young horses should continue to be fed high protein rations free choice, regardless of their weight. We prefer to stay on the safe side by feeding one pound of 13 percent feed per hundred pounds of body weight, plus a mixed hay free choice.

By the time a horse is one year old, he has put on about one half of his adult weight. Although he still has much growing to do, the fastest rate is from birth to one year.

There is some evidence that young horses that are fat and fed too much grain can develop epiphysitis. This is a problem which affects the cartilage as it changes to bone. It involves the growing ends of the bones and perhaps occurs because of too much weight coupled with an excessive growth rate. In other words, nature might not have intended for a horse's skeletal structure to develop in two or three years as we try to force it to do for reasons of economics and vanity. Rapid growth in animals intended for slaughter is sensible, but our aim is to develop a horse which will stay healthy and sound for twenty years or more.

With this purpose in mind, we provide our young horses good pasture or hay, plus a 13 percent ration at the rate of one pound per day per hundred pounds of body weight. We know of show colts and fillies which receive two or three times this amount of grain, but in our opinion it is not in the best long-range interest of the horse.

As the horse nears his second birthday, we feel we can safely reduce the protein level of the feed and if he is in good condition, reduce the quantity to ¾ pound per one hundred pounds of body weight. Along with the grain ration, we provide good pasture or mixed hay, as well as adequate salt, minerals and water.

STALLIONS

During the winter months, stallions should be kept in good flesh. Then, when breeding season begins in February, he'll be ready. As a matter of fact, it's almost impossible to put weight on a stallion during breeding season. Usually he will end up losing a little.

During breeding season, a stallion requires a pound of 10 percent protein ration and 1 to 1 ¼ pounds of hay per hundred pounds of body weight. Stallions vary greatly in temperament, which in turn affects their energy consumption, so their condition should be carefully watched and their feed regulated accordingly. When breeding season ends, he should be fed as you would any other horse.

MATURE HORSES

Mature, idle horses can get along quite well on pasture or hay alone. If they are put to work, some grain may be added.

A horse at light to medium work, requires from one half to one pound of 10 percent grain ration per hundred pounds of body weight. Hard working horses may need as much as a pound and a half.

MORE NOTES ON FEEDING

EQUIPMENT

To begin, remember that all feed must be kept dry. Grain must be stored in water tight containers. Remember to keep these containers where your horse cannot accidentally get at them. A locked grain room is best. Also, we keep our grain containers on wooden skids so they won't absorb moisture from the floor.

To accurately measure the grain, you can use a specially made grain scoop. To be honest, though, for most people the coffee can has just about replaced the grain scoop. Just remember that horses are fed by weight, not volume. While a two pound coffee can holds about two pounds of most grain, pelleted feed is much heavier, as is corn. Weigh your can when it is filled with feed, then you'll know exactly how much you're feeding each day.

While you won't need much room to store grain, you will need lots of room for hay. Older barns often have lofts, but since today they are quite costly to build, most of us must do without. Hay should be stored in a dry barn, or at least under a plastic sheet. These sheets aren't particularly recommended, however, as some hay almost always gets wet.

WATER

The best feed in the world will be of no value to your horse unless he drinks enough water to help him digest his food. A mature horse drinks an average of twelve gallons of water a day. Obviously, there are many variables so that working at fast paces, nursing and hot days will increase water consumption.

Automatic waterers are great for stalled horses, as are clear running streams for pastured horses. At the very least, a horse should be watered twice daily. If you water infrequently you're asking for trouble because your overly thirsty horse will be inclined to gorge himself.

Remember, too, not to water your horse right after heavy exercise. Allow him just a few sips at a time until his thirst is quenched.

COMMERCIAL FEEDS

Commercial feeds are usually composed of a mixture of grains with enough molasses to hold the ingredients together. The feeds, with high protein levels, have a supplement such as soybean meal added. Many also have trace minerals added, so further supplements aren't necessary.

In order for commercial feed to be sold across state lines, it must display a tag listing the ingredients, protein level and fiber level. The ingredients are listed in order of quantity, so the main ingredient is listed first and so on.

Although commercial feeds are often higher priced than the separate ingredients, they often are more economical for the one- or two-horse owner who would have no facilities for mixing his own.

If you have several horses, you might be able to save money by having a feed mill mix your feed from the formula given. Of course, you'll probably find the cost almost as much as a commercially prepared feed.

An important thing to remember about commercial feeds is that they vary greatly in quality. A very inexpensive ration can be made to look and smell good by adding molasses, but it may provide very little nutrition. Always check the tag so you know what you're getting. Some manufacturers provide a complete range of feeds from 10 percent to 16 percent protein levels. They might also market complete feeds, as well as supplements. From these many products, you are sure to find one that suits your horse.

Since money is so often a factor, initially you can select several products and compare their ingredients with their selling price. As with any business, a high advertising budget is passed on to the consumer. If you shop around carefully, you might find a lesser known but good quality feed at a lesser price.

Another way to save is not to feed a higher protein ration than your horse needs. Mature horses that seldom work don't need grain containing more than 10 percent protein.

American horsemen have an overwhelming number of supplements to choose from. Many of these are costly and quite unnecessary. Just as with people, the food should provide everything a horse needs to function. Unless a horse is growing, breeding or subject to extreme stress, he'll probably do just as well without supplements.

TEN TIPS

1) Rather than feeding from a standard formula, feed each horse as an individual by carefully observing his condition.
2) Feed by weight, not by volume.
3) Feed at the same time each day and feed in the same order.
4) Change feeds gradually over a period of several days.
5) If possible, keep water available at all times. Otherwise, water at least twice daily.
6) Keep water buckets and feed containers clean. Don't feed from the stall floor or the ground.
7) Never feed dusty, moldy or finely ground feed.
8) Don't feed for one hour before or after a horse is exercised.
9) Remember, poor quality hay is never a bargain. Coarse, stemmy, overly mature hay or weedy hay is not a good investment because it doesn't have the nutritional level of good hay.
10) Always provide free access to salt.

CHAPTER 6

Your Horse's Health

With good everyday care it should really be quite easy for you to keep your horse in excellent health. As a matter of fact, just remember that horses were able to get along quite well for many thousands of years without any help at all from man. But because we've made a drastic change in his lifestyle from when he roamed free, today's horse is subject to more hazards than ever before. A wild horse had only to fear an occasional mountain lion while he grazed continuously from fertile soil and drank pure stream water; he seldom had to run at full speed. Today, we confine these free moving animals in tiny stalls for long periods of time, feed them at our own convenience, then ask them to jump high or run fast with our weight on their backs. We transport them all over the country and make them graze over the same worm infested ground surrounded by dangerous wire fences. With all of this in mind, it is no wonder that many equine injuries and diseases result

129

from domestication. Of course, with proper care on our part, we can do a great deal to eliminate them.

As a horseowner, our first job in keeping a horse healthy is thus one of prevention. And the first step to take is to check for any obvious hazards in your horse's stall and pasture. Hammer flat any protruding nails and remove any sharp boards or debris of any kind, all of which can cause disfiguring or dangerous injuries. Next, be sure the fence is in good shape, so your horse can't get out. If the gates don't have secure latches, go out and buy some! Just recently a neighbor's horse was killed by a car after he opened a gate and let himself out during the night. If you have barbed wire fences, all we can say is good luck. We've seen many horses scarred by barbed wire, leading us to feel that it should be avoided if at all possible.

Once you think your pasture and barn are safe, review your stabling and feeding procedures. If you keep your horse in a stall, be sure he gets out for some daily exercise. We've seen many horses that have been stalled for a long period of time charge blindly out of their stalls in their eagerness to be turned loose. Horses need exercise to maintain their muscle tone as well as improve their disposition.

It's probably safe to say that improper feeding has caused as many problems for horses as anything else humans inflict on them. To begin, make sure your horse eats only what you feed him by making sure he can't get to the feed bin. Don't store your feed in an aisleway unless you have to, but if you must, make sure it's in a horse-proof container. Horses will eat until they make themselves quite sick, so this is essential.

Next, feed your horse regularly, at least twice a day. Remember, in the wild state horses grazed continuously and their digestive system can only handle small amounts of feed at one time. If you give them too much food once a day, they'll only eat themselves sick. Horses need two or even three meals a day.

The ration of food should be enough to maintain the horse, but not so much that he gets fat. Keep an eye on your horse. If he starts to get fat, cut back his ration. It's just as unhealthy for a horse to be overweight as it is for his owner. Remember, you expect your horse to be an athlete. A common complaint among ranchers and others who work regularly around horses is that most amateurs overfeed their horses.

Make sure the feed you give your horse is relatively clean and fresh.

Never feed hay which has even a trace of mold. Finally, at the same time you are exercising care in feeding your horse, make sure he has plenty of clean water to drink.

It's also very important that you plan a sound inoculation and worming program with your veterinarian. The inoculation program must begin soon after a foal is born. While some veterinarians believe that the colostrum in the dam's milk will protect the foal sufficiently, others temporarily inoculate the foal for tetanus. This is something you'll need to work out with your veterinarian.

All horses should be inoculated for tetanus, rhinitus and encephilitis.

FIRST AID KIT

If you keep your own horse at home, you really need to have a few basic first aid items on hand. Otherwise, you're sure to need something when all of the stores are closed and you can't reach your veterinarian. Keep all of your supplies together, so you'll know right where they are when you need them. One suggestion might be to keep them in an old discarded medicine cabinet. Another possibility is to use an old kitchen cabinet. If you can't find either of these, just label and use a box that has a lid to keep out the dirt.

Items needed:

Rectal thermometer	Sulfa based powder
Twitch for restraint	Furacin ointment
Knit wraps	Surgical soap
Elastic wraps	Colic remedy
Scissors	Liniment
Opthalmolic ointment	Petroleum jelly

Also, if you are able to give intramuscular injections, include:

100 c.c. bottle of antibiotic	Disposable needles
Dose of tetanus antitoxin	Disposable 12 c.c. syringe

PULSE—TEMPERATURE—RESPIRATION

These are three vital signs that indicate the general well-being of a horse. The temperature of a healthy horse is 100.5° F. Just as with people, an above normal temperature is usually a sign of infection or some other problem. As a horseowner, you should have a rectal themometer in your first aid kit. Then you'll be sure to have one when you need it. An animal thermometer is only slightly larger than one for human use. It has a hole on the upper end so that a string can be attached. With a string attached, it can't be lost in the rectum. You can even tie the string to the tail if you like. Before inserting the thermometer, shake it down and lubricate it with petroleum jelly. After a couple of minutes or so, gently remove it. If it reads over 100.5°, consult your veterinarian so that he can further evaluate the situation.

The pulse rate of a healthy horse ranges from 32 to 44 per minute. A more rapid pulse can be a sign of illness. The pulse rate can be determined by feeling the carotid artery, where it crosses over from the inner side of the jaw to the outside.

A healthy horse breathes an average of 8 to 16 times per minute. Of course, exertion can increase the rate, as can excitement, pain and weakness.

HORSE AILMENTS

TETANUS

Tetanus, which is also known as lockjaw, is one disease which is entirely preventable by inoculation. The organism which causes the disease lives in dung and the soil and is only able to infect an animal through a wound. Since the germs grow in an oxygen-free atmosphere, they thrive in puncture wounds which heal over quickly on the outside, closing off the air. Once inside the body, they proceed to attack the nervous system.

The first noticeable symptoms of tetanus include a stiffness of the joints when walking or a stiffness about the head, hence the name lockjaw. The disease progresses rapidly with the horse having tremors at the slightest noise or sign of activity. The outlook once a horse has tetanus is not favorable, with death the usual result.

Fortunately, tetanus is one disease horsemen need not worry about. All horses should receive a permanent inoculation, with booster shots given annually. The permanent inoculation requires an initial injection of tetanus toxoid, followed by a second injection about a month later. After this is completed, a booster should be given annually to insure protection.

Finally, in case the horse injures himself, it's a good idea to give him antitoxin at that time to make sure he is protected. This antitoxin immediately boosts the horse's resistance to the disease.

If you buy a horse with an unknown history of inoculations, don't hesitate to go ahead and administer the toxoid. It's not a good idea to wait until the horse is injured and then use an antitoxin. We are probably extra cautious about tetanus, however, knowing of several horses that quite needlessly died from this disease. In one case, no wound was ever found and although it was felt the horse must have had a puncture wound in his foot, this was little consolation for his heartbroken owner.

If a horse gets tetanus the outlook is grim. Massive doses of antitoxin must be administered as well as good supportive care. Although the mortality rate is high, some horses do recover.

EQUINE INFECTIOUS ANEMIA

E.I.A., as this disease is commonly referred to, is a very serious disease of the blood that usually results in the death of the horse. It is characterized by fever, lethargy, a general weakness and loss of weight. E.I.A. is also known as swamp fever, a name it earned because it appears most commonly in the lowlands of the South and Southwest.

While this disease is contagious, it doesn't affect all horses, and some horses carry the germs without showing any symptoms. Fortunately, a test has been devised which can determine if a horse is a carrier, so it can be isolated before it infects others. This test, called a Coggins Test, involves a procedure whereby a veterinarian draws a sample of blood from the horse. The sample is then sent to a laboratory for evaluation. A negative result indicates the horse is not a carrier of E.I.A., while a positive result indicates the horse might be a carrier.

The states now vary in their requirements for a Coggins Test. Many require that all horses entering the state have a negative Coggins, so to be safe all horses being transported between states should have had a negative Coggins in the last 12 months. If you are considering the purchase of a horse, be certain you have a negative Coggins before the transaction is final. The only time a horse doesn't need a Coggins is while it's a foal, in which case the dam's test is sufficient.

Although it is a controversial procedure, horses that test positive are ordinarily destroyed in an effort to eradicate the disease. Those horses which contract E.I.A. usually succumb to the disease as there is no known cure.

DISTEMPER OR STRANGLES

This is a common contagious disease that affects horses, particularly while they are young. However, just like many human childhood diseases, once a horse gets over a bout with strangles, he is usually immune for life. Strangles is most likely to occur when a horse is being moved to new surroundings or where large numbers of horses are stabled, such as at a race track or a breeding farm.

The first symptoms of strangles include a loss of appetite and general apathy, followed by a thick whitish nasal discharge and a cough. Soon after these symptoms appear, the lymph nodes in the horse's head start to swell. The nodes usually affected are under the jaw; however, in some more serious cases, those all over the body swell, too. The swollen nodes are very painful and eventually will break open and allow the pus trapped inside to drain, relieving the pain.

If you suspect your horse has strangles, call your veterinarian right away so that treatment can begin. This treatment will consist of giving the horse medication, along with a recommendation that you keep him in a clean, quiet shelter, out of drafts and provide adequate water and good feed. Because strangles is contagious, any horse suspected of having the disease must be isolated. All the tack and equipment used on the infected horse should be carefully disinfected, as should his stall. Finally, as a further preventative measure, burn the bedding from his stall.

INFLUENZA

As with people, influenza, or flu as we usually call it, is rarely fatal among horses, although it can make them quite ill. It is most common among young horses, and after they recover they will usually have some immunity. Flu is contagious and most commonly found where groups of horses are kept together.

The symptoms associated with flu occur about a week after the horse has been exposed. They include a fever, loss of appetite, a cough and a watery nasal discharge. Horses showing any signs of flu must be rested immediately to prevent the likelihood of complications. They should not return to work until they are free of all symptoms including the cough, which may continue for some time.

If you suspect your horse has the flu, ask your veterinarian about his suggestions for treatment. Some veterinarians will treat the horse with antibiotics to prevent the possibility of any secondary infections.

Although it's not usually suggested as necessary for all horses, there is a vaccine that offers protection against some strains of flu. Horses that need to be protected include those that are in training, on the show circuit or are about to be transported for a long distance. It appears that the trauma associated with shipping lowers the horse's resistance to flu and other diseases.

LAMINITIS

Laminitis, or founder as it is more commonly called, is an all too common affliction of horses that can usually be prevented. The term laminitis simply refers to an inflammation of the laminae which are located between the horny wall and the coffin bone in the hoof. When a horse founders himself, the laminae becomes swollen and inflamed. Because the hoof wall is unyielding, the pressure builds up and causes extreme pain, similar to what we feel when we hit our fingernail with a hammer.

Founder has several causes, most of which are preventable by simple good horse care. These causes include:

1) Retention of part of the placenta after foaling.
2) Excessive feedings of grains such as corn, especially after heavy work.
3) Allowing a horse to drink too much cold water, particularly when he is hot.
4) Overeating succulent green grass.
5) Overwork, especially on hard pavement, causing road founder.

6) Being overweight, which predisposes a horse or particularly a pony to founder.

Signs of founder include a rise in temperature, a reluctance to move, heat in the feet and an obvious pain when a hoof tester or hammer is used on it. When you try to get a horse with founder to move, he will stretch out his neck and put his hind legs quite far under his body in order to take weight off his sore front feet.

If the inflammation of the laminae continues for some time, the laminae can become detached. Then the coffin bone rotates downward and causes the sole to become flat, rather than concave. In extreme cases, the bone will actually puncture the sole. Along with these internal changes in the hoof, the outer horny wall develops horizontal ridges instead of being smooth.

If you suspect founder, call your veterinarian immediately. He can administer cortisone or antihistimines to reduce swelling, if he feels this is required. In the meantime, don't feed the horse any grain, remove his shoes and run cold water over the affected feet to cool them or stand the horse in cool mud.

In cases of mild founder, the outcome is usually quite favorable if it is treated promptly. If bone rotation and destruction of the sole occurs, the horse can be crippled for life.

NAVICULAR

Navicular disease, as its name implies, affects the navicular bone which is located toward the back of the hoof. The deep flexor tendon glides over this bone and the disease can damage this tendon and the surrounding cartilage as well as causing disintegration of the bone itself.

The symptoms of navicular include lameness, a short stubby stride and pointing, which is standing with one forefoot ahead of the other while the horse is resting. The lameness associated with navicular is sporadic at first, but eventually becomes more and more frequent.

If you suspect navicular, call your veterinarian promptly. He will apply a hoof tester to see if there is pain in the area of the navicular bone. He also might have the hoof x-rayed if he feels this is necessary.

Navicular primarily affects a horse's forefeet. It is most common among those with short, upright pasterns and small feet. In such

136

cases, the weight of the horse is directly over the vulnerable navicular area. Also, on horses with this conformation, there is more jarring when the horse moves. Frequent riding on hard surfaces increases the chances of developing navicular disease, as does jumping.

Sadly enough, complete recovery from navicular rarely occurs. In the first place, you can't take a horse off his feet to rest the injured area, which would allow healing to occur. The major treatment consists of corrective shoeing and trimming to try to take the weight off the heel, where the navicular is located. When this is unsuccessful, the horse can be "nerved" surgically. This means the nerves leading to the hoof are cut. Of course, this cuts off all feeling to the hoof making it possible for the horse to injure the hoof and not show any symptoms.

Possibly the best way to prevent navicular is by breeding and selecting horses with sufficiently long pasterns (feet large enough to support their weight) as well as by recognizing the physical limitations of the horse.

SOFT SWELLINGS

Synovial fluid is a thick, yellowish material used to lubricate the joints. Because of its function, oldtimers used to call it joint oil. Sometimes a strain will cause overproduction of synovial fluid. When this happens, a soft swelling occurs. These swellings, although disfiguring, are relatively harmless. Depending on the site, the swellings are referred to as thoroughpin, capped hock, bog spavin, curb, and windgalls.

It is difficult to completely reduce these swellings once they occur. When additional synovial fluid is secreted, the surrounding joint capsule enlarges to accommodate it. From that point on, even if the fluid is aspirated, there will always be a tendency for the capsule to refill.

Although synovial swellings are unattractive, they seldom cause any real problems for the horse.

Curb

A curb is a swelling at the lower back of the hock where the cannon joins the hock. It is actually a strain of the ligament which runs

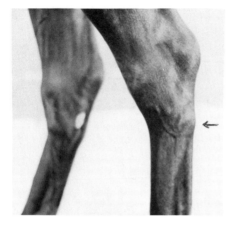
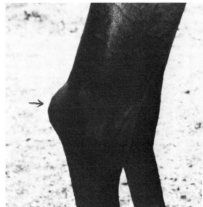

Curb.   *Capped hock.*

from the hock down the back of the cannon bone. Most often it occurs in young horses, especially those that are sickle hocked or stand with their hind feet too far under their body. The excessive strain caused by this conformation defect predisposes a horse toward curb.

As the curb develops, the ligament becomes inflamed and there may be some pain and lameness. Whenever a curb is suspected, the horse should be rested for a few weeks, after which time work can be resumed. Of course the horse will be left with a permanent blemish.

Thoroughpin

Thoroughpin is a soft swelling of synovial fluid at the top of the hock near the back. A thoroughpin is a blemish, not an unsoundness. Because this doesn't cause lameness, no treatment is indicated.

Capped Hock

Capped hock is an enlargement of the point of the hock. This condition occurs when a horse repeatedly kicks at the stall wall or bumps his hocks when he gets up and down in his stall.

While capped hocks are unsightly, they seldom cause lameness. Because of this, they are considered a blemish rather than an unsoundness, which means that while they don't look good, they do not physically affect the horse.

Bog Spavin

Bog spavin is a soft swelling on the inside front of the hock caused by a sudden strain. A bog fills the natural depression in the hock with joint oil or synovial fluid.

Although a bog is unsightly, because there is no bone involvement it rarely causes lameness. If you are bothered by the appearance of a bog, your veterinarian can give you something to help reduce it.

Capped Elbow

A bursa is found at the back of the horse's elbow and when it becomes inflamed, it is called a capped elbow.

A capped elbow generally occurs on horses that are shod. It is caused by repeated bruising of the elbow when the horse gets up and down or by contact with a shoe when a horse is lying down. To protect horses that tend to do this, care should be taken so that the ends of the shoes do not project beyond the end of the foot. Also a large padded donut shaped device can be buckled above the elbow for protection.

Windgalls

A windgall is another kind of synovial swelling that occurs on each side of and above the fetlock. Windgalls are considered to be a blemish and as such are of little consequence. Windgalls, or windpuffs as they are sometimes called, can be found on both the fore and hind legs. They are found particularly on horses that are worked hard and may even be considered a sign of a good honest horse, for they certainly weren't produced standing in a stall.

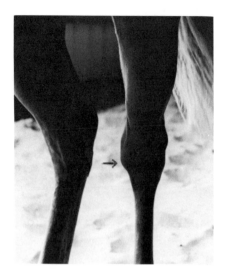

Bog spavin.

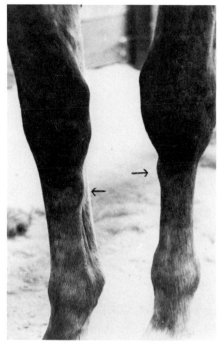

High splints.

SPLINT

A splint is a hard swelling on the cannon that usually occurs on the upper half of the inside of the foreleg. Splints can vary in size from those barely visible to those four or five inches in length. They are generally found on young horses shortly after serious work begins.

At first, the inflammation associated with a splint will cause pain and lameness. Then, as the tissue hardens, the pain will subside. The horse will be blemished, but the splint generally causes no more trouble unless it is located near a knee where it can interfere with movement.

The usual treatment for a splint is simply to rest the horse while the splint is developing. If the splint is severe, other treatment may be elected by your veterinarian who should be consulted if the pain appears quite serious.

BOWED TENDONS

The flexor tendons that run down the back of the cannon bone are often subjected to serious strain, especially when a horse lands on his forelegs after a jump.

When a tendon is sprained, it becomes inflamed, painful to the touch and the horse will be quite lame. The tendon will fill with fluid and bow-out, hence the name bowed tendon. In case of severe strain, the tendon can rupture and the situation become quite hopeless as the fetlock, which is no longer supported, touches the ground.

The treatment of a bowed tendon varies, but a long period of rest is always required. A veterinarian should be called immediately so treatment can begin. This treatment can include cortisone injections to reduce swelling, bandaging, ice packs, or possibly blistering and firing. The object of the latter two treatments is to encourage healing by bringing more blood to the area to hasten the process of repair.

Once a tendon has been sprained, it loses its original elasticity and never quite returns to normal. Horses that have this kind of injury may resume light work, but will probably never be sound enough for strenuous work.

BONE SPAVIN

Bone spavin is a serious unsoundness of the hock that results from a strain on the hock. It is thought some horses have a hereditary predisposition to this condition.

A bone spavin occurs low on the inside of the hock where it joins the cannon bone. The hock is actually made up of several bones and a bone spavin is nature's attempt to heal an injury. New bone is formed which sometimes interferes with the movement of the joint by fusing some of these bones together.

When this happens, the bone spavin will cause lameness. A veterinarian should be called at once. He can confirm this diagnosis with an x-ray once the new bone is formed.

In the past, the outlook for a spavined horse was not hopeful. Now, with new methods of treatment, the future is much brighter.

RINGBONE

Ringbone is a hard swelling on the pastern that results from an injury or a blow of some sort. It is called high or low ringbone depending upon where it's found on the pastern. High ringbone involves the long pastern bone, while low ringbone is visible close to the hoof and involves the short pastern bone.

Ringbone is actually new bone which grows on top of the normal bone. If it occurs in a joint, it is called articular ringbone and is quite serious as it interferes with movement.

Symptoms of ringbone include lameness and a swelling of the affected area. Once the new bone is formed, the lameness will probably disappear, unless it involves a joint. In any event, once ringbone is suspected, your veterinarian should be called to determine the extent of the damage and begin treatment.

HOOF PROBLEMS

Corns

A corn is a bruise on the bottom of a horse's foot that can cause lameness. Corns are found between the bars of the hoof and the hoof wall and are indicated by a bloody stain on the sole.

Corns are caused by riding on rocky ground or by shoes which don't fit properly at the heels. Whenever a corn is found, the injured tissue should be pared away by a farrier.

When a corn becomes infected it is called a supperating corn. Such cases will require antibiotics to clear up the infection in addition to cutting away the damaged tissue.

Puncture Wounds

No matter how careful we might be in keeping our pasture clean of debris, a horse might step on a sharp object, puncturing his sole. Such an injury may be too small to notice, but the horse can still become slightly lame. If the wound infects, the lameness might disappear for a short time, but eventually the lower leg will swell and the horse will be acutely lame.

In most such cases of injury, a veterinarian will apply a hoof tester to determine the actual site of the injury. He will then pare away the sole at the point of injury. This allows the accumulated pus to drain, relieving the pressure. The horse must be given a tetanus shot immediately and an antibiotic injection to reduce the infection. Often the veterinarian will also inject penicillin directly into the wound.

It is vital that such an injury be treated immediately not only because of the danger of tetanus, but also because the infection can destroy tissue in the hoof.

Thrush

Thrush is a fungus infection of the frog of the hoof. It is easily diagnosed by its foul smell and requires immediate treatment because it causes deterioration of the frog. A normal healthy frog is rubbery, while one diseased by thrush is soft, spongy and often oozing.

Many remedies are available for thrush. They are applied directly to the frog at prescribed intervals until healing occurs. Thrush can much more easily be prevented than cured. It is primarily caused by allowing a horse to stand in a filthy stall. Thrush is a very good reason to pick out the hoofs of stalled horses daily, as well as to clean stalls frequently.

Cracked Hoofs

A healthy hoof is strong and pliable and expands slightly with each step. The periople at the top of the hoof secretes a varnish-like substance which encases the hoof wall, sealing in moisture. In their wild state, horses roamed free and their hoofs wore down naturally. With domestication and more confined conditions, hoofs don't wear off and must be routinely trimmed. If they are not trimmed at least every two months, the hoofs will grow too long and eventually break off or split. A split on the side of the wall is referred to as a quarter crack, while one on the front is called a toe crack.

Cracks in the hoof wall are usually caused by hoofs that are either too long or too dry. The problem is that these cracks can't heal by themselves because of the natural expansion and contraction of the hoof. To repair this damage, the hoof must first be trimmed to its natural length. The horse can then be shod in a normal manner, which will allow the crack to grow out. If the horse is not to be shod, the bottom of the crack should be filed to a V-shape to keep the weight of the horse off of it.

Seedy Toe

When the hoof wall separates from the laminae at the toe, it is called seedy toe. This separation allows dirt to enter the crevice which causes pain and a slight lameness. Seedy toe can readily be seen on the bottom of the hoof as a dark line on the inner edge of the hoof wall.

This condition is common among horses that have been foundered. Treatment consists of simply keeping the hoofs trimmed and shod.

Gravel

Occasionally a small piece of gravel will lodge between the hoof wall and the laminae. The horse will become quite lame, but there is nothing to do but wait. Eventually the gravel will travel from the entry point in the sole, up the hoof wall to the coronary band. Here it will erupt, relieving the pain and making the horse usable again.

SADDLE SORES

When a horse wears a saddle for any period of time, the blood supply to the area covered by the saddle is reduced. If the saddle rubs back and forth or if there is undue pressure caused by a poorly fitting saddle or because the pad used wasn't heavy enough, a saddle sore can develop.

These sores heal very slowly. As with most injuries, they are easier to prevent than to treat. A horse with a saddle sore must be rested until it is completely healed and an antiseptic should be applied daily.

Then, the cause of the saddle sore must be determined and an effort made to correct it. Always use clean and dry pads under your saddle. Make sure the hair under the pad lies in the same direction that it grows. If your saddle doesn't fit your horse, trade it in for one that does. If your horse chafes behind the elbows, buy a pair of sheepskin cinch guards. If he starts to gall under the girth, buy a girth cover, keep it clean and use it when you ride.

SKIN DISORDERS

Ringworm

Ringworm is a commonly found disorder caused by a fungus. It is more common among stabled horses than among those that are pastured. Although ringworm is unsightly, it is seldom dangerous. It starts out as a small, round, scaly patch on the skin in which the hair falls out. The skin will then become crusty and itching may occur. If the ringworm is not treated, the affected areas will become larger. If you discover ringworm on your horse, your veterinarian should be able to recommend a good fungus remedy to clear it up.

Protein Bumps

Occasionally, small to medium size bumps will occur on the neck and shoulders of overfed horses. These are commonly referred to as "protein bumps." By reducing the alfalfa hay or the high protein level of the feed concentrate, the bumps will soon disappear.

Warts

Sometimes young horses develop unsightly warts on their nose. They are caused by a virus and there is little that can be done. Warts seem to bother the horse-owner more than the horse, who is hardly even aware of them. As a matter of fact, as soon as there is a good killing frost, the warts will disappear. Warts are most common where many young horses are kept together. They rarely occur after three years of age.

WOUNDS

No matter how careful you might try to be, you still can be confronted by a wounded horse sooner or later. The saving feature is, however, that wounds vary greatly in severity and are seldom fatal no matter how terrible they look.

If your horse injures himself, the first thing to check is loss of blood. Since a horse has a lot of blood, however, he can afford to lose several pints without any ill effects. So, though a small amount of pooled blood can look like a lot, don't panic. Notice if the blood is oozing or spurting out of the wound. If it is oozing, it is from a vein and you should be able to stop the bleeding yourself. If it is spurting, it is arterial bleeding and must be stopped without delay. One way to do this is by the application of a tourniquet between the heart and the wound. Call your veterinarian immediately in case of arterial bleeding! He can give you exact instructions on what to do until he arrives.

Next, all wounds should be cleaned thoroughly to remove the dirt. Use warm water, mild soap and sterile gauze. Once the wound is clean, examine it carefully. If it appears superficial with the skin only broken, dry the wound and apply an antiseptic ointment. Larger, deeper wounds may need professional care, such as stitches. If you are in doubt, it's obviously better for your veterinarian to say nothing further needs to be done than for your horse to get worse for lack of care.

The big problem with injured horses is that they make terrible patients. They can't be immobilized very well, which means they will move around, delaying healing, tearing out stitches and tearing off bandages.

Wounds that are low enough to pick up dirt and debris should be wrapped to prevent infection. We cover any wounds with an antiseptic solution and then wrap it using a large roll of gauze which we get from

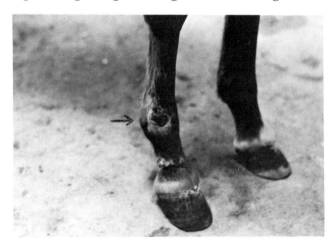

Severe laceration.

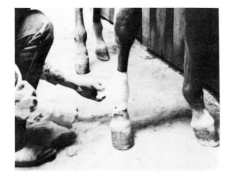

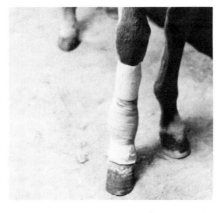

Bandaging a leg. These photographs show gauze wrap (above left) and then elastic wrap (above right) being applied and the completed bandage.

our veterinarian because people gauze isn't large enough. Next, we cover the gauze dressing with a knitted leg wrap or elasticized adhesive tape. The dressing is then changed daily until the wound is healed.

Puncture wounds should be carefully inspected to make sure nothing is left in them to prevent healing or cause infection. While not as evil looking as lacerations, punctures should not be taken lightly. Although the wound itself may not be as serious, a puncture is the kind of wound which invites tetanus. Even if your horse has had his permanent tetanus shots and annual booster, if you find a puncture wound, it's always a good idea to give him an antitoxin shot as a precautionary measure.

Wounds which are near joints can be particularly serious, especially if they ooze a thick, yellow joint fluid. Since infection can be a problem in such an injury, the horse should be given antibiotic injections. With other deep wounds, antibiotic shots may also be a good idea.

147

Proud Flesh

One complication that affects the healing process is called proud flesh. In any wound, the two severed parts must eventually grow back together and meet for healing to take place. Proud flesh is a pinkish, granular looking tissue which fills up a wound, preventing the ends from meeting. Usually, it continues to grow beyond the skin line. Medications are available to remove proud flesh and should be used if it begins to form. Otherwise, it will have to be cut out by a veterinarian.

Infection

Naturally, a wound may become infected despite our best efforts. If a wound fails to heal, is extremely sensitive to the touch or oozes continuously, an infection most likely has set in. Intramuscular injections of an antibiotic will most likely be prescribed by your veterinarian in such cases.

Steps Involved in Wound Care

1) Stop any bleeding.
2) Cleanse the wound thoroughly, removing all dirt and foreign particles.
3) Apply antiseptic ointment or powder.
4) Wrap if required.
5) Administer tetanus antitoxin.
6) If danger of infection exists, give antibiotic injection.

Call the Veterinarian

1) If you suspect arterial bleeding or cannot get bleeding stopped.
2) If the injury involves a joint and is oozing a thick, yellow fluid.
3) If the horse appears to be in shock. That is, if his breathing is shallow and rapid, his pulse shallow, his eyes glazed and his extremities cold to the touch.
4) If the wound is very large or deep and you feel stitches would help.
5) If infection occurs.

148

COLIC

Colic is a general term used to describe almost any stomach ailment a horse might have. Because of the peculiar nature of the horse's stomach, these ailments are quite common and unfortunately take a considerable toll on horses each year. The problem with a horse's digestive system is that he is unable to regurgitate, has a very small stomach for an animal of this size, not to mention the fact that the cecum, or fermentation vat, is located after the small intestine, thus causing less efficient digestion. The stomach is simply not capable of handling even such seemingly minor problems as overeating or slightly spoiled hay, thus making colic a major concern of most horsemen.

If the stomach of a horse is painfully distended with gas or if solid waste matter is not passed through the rectum, he suffers from colic. The symptoms associated with this ailment include pawing, looking at or biting the flank, repeatedly getting up and lying down, and rolling.

If you suspect your horse has colic, remove his feed and take his temperature immediately. Next, look to see if he has had a bowel movement recently. If his temperature seems higher than normal or it appears he hasn't had a recent bowel movement, call your veterinarian immediately. He will administer a pain relieving drug and treat the colic directly. One remedy he might use would be to pass a tube into the horse's stomach and pump oil through the tube. This acts as a laxative and helps any impacted matter pass through the digestive system.

While the causes of colic are many and it is impossible to completely prevent a horse from contracting it, there are some general principles to follow which should reduce the likelihood at least.

1) Worm your horses frequently. Worms cause aneurisms in the intestines which slow down the digestive process.
2) Feed your horses at frequent intervals at least twice a day and make sure the hay is mold-free.
3) Don't feed excessive amounts of grain to a horse or feed any grain to one that is hot and tired.
4) When you change kinds of feeds, do it gradually over a couple of days.
5) Water your horse at least twice a day. Water aids digestion.
6) If you put your horse in a lush, green pasture, do it gradually.

While most horses generally recover from colic, an all too frequent complication that can be deadly is a twisted intestine. In cases where this happens, the intestine literally twists around itself and causes a painful death. A horse suffering from a twisted intestine will have a very high fever and be in obvious distress.

The only remedy for a twisted intestine is immediate surgery. Although this is still not a common procedure, more and more favorable results are being obtained. Of course, time is of the essence. Since the blood supply to the affected area is cut off, gangrene will soon occur. When this happens, the tissue has died and cannot recover.

ENCEPHALOMYELITIS

There are three different strains of EEC, as this disease is commonly referred to, which effect horses. These are the Western, Eastern and Venezuelan, each of which is serious and can possibly result in death.

Sleeping sickness is a disease of the brain during which the affected horse at first stumbles about and then appears very sleepy, as the name implies. The horse's head is usually lowered and later the horse may lie down completely. If the horse recovers, he may be completely well or he might have suffered brain damage.

As with most diseases, sleeping sickness is best prevented, rather than cured. Vaccines are available and are most commonly administered in the early spring. This will protect the horse during the summer months when most outbreaks occur. Since mosquitoes are the most likely carrier of the disease, prevention must include a good sanitation program in which the insect breeding grounds are eliminated as much as possible.

FISTULA AND POLL EVIL

A sudden sharp blow to the body of a horse or an ill fitting saddle can cause a painful abscess or fistula at the withers. A fistula might also be caused by the horse rolling on a stone or some other sharp object.

While fistulas used to be very slow in healing, penicillin can now help immediately if it is injected directly into the wound by using a syringe with a long plastic needle. A fistula will cause such extreme pain that the horse will resist putting any pressure on the area. At first, there may be only a swelling or slight sore and the abscess may even seem to heal over, but the tenderness will still be apparent. Antibiotics, such as the penicillin we just mentioned, when injected into the wound should take care of the problem.

The only cases of fistula we've seen have been caused by poorly fitting saddles. If you aren't sure your saddle fits, check to make sure there is at least an inch or two clearance at the withers.

Poll evil is the name for a similar abscess which forms at the horse's poll.

PNEUMONIA

Pneumonia can be a very serious disease among horses and it can come as an aftermath of influenza or strangles. It most frequently affects young horses or those subjected to stressful conditions. As with humans, pneumonia is not as much a cause for concern as it was before the use of penicillin. When a horse contracts this disease, he will run a temperature, which will reach sometimes as high as 105°. He will be listless and not inclined to eat or move around very much. He will also have difficulty breathing and have a thick nasal discharge.

If you suspect your horse might have pneumonia, call your veterinarian immediately. Prompt treatment will insure a quick recovery. In the meantime, put your horse in his stall with a generous amount of bedding. Make sure he has a clean bucket of water and keep him out of drafts. If it is very cold, you might have to put a blanket on him so he doesn't get chilled. This, of course, is just supportive treatment and the horse will undoubtedly need several injections of antibiotics and a lengthy period of recovery before he is well again.

BROKEN WIND OR HEAVES

Broken wind is another names for heaves. It is a condition which causes a breakdown of the lungs due to too much strain being put on them. The damage done is largely irreversible, much as with emphysema in people. Heaves may be an aftereffect of severe pneumonia, pleurisy or simply being run too hard. In the beginning stages, the horse will have a chronic cough and his breathing will be labored after only moderate exercise.

With heaves, a horse inhales in the usual manner, but due to a breakdown in his lungs, he is unable to exhale the air in one breath. Instead, he exhales or "heaves" twice.

A horse with chronic heaves develops a heave line or ridge along the flank. There is no cure for heaves, but with good care, the horse can be used lightly as a pleasure horse. Any hay he is fed should be first watered lightly to keep down the dust.

EYE PROBLEMS

Horses sometimes develop an inflammation of the membrane covering the eye. This condition is known as conjunctivitis. The affected eye will exude a whitish pus. An application of opthalmolic ointment, which you can get from your veterinarian, should clear it up.

If an eye contains a particle of foreign matter, it will water frequently and be red around the edge. If this is the case, call your veterinarian so he can determine the seriousness of the problem and decide on a plan of action.

Cataracts are sometimes a problem for horses just as they are for people. They grow over the lens of the eye and cloud it. As they seriously impair vision, cataracts are most serious and require the attention of a veterinarian.

The eye can also be a good indicator of the general well-being of a horse. If he's healthy, his eyes will be clear and surrounded by a pinkish membrane. Signs of trouble include a watery or pussy discharge, a cloudy appearance, swelling, closing the eye in sunlight, or if the membrane around the eye is red.

TEETH

Horses grind their food with their molars. If you notice the shape of a horse's head, you'll find that it tapers or narrows from the top to the bottom. Following this shape of the face, a horse's molars do not meet evenly. The outer edge of the upper teeth protrude outward beyond the lower teeth. In turn, the inside edge of the lower molars extend inside the upper ones.

This works well enough, except that the outer edge of the upper teeth and the inside edge of the lower teeth aren't subject to wear. Because of this, it sometimes happens that quite large, sharp points on the molars interfere with proper chewing. If the points are on the upper teeth, they can cause sore cheeks, while the lower edges can even puncture the tongue.

Now, while all of this may seem quite confusing, it simply means that you need to have your horse's teeth checked annually by a veterinarian. He will examine the teeth to see if there are any of these sharp projections. If he feels it necessary, he can rasp or float the teeth. To float teeth, a veterinarian uses a large metal file with a long handle. With these sharp edges removed, the horse can then chew his food more thoroughly and make the best use of his feed.

In between these annual checks by a veterinarian, if your horse slobbers excessively when he eats or if he chews with his head held to one side, it could mean that he has problems with his teeth and that they should be checked.

PARASITES

A parasite is an organism that lives off another host animal. Unfortunately, horses are plagued with many different varieties of both internal and external parasites. Some internal parasites include the many varieties of worms as well as the larvae of the bot fly. External parasites include lice, mites, ticks, and flies.

EXTERNAL PARASITES

By using good stable and grooming management practices, we should be able to keep our horses virtually free of external parasites.

Flies

Flies can be a terrible nuisance during the summer months, bothering horses whether they are in a stall or in a pasture. Fortunately, there are many varieties of insecticides that control these pests. For stable use, we have received excellent results from the wall units that automatically dispense a prescribed amount of insecticide at regular intervals.

153

Simply keeping stalls clear of manure can do a great deal in reducing the number of flies, as will frequent removal of the manure pile, which is a favorite breeding ground for flies and mosquitoes.

There are many commercial insecticides now on the market which are sprayed or wiped directly on the horse. We highly recommend using them each time you ride during the fly season. Your horse will be more content if he's not bothered by flies and can concentrate more on what you are asking him to do.

Lice

Lice are particularly loathsome insects which often infest horses. Horses are particularly susceptible to them. On the other hand, it is relatively easy to prevent lice and they are rare among well cared for horses that have the benefit of good sanitation, good nutrition and frequent grooming.

Lice live on the body of the host animal. The females lay their eggs close to the host's skin where they hatch and proceed to produce more generations. These lice will then bite their host and can drive him almost to distraction.

The hair of an infested horse will lose its luster. Further, the horse will continually rub the infested location and eventually cause the hair to fall out. Some lice also suck on their host and can cause him to lose his vigor.

Lice are most often evident in winter and early spring before the long hair is shed. They often concentrate at the base of the tail, inside the thighs and along the neck and shoulders. Scabs associated with lice are most often caused by the animal gnawing and rubbing.

Lice are quickly spread from one horse to another, so if you suspect a horse has lice, isolate him immediately and call your veterinarian. Don't use that horse's grooming equipment on any other horse until a diagnosis has been made.

If your horse has lice, your veterinarian will prescribe an insecticide to kill them. On your part, to prevent future outbreaks simply be sure to groom your horses frequently and feed them adequately.

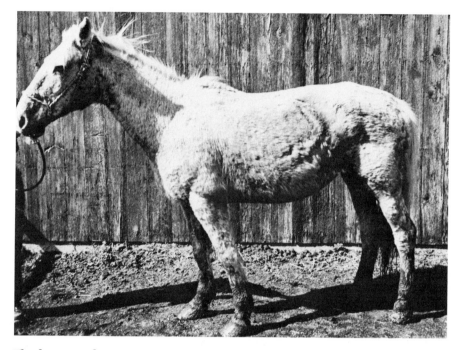

The horse in this picture is suffering from a severe case of mange. Note the unthrifty condition and the loss of large clumps of hair.

Mites

Another kind of external parasite that frequently infests horses are mites. These mites produce a specific ailment known as mange.

As with lice, poorly cared for horses are more likely to suffer from mange than are those that are well cared for. As a matter of fact, both mites and lice are often found on the same host animal.

Some kinds of mites burrow into the skin, while others bite and suck blood. Neither of these types, of course, is very desirable. Burrowing mites, called sarcoptic mites, are particularly loathsome because of an irritating substance they secrete.

Horses with mange suffer from scabs, severe itching and loss of hair. The skin first becomes crusty and then becomes tough looking and wrinkled. Mange is best prevented by using sound management practices. If you suspect your horse has mange, isolate him immediately and call your veterinarian. He will recommend a dip or spray to kill the mites as well as a soothing medication to relieve the itching.

Ticks

Ticks are another external parasite that sometimes infest horses. They are most commonly found among pastured horses during the summer months. Ticks often attach themselves to the base of the forelock, the mane and the tail. Once attached, they feed on the blood of the host animal.

Ticks cause severe itching, sores and sometimes secondary infections. If you suspect or find ticks on your horse, your veterinarian can recommend a dip or spray to kill them.

INTERNAL PARASITES

It is pretty much a matter of fact that all horses are infested with internal parasites, or worms as they are commonly called. No other domestic animal is infested by such a wide variety of parasites, nor in such large numbers as is the horse. Because of the severe damage that can be caused by worms, horseowners must develop a comprehensive program to keep these pests at a minimum. This program is particularly important for performance horses and young horses that are still growing.

The major parasites that affect horses and ponies include: large strongyles, small strongyles, roundworms, pinworms and bots.

Large and Small Strongyles

Strongyles infest the large intestine of the horse. Here, these worms mate and the resulting eggs are passed out with the manure. After about a day, the eggs hatch and in a week or two are mature enough to infest another horse.

The new infestation occurs when the larvae are eaten by a horse grazing in a contaminated pasture or by eating feed that has come in contact with contaminated manure.

The larvae are quite hardy, not at all bothered by cold or freezing, and may live outside up to a year. The only way they can be killed is by exposure to heat and sunlight.

Once the larvae are eaten, they enter the intestines, penetrate the

156

intestinal wall and migrate through the body. During this period of migration, the worms are not affected by any worm medication given to the horse.

Once the worms reach the large intestine, they mature in four to eleven months and begin the process all over again. To give you an idea of the magnitude of the problem, when a horse manures he can deposit hundreds of thousands of strongyle eggs at a time.

Horses that are infested with strongyles make poor use of their feed and are not as vigorous as they should be. They tend to have rough hair coats, shallow flanks and light colored mucous membranes.

Roundworms or Ascarids

Roundworms or ascarids are large white worms which at maturity can be up to twenty-two inches long and as thick as a lead pencil. They primarily infest young horses and are seldom a problem after the age of five or six.

The adult roundworm lays eggs in the large intestine and these eggs are thus passed out in the manure. The eggs do not hatch until another horse ingests them and they lodge in the small intestine. Once the larvae are hatched, they then migrate through the organs and eventually return to the small intestine.

Roundworms are a serious problem because they can damage the liver and lungs of a horse. Because of their large size, they can completely block the small intestine. Foals with pot bellies, rough hair coats, repeated attacks of diarrhea and a poor growth rate should definitely be suspected of having roundworms and treated immediately.

Pinworms

Pinworms, although troublesome, are not as serious a problem as strongyles or ascarids. These worms mature in the large intestine and subsequently crawl out the horse's anus, where the female will deposit her eggs under the tail. The eggs then drop off to the ground where they can be eaten by another horse and the cycle repeated. Pinworms travel directly through the intestines and do not migrate to other organs as do strongyles and ascarids. Pinworms should be suspected whenever a horse is found repeatedly rubbing his tail.

Bots

Bots are not worms, but another type of internal parasite, the larvae of the bot fly. In the late summer, female bot flies will lay their eggs on the chin, nose and legs of a horse. These flies can be seen following horses as they graze. They dart repeatedly toward the horse and lay an egg each time. The eggs then cling to the ends of the hair and can neither be brushed or washed off very easily.

The bot egg enters the horse's mouth when the horse rubs itself. From there, the eggs enter the stomach where they mature. The resulting larvae attach themselves to the lining of the stomach where they spend the winter. Then, in the spring, the larvae pass through the horse. After a month or two they mature into flies and the process is repeated.

CONTROL OF INTERNAL PARASITES

The close confinement of horses undoubtedly increases problems associated with worms. Periodic "worming" (which is the term used for the process of de-worming a horse) usually doesn't totally rid a horse of these parasites, but it should help keep them at a minimum. Following are some general steps you can take to help ease the problem.

1) First, feed and water from clean tubs and buckets.
2) Feed hay from hay racks instead of the stall floor so that it doesn't get contaminated with manure.
3) Remove the manure from stalls daily so the horse has minimal contact with it.
4) Frequently chain-harrow pastures so the manure and worms are exposed to sunlight.
5) Rotate your horses among different pastures if possible.
6) Don't allow your horses to overgraze a pasture. This forces them to graze close to the ground where the worm eggs are.
7) As soon as the bot eggs appear on your horse, clip the hair with an electric clipper. Our feeling is that it's best to prevent the infestation, rather than having to kill the parasite inside the horse.

How often you worm your horse depends on the age of the horse, how he's being used and how many horses are confined together. Again, remember that when a horseman refers to worming a horse, he's actually referring to the procedure of de-worming.

As a starting point, first have your veterinarian check a fresh deposit of manure for worms. By using a microscope he can see the worm eggs and determine the severity of infestation. Remember, even horses that appear healthy can have large numbers of worms, so don't be negligent, even if your horse appears relatively worm free.

Based on the findings, your veterinarian can recommend a worming program. Medication for worms can be administered by stomach tube, in the feed, or in a gel or paste form. The way in which the medication is given is not nearly so important as what is given. In the past, it was recommended that horses be tubed because you couldn't always be certain that a finicky eater would eat the feed that contained his medication. We've solved this problem by mixing the medication with a small amount of feed molasses. This makes the mixture much tastier and better smelling, too. Our horses accept it reasonably well.

The gel method of worming is so simple, it is certainly recommended. Passing a stomach tube is quite effective, but is a rather harsh procedure. In most cases the horse will have to be twitched before the veterinarian can pass the tube, which must go through the nose, down the esophagus and into the stomach.

Once you've decided on the method of worming you wish to use, then the type of medication must be chosen. You will find a wide variety of equine worm remedies available from which to chose. You are safest to have your veterinarian help you. Have your veterinarian help you chose the right medication. He'll undoubtedly recommend changing medications regularly as there is much evidence that parasites become immune to any medication that is repeatedly used.

After the initial worming, you'll probably be advised to follow up again in one or two months. Then, depending on the conditions, you should worm your horses every two to four months. Although you may think this is a needless bother and expense, you'll be rewarded with a more vigorous, easy keeping horse. He'll have a good hair coat and will be less subject to colic than his worm infested neighbors.

We first worm foals when they are two months old. Earlier worming is useless because the worms haven't yet reached maturity. Before they begin eating solid food, foals will nibble their mother's manure, so it's essential that the mare be kept as worm free as possible. Although there are wormers that are safe for mares in late pregnancy, be sure to first check with your veterinarian before using any.

159

OTHER HEALTH CONCERNS

Realistically, any mature horse can do just about anything he wants to do. Thus, restraining horses is necessary if we want to do something to them about which they aren't too enthusiastic. Many different methods of restraint are used by horsemen, depending on the horse and the situation.

Simple restraints include tying a horse with a rope or confining him to a small enclosure such as a breeding or examining chute. Another simple restraint requires simply lifting a foreleg. This is an easy way to keep a horse from moving around, and since he needs all three other legs to stand on he won't be picking them up. We do this when we are trying to wrap a leg of a fidgety horse or treat one for a leg injury.

Blindfolds are sometimes used to quiet a nervous horse. All of us who have read the book *Black Beauty* remember that the horses were blindfolded before being led from the burning barn. The idea behind a blindfold is that a horse won't be frightened by something he can't see. The problem we've found with blindfolds, however, is that they can come loose. So if you use one, be sure it's fastened securely.

Twitches are another commonly used form of restraint. Many beginning horsemen are shocked by their use, but it's safer to use a twitch than to have the horse hurt himself or his handlers by doing something stupid. Twitches should only be used when they are necessary, but are a real help then.

The idea behind a twitch is to cause a horse some discomfort, either with or without a mechanical device. If he feels discomfort in one part of his body, he'll be thinking about that and not be concerned with the discomfort you may have to cause in another part of his body.

One form of twitch involves twisting an ear. Another is to pinch a fold of neck skin. Either of these are good to use if a horse is excited about an injection or something else that only takes a short time.

A mechanical nose twitch is a pliers-like metal device which squeezes the skin of the nose. Another type has a wooden handle and a circular leather thong that is twisted around the nose. Either of these works well. We use a nose twitch on a horse that doesn't want his ears

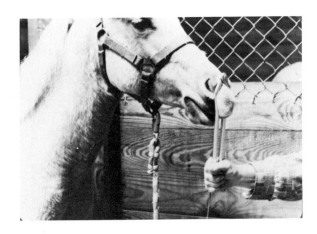

Twitched horse.

clipped or won't let us examine an injury. Other than that, we prefer not to use a twitch.

Other forms of restraint include chains or war bridles. These are mainly used on very unruly horses. Chains over the nose or under the chin will make an exuberant horse easier to handle. A chain can be run through the mouth, but there is always the danger of cutting the lips. In more extreme cases, a chain can be run across the upper gums. This should only be used if the horse requires severe discipline.

War bridles are simply made with cotton rope. They are put on in different ways and apply pressure to the poll or mouth area.

STABLE VICES

Stable vices, as they are referred to by horsemen, include a number of peculiar kinds of behavior that can injure a horse's health. Most result simply from boredom and perhaps can be prevented, but they are seldom cured. We have noticed that most stable vices occur among stalled, highly fed horses.

Wood Chewing

Wood chewing is all too common among stalled horses. Although it

161

is not usually serious to the horse, it can be a very expensive way for him to spend his time.

Confirmed wood chewers can really destroy their surroundings bite by bite. It has been suggested that a mineral imbalance plays a part in this behavior, but it has not been proven. We've had a stable full of horses on the same diet and some chewed the wood while others didn't.

We suspect that wood chewing is caused by a combination of boredom and the horse's temperament. Since wood chewers prefer soft woods, use hard woods in your stalls. Cover the edges of the wood with metal stripping, making it harder for your wood chewer to find a place to sink his teeth into. Paint all of the wood with creosote to give it an unpleasant taste. This also discourages insects and helps preserve the wood. Exercising stalled horses may also ease the problem.

Cribbing

More serious than wood chewing is the disagreeable habit of cribbing. When a horse cribs, he bites down on a hard surface and sucks in air. Although this is less damaging to his surroundings, it is definitely not good for the horse. Such a horse will usually not stay in as good a condition as one that does not crib. Cribbers are also more subject to colic. Finally, confirmed cribbers do their thing wherever they are. Wood chewing can be stopped by removing their supply. Cribbers are active in and out of their stalls. We've even seen them crib on metal gates in a pasture.

A cribbing collar is an ingenious device designed to eliminate this habit. It is a circular collar which fastens around the horse's throat. A metal hinged part is designed to cut off the passage of air through the windpipe whenever the horse tenses up and tries to suck in air. These collars can be somewhat effective. Those with spikes are intended to cause pain whenever the horse sucks in. The problem with spikes is that they can break the skin and cause sores. All in all, unless a horse is perfect in every other way, we'd rather not own a cribber.

Stall Weaving

Another habit that occurs among stalled horses is stall weaving, which is a rhythmical swaying from side to side. Weavers expend a lot of energy doing this and are said to be difficult to keep in condition. It is likely that this is more common among nervous horses.

We have a favorite gelding that weaves when he wants to be let out or if he's impatient for his dinner. It hasn't done him much harm and in this case his good points more than outweigh this one problem.

Kicking and Pawing

Horses that continually bang away at their stall walls are a real nuisance. Not only can they injure themselves, they can destroy their surroundings board by board.

We're not going to waste any time discussing horses that maliciously kick at people. Such animals should not be tolerated. Horses that kick at their stall may simply be annoyed with their neighbor. Whenever a new horse arrives, we carefully shift the horses around until we find an arrangement that pleases everyone. This saves wear and tear on us as well as on the horses and the stalls. Some horses kick at their neighbors at feeding time, but this usually isn't too serious. If you have a confirmed stall kicker you want to keep, about all you can do is wrap his hind legs to keep him from injuring himself.

Pawing horses are also a nuisance. Chains about a foot long can be fastened to the front pasterns to prevent pawing. If the horse tries to paw, the dangling chain slaps him on the leg. If you use chains, his front legs should be wrapped. The wraps will keep him from injuring himself. The treatment is much preferable to having the horse rearrange his stall floor every night.

Other than exercise, a way to occupy stalled horses is to give them something to play with. You can hang up a rubber tire or plastic horse as an amusement. Something else we've seen that works well is a piece of innertube about one foot by two feet. The horse tossed it around vigorously. In no way could it harm him, and it allowed the horse to release his frustration.

PROBLEMS WITH FOALS

Just as young children are subject to childhood diseases, young foals are also susceptible to quite an array of diseases. They come down with colds and other minor diseases, as well as being more prone to injury than older horses.

Once the foal is over the first few days of his life, his mother's milk will provide antibodies which will give him initial protection from disease. Shortly after birth, however, he should be given a tetanus shot as a precautionary measure.

In the chapter on breeding, we mention that the stump of a foal's navel should be treated with iodine immediately after birth. The umbilical cord supplied the foal with nutrients and carried away waste materials while he was in his mother's womb. Shortly after birth, this cord breaks and leaves an open wound that germs can enter and cause navel or joint ill. This is an extremely serious disease in which infection enters the joints and causes lameness and swelling of the joints.

The treatment for navel ill consists of injections of large quantities of antibiotics. The sooner it is treated the better, as permanent damage can result. In any case, if navel ill is suspected, a veterinarian should be called immediately.

A newly born foal should be housed in safe and clean quarters. He should have access to a pasture each day so he can run and play. The only time we keep new foals in a stall is in bitter cold or very damp rainy weather.

Foals need to be protected from extreme changes in weather. Although many horsemen transport and show their young foals, we prefer to keep them at home and avoid the stress of trailering.

Other than exercise and fresh air, give a young foal as much grain as he will eat. Keep his feet trimmed and worm him often, at least every two months.

CASTRATION

The most frequent operation performed on horses is castration. During this procedure, the testicles of a male horse are removed, leaving him impotent. Not only is he impotent, his production of the male hormone testosterone stops and along with it, his stallion-like behavior will end.

Gelding a young horse will largely eliminate biting and rearing problems, as well as leaving him more placid and easily managed. Also, as a gelding he will be less excitable around other horses and appear generally more content. To those who think castration deprives a horse, we suggest they think about the frustrations of a stallion that can't be turned out with other horses and seldom, if ever, gets to breed a mare.

The best age for castration largely depends on the convenience of the owner. Colts are sometimes castrated as early as five months, shortly after they have been weaned. Other owners wait until the colt is two years old, with no adverse affects.

It has been our experience that some colts mature sexually much earlier than others. We once had a colt that made such a nuisance of himself that he had to be gelded at eleven months of age. Other colts of ours were docile well into their second year.

It is possible for a colt under one year of age to breed and possibly to settle a mare. For that reason, colts and fillies need to be separated from about eight months of age.

In the past, colts were allowed to develop until they were two years old before being gelded. At that time it was thought that secondary sexual characteristics such as a crested neck and deep jowl would develop. Now this is not commonly believed true, with many colts castrated as yearlings. It only seems logical that if you have a feisty colt, it's better to geld him as a yearling rather than to suffer through another year. This is especially true if you don't have facilities sturdy enough to handle a young stallion.

The actual operation can be performed by a veterinarian in a paddock or large stall. An anesthetic is administered and as soon as it takes effect, the veterinarian removes the testicles. The wound is not sutured so it will be able to drain properly. Within minutes, the horse will be back on his feet unaware of any changes in his anatomy. An antibiotic is usually administered to help prevent infection. The colt should then be watched, but in most cases the recovery will be quite uneventful. He should be allowed out in a pasture as soon as possible, at least during the day. This will force him to exercise and help keep the swelling to a minimum.

For a few days he will be stiff and sore in his hindquarters, but soon he will be as good as new, except in the breeding shed!

Occasionally, a colt's testicles do not descend into the scrotum, in which case he is called a cryptorchid. In this case, castration is a more serious procedure involving major surgery.

CHAPTER 7

Grooming and Shoeing Your Horse

The only way your horse will ever look his best is if you groom him frequently. You're probably thinking that this sounds like a lot of hard work. It is! The amazing thing, however, is that it all will seem worthwhile when you can stand back and, with a great sense of pride and accomplishment, admire your horse's glistening coat.

In this chapter we're going to discuss in detail the things you'll need to do to keep your horse looking his best. We'll also go over some of the more elaborate techniques used by professional grooms to make their horses really stand out. If you just have a backyard horse these things won't mean much to you now, but you'll be surprised at how quickly your tastes change. Perhaps next year you'll decide to enter a show and all of these things will be very necessary if you're to have any chance of winning.

WHEN TO GROOM YOUR HORSE

If you keep your horse in a stall and ride him pretty often, he'll need to be groomed regularly, even daily if you have the time. Grooming makes your horse's coat healthier by opening the pores and stimulating his circulation and oil glands. This is also a good time to check him over carefully for small cuts and sores so you can treat them before they cause much trouble.

If your horse is kept in a stall and not able to scratch, he'll love being groomed. He'll often show how much he likes it when you brush his favorite spot by stretching out his neck or upper lip and by trying to scratch you back. This can soon get out of hand, so if he starts being a pest, make him stop.

Your horse will particularly like being groomed when he's shedding his winter coat. At this time his thick, heavy coat is itchy and he'll want to scratch a lot. Frequent brushing will get rid of much of the dead hair that makes him itch and he'll be more comfortable. To help him shed, you can use a rubber curry or a shedding blade, but remember to be careful as these tools are harsh and can bother sensitive horses.

WHAT TOOLS ARE NEEDED?

The tools you'll need to groom your horse include:

> a rubber curry
> a stiff body brush
> a soft dandy brush
> some soft cloths (old towels are fine)
> a hoof pick

Rice root brushes work very well as a dandy brush. Although they are a little more costly, they last longer and do a more thorough job. Body brushes are softer and are used as a finishing brush. We've purposely omitted metal currys from our list of grooming tools because we don't use them and feel they are too harsh for most horses. All of the supplies listed can be found at most tack shops.

HOW TO GROOM YOUR HORSE

Most horses can be groomed in their stall; however, if your horse is nervous and excitable you should put him in crossties. This isn't always necessary, but it can make grooming him a lot easier.

Before you start, be sure your horse's coat is completely dry. Brushing a wet horse is simply a waste of time. If he is wet, go over his coat with a sweat scraper, rub him with a towel and walk him until he's completely dry.

If there's any caked mud or dirt on him, you'll need to remove it with a rubber curry. Simply rub the curry in large circles. The dirt will collect in the center and from time to time you should get rid of it by tapping the curry on a hard surface like the heel of your shoe. Don't use a curry on your horse's face or legs as these areas are very sensitive. Some

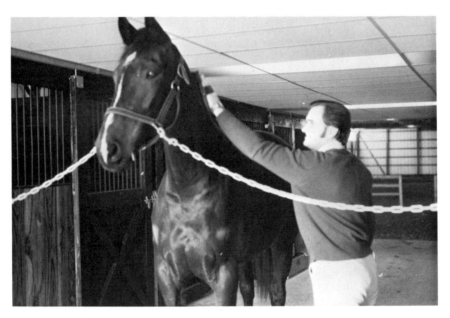

A horse in crossties being groomed with a body brush.

horses even resent a stiff brush, so be careful not to cause any unnecessary irritation.

Continue by brushing vigorously with the stiff body brush and remove the dirt you just loosened with the curry. Brush with the lay of the hair and be sure to brush hard so you really get rid of the dirt. You'll do even better if you snap your wrist up after each stroke. This helps lift the dirt off the horse rather than just spreading it around. Since you can't clean a horse with a dirty brush, clean it periodically as you work by running the rubber curry through it.

Next, you'll want to go over the whole coat with a softer body brush. This will get out the smaller bits of dirt and make the coat shine by opening the pores and bringing the oil to the surface. Be sure not to miss such places as between the front legs, the belly and the back of the pasterns.

To get a deeper shine and to get rid of any lingering dust, use a rub rag for a finishing touch. Simply polish his coat like you would anything else and continue until you're satisfied with the way he looks.

With most horses you'll also want to brush their mane and tail. While you can buy brushes and combs made especially for horses, something that works quite well is a hairbrush made for humans. It is usually a little more gentle and won't break off as much hair. Brushing manes and tails is a lot easier if the brush is damp and if you do a small section at a time, you'll do a better job. Begin brushing with the ends of the mane and tail hair and work upward toward the roots as it untangles. In this way fewer strands of hair will be pulled out. If the mane is very thick, you'll need to take extra care and be sure to brush all the hair on the underside. Some breeds need special ways of grooming manes and tails and we'll discuss these later in the chapter.

Picking Your Horse's Hoofs

If your horse is kept in a stall, you'll need to pick the manure and other litter out of his hoofs. If it's left to accumulate, it could cause a serious hoof disease known as thrush. Pastured horses don't need this special attention as their hoofs get packed with mud in wet weather and this keeps them healthy and natural. It is possible, however, for a pastured horse to pick up a rock in his hoof, so if you see any signs of lameness, check his hoofs first.

169

To be able to clean your horse's hoof, you first have to get him to pick it up. Horses are supposed to lift a hoof if you face the rear, push against the leg you want to lift and place your hand on the lower part of the leg. Of course, some horses will be stubborn and just stand there with their feet planted firmly on the ground. This happens to all of us, so don't be embarrassed. Grumble like we all do, and keep after him until he picks it up. By all means don't give up and let him get away with being stubborn. It will be twice as hard the next time. Once he's learned you're not going to give up, he'll give in sooner.

Now that you have the hoof up, pick out the dirt by scraping with a hoof pick from the heel toward the toe. Be sure to clean thoroughly the groove between the frog and the bars where the hoof wall turns in. The sole of the hoof is quite tough, so don't be afraid to scrape hard and really do a good job. This is also a good time to check for any hoof problems such as cracked hoofs, loose shoes or thrush. You can tell if thrush is present by a rotting of the frog or a discharge of a dark, foul smelling liquid. If a hoof seems especially dry and brittle, you should apply some sort of commercially prepared hoof dressing.

Scrape the hooves of stalled horses periodically with a hoof pick.

GROOMING A PASTURED HORSE

Pastured horses don't need as much care as stalled horses, but they do need attention once in a while to make sure any serious problems aren't developing. It's a good idea at least to check pastured horses every day.

In hot weather, the inside of the ears of a pastured horse can get infested with troublesome gnats. You can help prevent this by cleaning out any crusted matter with a damp cloth and smearing petroleum jelly lightly in the ears to help protect them.

If ticks are a problem in your area, be sure to check for them often, particularly in the root of the foretop, the mane and the tail. Ticks burrow into the skin and can cause severe itching and even infection.

Many horseowners neglect the belly and the elbows of pastured horses, yet these areas can become itchy and sore from gnats. You can soothe any of these raw spots by lightly smearing them with petroleum jelly.

BATHING YOUR HORSE

In most cases you will never have to give your horse a bath and some horsemen recommend avoiding it entirely. Bathing does remove the natural oil from the horse's coat and this oil gives him important protection that's essential if he's kept in a pasture.

So many horses go their entire life without getting a bath and this is fine—unless a situation arises when you decide to take your horse to a parade or a show and find he's spent the morning rolling in the mud. Natural oil is fine, but the only way he'll look his best is if you give him a bath.

In the way of equipment, you'll need a bucket of warm water, shampoo, a sponge, and a brush. Now find a warm, draft-free spot in which to bathe your horse. Sunny summer days are ideal. If the bath is a first for you and your horse, allow plenty of time for both of you to get used to the situation. If he's like most horses, he'll soon learn to enjoy his bath, but the idea will have to grow on him. He's bound to act a little silly at first, particularly when you begin spraying him with water, but keep at it for a time and he'll soon learn that it's not going to hurt him. It might even feel good, especially on a hot summer day. Also, it's a good idea to have someone around to help hold your horse, at least for the first time or two.

First, you'll need to soak completely his legs, body and neck with water from the hose. Some horses are afraid of the spray at first, so move gently and gradually. Start by dampening his legs with a small stream of water and as he gets used to it, increase the force and soak the rest of him.

Be very careful always to spray away from his head. If you get any water in his ears there's no way to get it out and just a small amount can cause him to lose his sense of balance.

After he's completely soaked, start sponging him with the warm, soapy water. A sponge works fine on most places, but if you find a stubborn spot, scrub it with the brush. Be sure to wet and lather the mane and tail all the way to the roots. You can wash the tail by sponging the tailhead and dipping the rest of it in a bucket of water. The tailbone is very sensitive, so try to avoid getting it in the water.

Once your horse is scrubbed completely, start rinsing him with water from the hose. Again, remember to spray away from his head. Be sure to rinse him thoroughly and you might want to go over him again to be sure you remove all of the soap. Any soap left in his coat will collect dirt quite easily.

Finally, scrape off any excess water with the sweat scraper and walk him until he's completely dry before you put him away.

CLIPPING YOUR HORSE

Obviously, your horse can get along fine without your ever trimming any excess hair, but it certainly can make him look a lot better and is necessary if you ever show him. On the other hand, if your horse stays in a pasture all the time, he needs this hair to protect him. The shaggy hair on his fetlocks acts as a natural drain by keeping the water from running down his heels and chapping them, while the hair in his ears protects him from insect bites.

Professional grooms use trimming to highlight the smooth graceful lines of their horses and accent the good points they want people to notice. Saddlebred show horses even have their eyelashes trimmed to give them the desired "wide-awake" look.

Although you can use scissors, clippers do a much neater job and

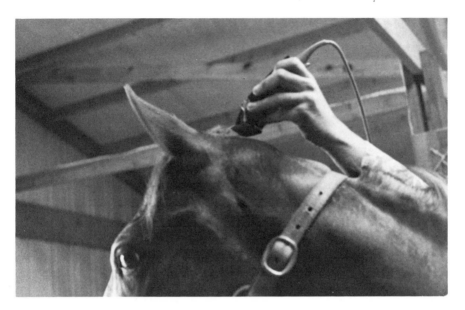

Trimming the bridle path with electric clippers.

even though they cost more they are usually worth the investment. Probably the handiest are the small electric clippers similar to those used on dogs. They have the advantage of being small and easily handled and are relatively quiet, which helps when trimming nervous horses around the ears. The larger models are bulky, quite noisy and not necessary unless you plan to clip a lot of horses or the entire body. The smaller, hand operated models can be quite awkward and can't be counted on to do as neat a job.

If you can't afford clippers, a pair of scissors with blunt points can be used to trim excess fetlock hair and even to clip the mane for the bridle path.

If you just want your horse to look a little neater, there are a few places to trim that can really improve his appearance. Beginning with the face, very carefully remove the whiskers around the muzzle and eyes. Then lift the forelock and clip any excess hair you find there. This will make the forelock lie smoothly without cutting it shorter. Also, trim any long hair growing on the cheeks and jowls.

Next, trim all the hair from the inside of the ears and go over the edges to smooth the outline. Many horses don't like having their ears clipped, so you might have to use a twitch. The mane is ordinarily clipped at the poll. This clipped portion is called the bridle path and its purpose is to allow the crownpiece of the bridle to lie flat.

Now, to finish, trim the hair around the coronary band or the top of the hoof as well as all long hair on the back of the pasterns, fetlocks and cannons.

While most horses never have their bodies clipped, you should know that in places where hunting and jumping are common, it's customary to clip the entire body of the horse during the winter. If a horse is worked hard, he'll cool out more quickly if he's been clipped, than if he has a long, shaggy coat soaked with sweat. Also, horses with heavy winter coats tend to lose condition rapidly if they're worked hard. Sometimes, hunters will have their bodies clipped, but their legs are allowed to grow shaggy to protect them from the brush. Once a horse has his body clipped, his natural protection against the weather is gone and he must be blanketed so he doesn't become chilled.

In most cases, however, if a horse is blanketed and kept inside as soon as it starts to get cold, he probably won't grow a long coat, making clipping the body unnecessary.

GROOMING FOR A SHOW

If you decide to take your horse to a show or display him in public in any other way, you'll want him to look his very best. First you need to groom him very thoroughly, as we've already described. Then there are some additional techniques professional showmen use to make their horses really stand out.

A very important part of preparing for a show is to think ahead. You have to begin at least several weeks before the show to get your horse in good physical condition and his coat, mane and tail ready. He'll need sufficient feed to be in good flesh, as well as frequent grooming to improve his coat. Then, several days before the show, you should clip him carefully as we have just described. A shaggy horse may be fine in the pasture, but he'll look out of place among other well-trimmed horses in a show or parade.

Finally, on the day of the show, give your horse a bath and apply a coat dressing if you like. There are several of these on the market and they will help make his coat glisten without nearly as much rubbing. They work especially well on gray horses and can be found in any tack shop. Some grooms rub briskly over the horse's coat with the palms of their hands. The heat from the hands and the rubbing helps bring the oil to the surface and makes the coat shine.

If your horse's hoofs are black, you can go over them with a hoof blackener. There are several on the market now that make the hoofs shine without collecting dust. Now, clear hoof polish is available for white hoofs, too.

Just before you enter the ring or parade, you can smear baby oil or mineral oil around his muzzle, eyes and inside the ears. This makes them glisten, particularly at night under bright lights.

GROOMING THE MANE AND TAIL

You are going to see horses with their manes and tails in several different styles. The particular style depends on the breed or how the horse is used. Each style requires different ways of grooming. Styles vary even within a breed, such as the full mane of the five-gaited Saddlebred and the roached mane of the three-gaited Saddlebred. There's usually a reason for each style, whether it's a braided mane to prevent the reins from getting tangled or a roached mane to refine the appearance of the neck. If you plan to show your horse, find out what style is required and we'll give you some tips on taking care of it.

Full Length Manes and Tails

Hand picking is required whenever you want length, since it reduces the breaking and split ends you get from brushing and combing. This involves separating each strand individually so it doesn't break off. It's the only way to groom the mane and tail of a very fine-haired horse when you want them to grow long. As much as skill, hand picking requires a great deal of patience and care.

A horse that has a long tail might need it braided between shows and while he's in his stall. If his tail grows to the ground this will keep him from stepping on it and pulling the hair out.

175

Pulled Manes and Tails

Thoroughbreds usually wear pulled manes, while Quarter Horses often have both their manes and tails pulled. This is the best way to keep a mane short and neat. It involves pulling out any hair that grows longer than you want, which is usually about six inches. Pulling simply means jerking a few strands of hair out at a time. This makes the mane lie flat and requires only a light brushing to keep it looking neat. If some strands stray to the other side of the neck, a little water brushed in will weigh it down enough to keep it on the right side.

Some stock horses and hunters have their tails pulled until the tail is the length and shape that you want. Stock horses' tails are pulled and shaped the whole length, while for Thoroughbreds the hair is mostly removed from the base.

Thoroughbreds sometimes have their tail cut short or banged with scissors at about the point where it reaches the hock when the horse is in motion. Other than banging, scissors should not be used on a mane or tail because it gives them a very unnatural look, while pulling just removes straggly hair and makes them neat.

Roached or Hogged Manes

This kind of mane is simply clipped close to the root. It's required for three-gaited Saddlebreds so you can tell them from five-gaited Saddlebreds and it's also popular among stock horses. Quarter Horses all used to wear a hogged mane to refine the appearance of their neck. The forelock was left long and a lock of hair was left at the withers to make it more prominent. Now, most wear pulled manes.

Three-gaited Saddlebreds have their forelocks clipped with no tuft of hair at the withers. They also have the first few inches at the base of their tail clipped. Standardbreds have their manes left full, but the forelock is clipped to make putting on and taking off the harness easier.

Generally, hogging refines an otherwise heavy neck and reduces the grooming time between clipping. Once a horse's mane has been hogged, it must be reclipped about every two weeks to keep it looking neat. One note of caution, however; think about what you're doing be-

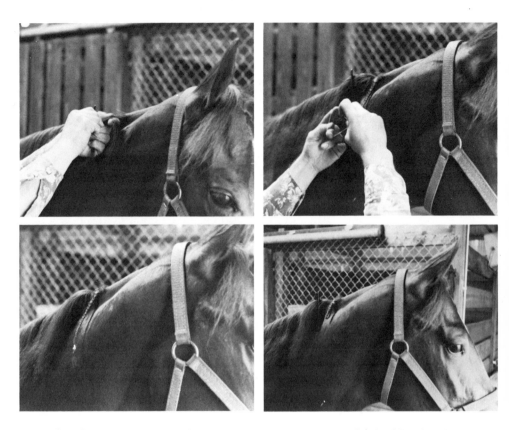

Mane braiding. Beginning to braid (top), and fastening with a rubber band. Completed braid fastened with rubber band (bottom), and completed braid tucked under.

fore hogging your horse's mane since it takes about a year before it grows out again.

Braiding Manes and Tails

Thoroughbred hunters and jumpers are usually shown with their manes and tails braided. A mare traditionally has an even number of braids in her mane, while a gelding has an odd number. Braids can improve the appearance of a horse, as many small braids will make the

177

neck look longer, while a few large braids make the neck appear shorter.

In order to braid a mane, you must first dampen it with water. This makes it more manageable. Then, beginning at the top, separate a narrow section of about three inches, divide this into three strands and proceed with a regular three-plait braid. When finished, the braid may be tied with a rubber band or with yarn, folded underneath to the base of the mane and fastened by sewing it with coarse thread and a blunt needle. The forelock should also be braided in the same way.

Tail braiding is pretty tough to do. It's a good idea to practice a few times before you get ready to go to a show. You should begin at the root by taking a strand of hair from underneath each side of the tail. Cross these strands and add a strand from the center. Braid these strands and continue down the tail alternately picking up strands from the left, right and center and braiding them together. As you work down the tail be sure to keep the hair strands snug. Continue until you reach the end of the dock, or tail bone. Tuck the last braid underneath the braids above it and sew them together with a blunt needle. The hair that's left forms a switch and is left long unless the horse is to be ridden in mud when it's tucked up to make a neat stub.

After the show, undo the braiding as soon as possible. If you don't, it will cause the horse to itch and he will rub, pulling his hair out.

HOOF CARE

It seems that one of the big worries of beginning horsemen is whether or not their horse needs shoes. There is no hard and fast rule. It depends on the kind of riding you expect to do. If you're going to ride over rough, rocky ground or pavement or even if you just ride a lot, then it's likely your horse will need to be shod. Shoes help protect your horse's hoofs and keep them from wearing too rapidly, so you need to decide whether the kind of riding you do makes them necessary. It's generally felt that white hoofs are not as durable as black, and this can make a difference as to whether or not your horse needs to be shod.

Aside from the question of shoeing, your horse's hoofs will grow up to one quarter of an inch every month, and because of this they need regular trimming. If you ignore the hoofs they might split or crack, leading to other more serious problems. There's nothing more frustrating than to get all ready to ride and find that your horse is lame because of something that could easily have been prevented with proper care.

Regardless of whether or not you decide to have your horse shod, you do need to have a farrier come every six to eight weeks at least to trim the hoofs. Some horsemen do the trimming themselves and this is something you might want to learn to do. If you have shoes put on, trimming is part of the job.

Because your horse's hoofs contribute to many problems that can result in lameness, you must be very careful in choosing a farrier. You'll find that people who shoe horses are called both farriers and horseshoers, but here we'll refer to them as farriers. Only a few states require a license and too often all that's needed is to hang out a sign and call yourself a farrier. Shoeing horses is a highly skilled craft that takes a lot of experience and someone that's not skilled can do more harm than good.

Probably the best way to find a good farrier is by asking the other horsemen in your area. Reputations, both good and bad, spread quickly and you'll find most people eager to talk about both. Be wary of farriers who spend a lot of time talking about how good they are. Judge them by the job they do, rather than by what they say they can do. Those that are good let their work speak for itself, so don't be misled by bragging.

It's a good idea to be around when the farrier comes. You can then watch the way he does his job as well as generally how he handles your horse. He should be firm, but not needlessly rough. You certainly don't want to have a battle with your horse every time a farrier comes simply because someone was once too rough. Also, if like most of us you have a lot of questions, your farrier should be glad to answer them.

It will be easier for everyone if you have your horse in crossties for either trimming or shoeing. Be sure to have a strong halter on your horse. Try to find a place where the farrier can easily get at each hoof.

Trimming involves first cutting off the excess hoof wall with a pair of nippers that look like big pliers. Then a special knife is used to trim the sole and outline the frog by cutting off the ragged, scaly outer surface. Both front feet and both hind feet should be trimmed to the same length and angle as well as setting level on the ground.

By trimming a little more off either the inside or the outside of the hoof, a farrier can help correct leg faults by making the horse stand straighter. This only works effectively on young horses, however, so be-

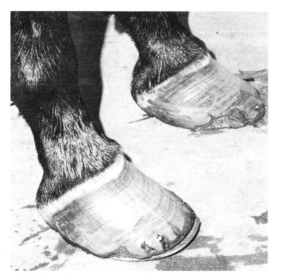

This horse wintered in a pasture and foot care was completely neglected. Note the extreme length of the hooves which cause the horse to stand unnaturally back on his heels. This series of photos shows the steps involved in caring for badly deteriorated hooves.

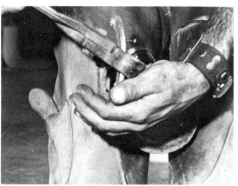

First, the horseshoer removes the old shoes from the horse's hooves.

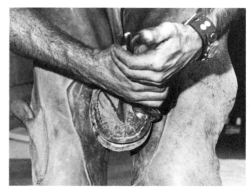

The farrier then trims the hoof wall so that the hoof is flat and angled properly.

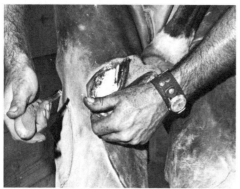

The sole of the hoof is trimmed to remove dead and decaying tissue.

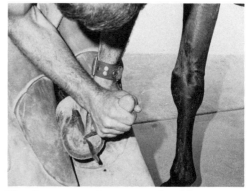

The frog is pared to expose healthy tissue and insure proper ground contact.

The hoof is then rasped to make it smooth and completely flat and level with the ground.

The farrier makes horse shoes from bar stock.

He shapes the shoe for a correct fit around the hoof wall and at the heel.

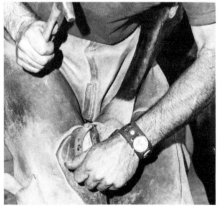

The shoe is nailed in place through the outer wall.

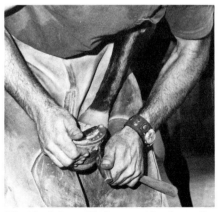

Clinched for added strength, the nails are rasped flat and smooth.

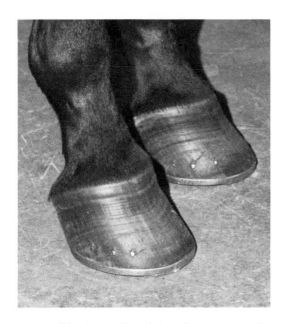

Finally the horse has hooves that have been trimmed correctly and shoes that fit well and will protect his feet.

ware of farriers who claim they can work miracles and instead might do more harm than good!

Once the hoof has been trimmed, if the farrier is going to put on shoes he'll next have either to pick out a pre-made shoe the proper size or begin to hand-forge a shoe to the proper shape and size. Although many farriers buy their shoes ready-made and pick out one to fit the hoof, some still forge their own from metal bars. This is preferred by most horsemen as the shoe can be made to fit the hoof a little better. A pre-made shoe can be made to fit quite adequately, however, so don't be concerned if this is all you can get. The metal in pre-made shoes is quite malleable and can be hammered into the proper shape. The most important thing is that the farrier be good at what he is doing.

Once the shoe has been made to fit properly, it will be attached to the hoof by using long nails that are driven through the hoof wall, twisted off, clinched on the outside and filed flush. It's important that the nails don't reach too high on the hoof wall where they could pierce the sensitive laminae and cause lameness or be too low where they could pull out of the hoof.

A properly fitting shoe will fit flush with the outside of the hoof all the way around. The fit should come from forming the shoe to fit the hoof and not by trimming the hoof to fit the shoe, which is an old but frequently used gimmick to save time. It is possible to trim the hoof so the shoe appears to fit, but once it begins to grow, the shoe will be too small and can cause discomfort.

Something fairly new that is certainly a good idea is the application of borium to the bottom of the shoe. It is a hard abrasive metal that is welded to the toe and heel. It adds a few dollars to the cost of the shoes, but it does prevent the horse from slipping, especially on slick pavement. Also, borium will help the shoes last longer and might even save you a little money since the cost of resetting shoes is less than the cost of replacing them.

Corrective Shoeing and Trimming

Through corrective shoeing and trimming, a good farrier can improve faulty conformation and action as well as change the length and height of stride. All this is accomplished by slightly changing the angle of the pastern and the hoof and by lengthening or shortening one side of the hoof or the other or by using weights.

It's particularly important that young horses have their feet trimmed often to keep any problems from developing. The hoof grows downward and eventually is worn, trimmed or broken off. If it's broken off, it will likely be uneven and result in a hoof that is not level. The horse will stand crookedly on this leg and if it's a foal with soft bones, minor leg faults can develop rather quickly. Becuase of their softer, more pliable bones, foals also respond better to corrective trimming than do older horses. It's important to have foals' hoofs trimmed regularly even if they have excellent legs in order to make sure they stay that way.

An excessively long toe causes a foal to start breaking off center as he moves. As this continues, the hoof wears unevenly, more on one side than the other. Eventually, the long side breaks off crookedly and makes the problem even worse.

A very common problem in horses is toeing out. This is helped by trimming the outside wall a little extra so the horse stands more evenly. The opposite, a pigeon-toed horse, should have extra trimmed off the inside wall to compensate for the excessive wear on the outside.

While minor problems in action won't make much difference to the average backyard horse, for horses that are used hard, such as race or show horses, even a minor problem can quickly cause the horse to break down. If he injures himself, such a horse wouldn't be much good for racing or showing.

If a performance horse isn't built correctly, he places additional stress on his legs. A skilled farrier can help this through the use of corrective shoeing. By the clever use of trimming and weights, the gait can be changed enough so one leg won't strike the other. When dealing with racehorses it's easy to see why a skilled farrier is in such demand.

If you have ever seen a five-gaited Saddlebred perform or watched a Tennessee Walker do his running walk, you might have wondered why the horses in your neighborhood don't move that way. Much of what you see in the show ring is created or at least helped a great deal by special shoeing. These horses have a lot of weight added to each shoe, Walkers up to seven pounds per foot, in order to achieve the overstride demanded by today's show competition. Then, too, these horses have extremely long hoofs so their action will be higher. Because the frog must be in contact with the ground, special pads are put between the shoe and the sole of the hoof so the frog will have pressure and not contract or cause other problems. With this extra hoof length, the horse must be ridden only on a smooth surface such as in a ring. Rough ground could cause severe tendon strain and permanent damage could result.

A horse's shoes can improve his performance by giving him added traction. Borium helps on slick surfaces such as asphalt. On natural yielding surfaces like dirt, special shoes with calks help the horse dig in and prevent slippage or falls.

Gaming horses, polo ponies, hunters, jumpers and racehorses all have to run fast on natural surfaces. Their shoes have rims so they can turn easier. Running racehorses wear the lightest shoes. These are called racing plates and each weighs less than six ounces. The emphasis is not on durability, but lightness and protection so as not to hinder the stride. Standardbreds sometimes require special shoeing techniques to help them to perfect their gait. Once in a while you'll see toe weights fastened into the front of the horse's hoof for added weight to lengthen the stride.

CHAPTER 8

Tack For Your Horse

Now that you've bought a horse, have a warm, comfortable place for him to stay and are keeping him healthy and fit, he's almost ready for what you bought him for—riding! As you've probably noticed though, you can't just jump on his back and go galloping off into the sunset. You'll need certain equipment to control your horse as well as make him a bit more comfortable to sit on.

A general term used to describe any horse-related equipment is "tack." This equipment is found in what are appropriately called tack shops. To the dismay of many new horseowners, tack can end up costing as much or more than their horse. Nevertheless, if your tack is well cared for, it should last for many years, proving to be a sound investment toward enjoying your horse. The saddle and bridle are what makes the horse and rider a team, and you'll both do better and enjoy each other more if the equipment fits well and is cared for properly.

While the most expensive tack is not necessarily the best, good

185

equipment does cost more initially, but proves its worth by lasting longer. On the other hand, gaudy trinkets can add much to the cost of a saddle or bridle, while adding nothing to its usefulness. Generally, quality tack is properly designed, fits well, is made of a prime grade of leather with good hardware; but more about this later.

ENGLISH TACK

SADDLES

While English style riding in the United States used to be centered almost entirely in the East, today it is popular all across the country. Even the Quarter Horse, long considered to be the symbol of Western riding, is being shown regularly in English tack.

English saddles come in a wide variety of styles and prices. They are necessary if you intend to compete in any English classes at horse shows or plan to attempt hunting and jumping or three day eventing. Also, the deep-seated English saddles are excellent for beginning

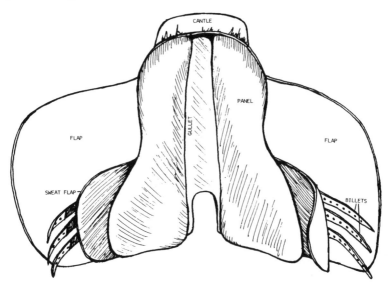

Underside of an English saddle.

young horses because they weigh little, while many people simply prefer them for pleasure or trail rides.

Because of their light weight, English saddles give the rider close contact with his horse and obviously are easier to lift on and off than the bulkier Western saddle. On the other hand, their relatively flat seat and light stirrups offer less security than a deeper Western saddle.

There are three basic types of English saddles to choose from. These are the cut-back, the forward seat or jumping saddle and the dressage saddle. The cut-back or "flat" saddle as it is sometimes called is the type used in saddle-seat riding on American Saddlebreds, Arabians and Morgans. The saddles get their name from a four inch cut-out at the pommel and the fact that they have a very shallow seat. They allow the rider to sit back on the horse while he tries to elevate or lift the forehand, emphasizing the action of the horse. Because of these features, cut-back saddles are found almost exclusively in the show ring.

Girths used with cut-back saddles have traditionally been white, but now are often color coordinated with the browband and caveson as well as with the rider's clothes to create a highly distinctive look.

A narrow full or "double" bridle is used with a cut-back saddle. Double bridles have both curb and snaffle bits, each with its own set of reins. These reins permit delicate communication between the horse and rider. Obviously such a bridle is not intended for a beginning horse or rider.

Another kind of English saddle is a forward seat or jumping saddle. They generally have a deeper seat than cut-backs. Instead of being vertical, the flaps on these saddles extend slightly forward. Some also have a padded roll at the front of the flap to keep the knee from slipping. These rolls can be covered with suede, although today the trend is toward close-contact saddles with small, plain knee rolls.

Forward seat saddles are used primarily on hunters, jumpers and on horses competing in hunt-seat classes at horse shows. Because of their deep seat, these saddles are fine for beginning as well as advanced riders. Girths used include string, leather and leather with elastic ends. Any of these work well enough, the choice being determined by the pocketbook and preference of the rider.

Forward seat saddle with suede knee rolls.   *Close contact forward seat saddle.*

Bridles for hunt-type saddles are sturdier than the fancy show bridles used in saddle seat riding. Especially for the hunt field, reins and bridle parts should be from three-quarters to one inch wide. Show bridles used in hunt seat classes are often only one half inch wide, but these are not sturdy enough for strenuous cross-country use. Hunt bridles are most often used with snaffle bits; however, kimberwick as well as pelham bits are sometimes seen.

A third type of English saddle is a dressage saddle. It has a deep seat, straight flaps and knee rolls. As with hunt saddles, the knee rolls are sometimes covered with suede or left plain. Dressage saddles have longer flaps and are ridden with a longer stirrup than are hunt saddles. A leather or string girth is commonly used. Bridles used are similar to the hunt type, except in shows, a fancy black and white browband is sometimes used.

Selecting an English Saddle

The type of English saddle you buy will largely depend on the kind of riding you do. That is, if you want to learn to jump, don't buy a cut-back saddle—it won't fill the bill!

If you are a beginner and just want an all-around English saddle, we prefer a deep-seated dressage or hunt-type saddle because of the security it offers.

Dressage saddle.

Seat sizes vary, beginning with 15 and 16 inch children's saddles. Adult sizes range from 16½ through 19 inches, with 17 and 17½ being the most popular. English saddles usually have the size printed in the billet guard. You can measure one yourself though by determining the distance from the center of the cantle to the nail head on either side of the pommel.

STIRRUPS

Unlike Western saddles, English saddles do not come equipped with stirrups or stirrup leathers. They must be purchased separately. English stirrup irons come in different qualities to fit every pocketbook and different sizes to fit every rider.

Stirrup size is determined by the inside measurement of the tread. The iron should be about one inch wider than the rider's foot so there is less chance of becoming caught in it in case of a spill.

The most expensive stirrup irons are made in Europe of stainless steel. These heavy irons tend to hang in place rather than swing wildly if your foot comes out of the stirrup while you are riding. Fine stainless steel irons are now made in Japan. Irons made of a never-rust alloy are not as shiny, but are very serviceable. Don't buy chrome plated irons as they tend to pit and rust.

For a modest additional price you can, and should, add a pair of rubber stirrup pads. They increase traction and are warmer on your feet in winter.

GIRTHS

There are several different kinds of girths used with English saddles, depending on how the saddle is going to be used and the size of the horse. Girth sizes vary from forty-two to fifty-two inches in two-inch increments. The small sizes are used for ponies and the large for hunter-type horses. The average riding horse takes a forty-six-inch girth.

The least expensive girths are made of white webbing. Even though these are economical, they tend to slip and are not recommended as they can break under extreme conditions.

String girths are quite practical, strong and not much more expensive than web girths. They can be made of mohair, nylon, cotton or even polypropylene plastic.

Leather girths are the most expensive. They are durable, strong and comfortable for the horse. The most popular leather girths have at least one elastic end and are narrower at the horse's elbow to prevent chafing. Imitation leather girths are available, too. They are less expensive, easy to care for, but probably won't last as long as the English- or German-made leather girths.

Fancy show girths used to be made of white cotton webbing, which didn't stay white very long. Now they are almost exclusively made of patent leather or vinyl. As with everything else, color is now in and white is out. You can customize your tack and buy a girth made in any imaginable color or colors. These girths all have a pimpled rubber backing inside to prevent slipping.

SADDLE PADS

To begin, the purpose of a saddle pad is to cushion the saddle, absorb sweat and keep the saddle clean. If you ride a horse without using a saddle pad, the saddle will soon get quite dirty and sweaty and if you ride long enough, the rubbing of the saddle on your horse's back will cause saddle sores.

English saddle pads used to be made exclusively of sheepskin and felt, but now the majority are made of imitation fleece. These pads

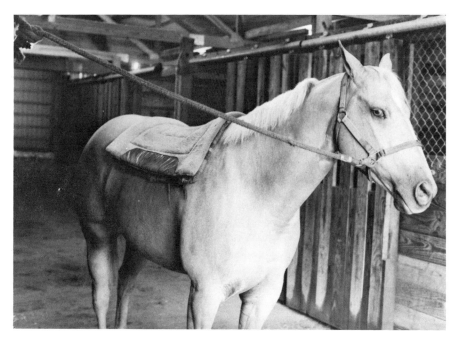

Horse in crossties with saddle pads that go under the saddle.

are used by most riders because they are relatively inexpensive, easily laundered and highly absorbent.

English saddle pads come in different shapes to fit all of the different types of saddles. The simplest pads are either made of felt or one layer of fleece. Single-ply fleece pads aren't as absorbent as the double-ply pads, but they can easily be cut out to fit the exact shape of the saddle. Be sure to remember that single-ply fleece pads are used with the fleece side down against the horse.

Double-ply fleece pads are more absorbent, but tend to slip slightly under the saddle. Olympic-style pads are single ply under the saddle, but have a two to three ply rolled edge around the outside. They are attractive, too, but most importantly, the edge helps keep the saddle from slipping. Currently, a successful jumper has introduced a foam rubber pad shaped to fit the outline of the saddle. For simple schooling purposes, we even use a Western style pad with our English saddles.

BRIDLES

English bridles are made up of several different parts, each of which has a special term used to describe it. Because it's likely that you'll hear horsemen use these terms, we'll give you a brief explanation of them. The bridle that we'll use as an example is a snaffle bridle which is one of the three most common English bridles. The parts of the others are basically the same with some special features for various purposes.

When looking at an English snaffle bridle while it is on a horse, at the very top is a strap that goes behind the ears and over the poll. This is the crownpiece. A few inches below the horse's ears the crownpiece splits to form the throatlatch, which as its name implies fastens under the throat. The throatlatch keeps the bridle from falling forward over the ears. In front of the ears and across the forehead is the browband, which keeps the crownpiece in place.

The crownpiece ends about midway down the cheek of the horse. There it is buckled on each side to the cheekpiece, which is the strap to which the bit is fastened. Although the bit used to be fastened to the cheekpiece with buckles, today hook and studs are used almost exclusively.

English bridles all have a noseband or caveson which fastens around the horse's nose so that he can't open his mouth to evade the bit or get his tongue over it. The noseband is held in place by a strap which runs up the cheek, through the browband and behind the ears.

Reins can be plain, laced or braided. Lacing or braiding begins about eighteen inches from the ends at the bit and is supposed to keep the rider's hands from slipping. Some work reins are made of webbing, which is strong and doesn't slip.

Pelham bridles are made in the same way as snaffles, but have two sets of reins; one for the upper ring of the bit and one for the lower. The lower, or curb reins, are slightly narrower than the snaffle reins so the rider doesn't confuse them.

Another type of English bridle is called a Weymouth, full, or double bridle. These are similar to those we've just described, but use

192

Horse wearing a full or Weymouth bridle.

two separate bits. To accommodate this extra bit, an additional strap called a bridoon strap is added to the bridle to which the snaffle bit is attached. The curb bit is then attached to the regular cheekpiece.

This type of bridle is not intended for a green horse or an inexperienced rider. It's used almost exclusively for saddle seat riding. This is because a saddle seat horse is required to be set up or flexed at the poll. A full bridle enables the rider to lift the horse's head with the snaffle bit and lower his head with the curb.

Pelham and snaffle bridles are used in most types of English riding. The width of the leather used in the bridle varies due to the type of riding. Those used for hunting and jumping must be strong and serviceable. Cheekpieces and reins should be from three quarters to one inch in width. Those used in showing are sometimes as narrow as one half inch. The most elaborate are often made of round, rolled leather. For dressage tests, a fancy black and white browband can be added.

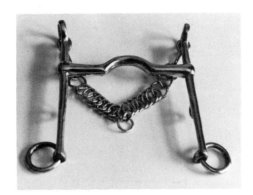

Bridoon.

An English Weymouth bit used with a bridoon.

Weymouth bridles often have very narrow straps. The most popular show models are only three eighths of an inch wide with reins three eighths and five eighths of an inch wide. Fancy colored browbands and cavesons are added to enhance the beauty of the horse's head and coordinate with the rider's clothing.

BITS

The purpose of any bit is to allow the rider to communicate with his horse. This communication can be gentle or powerful depending on the bit and the tactfulness of your hands on the reins.

A bit rests in the horse's mouth above the tongue in the space between his incisors and molars called the bars. Actually the bars are nothing more than gums. A young horse has tender, sensitive bars and thus it is easy to communicate with him through a bit. This condition can only be preserved by carefully selecting the proper bit and handling a horse gently. Rough handling and excessive pressure will eventually cause the buildup of scar tissue and loss of feeling. A horse with this condition is said to have a hard mouth. We've even seen one old gelding with a tough callous on each bar! You can imagine how responsive he was.

The bits we're going to talk about in this chapter should cover most riders' needs. Although there are endless variations, we think a properly fitted bit in the hands of a sensitive rider is more important than a new fad bit that everyone's using at the moment.

You should know that a snaffle bit with its direct pull tends to raise a horse's head, while a curb bit tends to lower it. Other than that, you'll just have to experiment until you find just which bit is right for you and the kind of riding you intend to do.

Selecting an English Bit

English bits are either made of stainless steel, a never-rust steel alloy or are chrome-plated. The least expensive bits are chrome-plated, but these tend to rust and pit rather easily and we don't consider them a good investment. Never-rust bits usually cost less than stainless steel and are quite practical. They aren't as shiny and do need polishing once in a while, but should provide many years of service. Stainless steel bits are the most expensive, are bright and shiny and wear quite well. The most expensive are made in England and Germany, but some good stainless steel bits now come from Korea and Japan.

The mouthpiece of the bit may be made from any of the above metals as well as copper and occasionally rubber. Copper is said to encourage salivation and thus is used on horses that tend to have dry mouths. Rubber mouthpiece bits are sometimes used with horses that have tender mouths.

Another point to notice is that well made bits flare out slightly at the upper cheekpieces to allow for the fact that the horse's head widens the farther up it goes.

Types of English Bits

There are three basic kinds of bits used with English bridles. These are the snaffle, pelham and curb. Because it is the mildest, the first bit used on a young horse is a snaffle. Snaffle bits commonly have a broken mouthpiece which is made up of two parts joined in the center. At the outer ends of the mouthpiece is a ring to which the bridle cheekpieces and the reins are attached. Snaffle bits are mild because the pressure felt by the horse is equal to that exerted by the rider on the reins. Curb and pelham bits have the addition of a lever which multiplies this pressure.

Snaffle bits act upon the lips and corners of the horse's mouth. They vary in severity according to the shape and size of the mouth-

Round ring snaffle.

Twisted wire snaffle.

Twisted mouth snaffle.

Full cheek snaffle.

Rubber D-ring snaffle.

Hollow mouth egg-butt snaffle.

piece, the mildest bit having the thickest mouthpiece. Although this surprises some people, it's easy to understand when you realize that if a given amount of pressure is exerted, it will be spread over a wider area with a thick mouthpiece and more concentrated with a thinner one.

An egg butt snaffle is an excellent bit for a young horse. These bits get their name from their rings which are egg-shaped. They have a thick mouthpiece which is sometimes hollow to reduce the weight.

D-ring snaffles are often used on the race track. They are simply snaffle bits with large D-shaped rings on each end. Wire and chain snaffles are more severe and are only recommended for hard pulling horses.

A pelham bit is actually a snaffle and curb combined into one. On each side of the mouthpiece is a ring to attach a set of reins and the cheekpiece of the bridle just like a snaffle. There is also a shank at the bottom to which another set of reins is attached. With this combination, the rider can choose to communicate with his horse delicately or strongly depending on the situation at hand.

Pelham bits are commonly used by hunt seat riders. If a horse tends to be a little strong or aggressive on a snaffle, a pelham will give the rider more control. Pelham bits come with a variety of different mouthpieces. A broken-mouth pelham has a mouthpiece similar to the snaffles just discussed. Mullen mouth pelhams have a gently arched mouthpiece that applies pressure on the bars of the horse's mouth, but arches enough to allow room for the tongue. Pelhams with a curb mouthpiece are the most severe and are not needed for sensitive horses.

The severity of a pelham bit is determined by the mouthpiece and the length of the shank. Mild Tom Thumb pelhams have short shanks only a couple of inches long, while more severe bits have shanks up to seven inches in length. Riders who have a pelham bit, but only want to use one set of reins, can buy a pelham converter strap which joins the two rings on each side of the bit. One rein on each side is then attached to this strap.

Jointed mouth pelham.

Mullen mouth pelham.

197

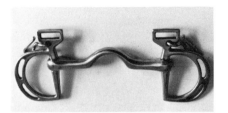

Kimberwick bit.

A kimberwick bit is in a classification by itself. It has a mouthpiece like a curb bit, but because it doesn't have a long shank like a curb, it acts by direct rein pressure rather than leverage. The curb mouthpiece makes it more severe than a snaffle because it acts on the bars and tongue of a horse's mouth rather than on the lips and corners. Over a long period of time this will make a horse less sensitive, but it can be good for a beginning rider mounted on a strong horse.

English curb bits are used primarily in saddle seat riding and with Walking Horses. They are more severe than snaffle bits because the pressure from the rider is exerted through a long shank or lever. The mouthpiece is one solid bar with a port in the middle which can vary from a gentle to a high arch. The severity of a curb bit depends on the port and the difference between the upper and lower cheek-pieces.

A curb bit rests in the horse's mouth and is supported by a curb chain which fits snugly in the chin groove. When the rider exerts rein pressure, the curb chain tightens under the chin with a vice-like effect. At the same time, the mouthpiece is pressed against the bars. If the mouthpiece has a high port, it can cause pressure on the roof of the mouth. If the mouthpiece is straight or slightly arched, the pressure is applied to the tongue. When the rider pulls the reins, the cheekpiece moves forward and a slight pressure is even felt on the poll.

English curb bits have a hook on the top of the cheekpiece where the curb chain fastens and a loop midway down the bottom cheek-piece where the lip strap fastens. By the way, if you use a curb or pelham bit, don't neglect to use a lip strap. It prevents the horse from grabbing the shank in his mouth; a disagreeable habit to be sure!

Bit Sizes

When you go to your local tack shop to buy a bit for your horse, not only will you find all of the different kinds of bits we're describing, but you'll also find that these bits come in different sizes. Although this variety may seem confusing at first, it really isn't that difficult to find the right bit for your horse.

Most average size riding horses require a five inch wide bit. Larger Thoroughbreds and hunters may need a wider one (5¼ to 5½ inches) while smaller Arabians and Morgans would probably use a slightly shorter (4¼ or 4¾ inch) bit.

A bit is measured from one inside end of the mouthpiece to the other. A snaffle bit should fit in the horse's mouth so that it causes a wrinkle or two in the lips. It should not be so small that it pinches the corners of the mouth nor should it extend more than one quarter of an inch beyond the corners of the mouth.

A curb bit should rest slightly lower in a horse's mouth than a snaffle. It should not wrinkle the lips, nor should it hang so low it touches the tushes or incisors. A curb should be wide enough not to pinch the corners of the mouth, but not so wide it slides in the horse's mouth.

Probably the best advice we can give is just to use common sense and look at how the bit fits in the mouth.

WESTERN TACK

SADDLES

The majority of American horsemen ride with what is known as a Western saddle. Everyone is familiar with these saddles from the many cowboy movies they have seen, but aside from their nostalgic value, Western saddles provide a comfortable and practical seat in which to ride.

While you'll find many variations of each of these types, most Western saddles are gaming, cutting horse, roping or pleasure saddles. Gaming, or barrel saddles as they are sometimes called, are used for barrel racing or flag racing or in any of the other gaming events found at rodeos or Western horse shows. They have very deep seats

Barrel or gaming saddle (top). Western work saddle (bottom left). Western show saddle (bottom right).

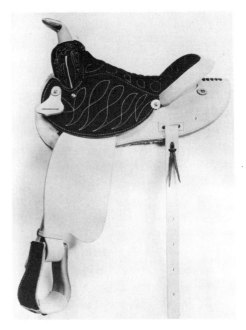

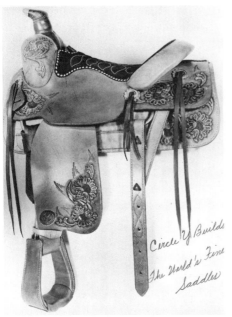

for security and often the seat and jockeys are covered with suede to give the rider a better grip. Gaming saddles usually have small rounded skirts to reduce weight so that often the entire saddle weighs less than thirty pounds.

Cutting horse saddles, as their name implies, are especially designed for use in cutting cattle. They have a deep seat like a gaming saddle; however, they have a wide fork which is undercut to keep the rider's legs in the saddle.

Roping saddles are rugged, heavy saddles that often weigh as much as fifty pounds. They have tough wooden trees that sometimes are covered twice with bullhide. The seat is not as deep as gaming or cutting horse saddles and the cantle can be lower to make it easier for the rider to dismount. Also, the fork in a roping saddle is gently rounded, which helps the rider dismount quickly. Roping saddles have large horns with thick necks, since the horn must hold a heavy steer or fighting calf that has just been roped.

In Western horse show pleasure classes any of these saddles may be found, but they will be much more decorative than working saddles. Show saddles are sometimes trimmed with white buckstitching or expensive silver trim. At the very least, show saddles are often ornately hand tooled.

Selecting a Western Saddle

Because of the many styles available, you must first find a saddle that appeals to you both in appearance and in its usefulness for the kind of riding you expect to do. Then, be sure to sit in it to make certain it's comfortable.

Saddles come in several different sizes as well as styles. The size of a saddle refers to the seat size, which is measured from the seam where the seat fabric is sewn to the cantle to the back of the fork. Small children use a twelve to thirteen inch seat. Ladies often prefer a fourteen inch seat, while an average size man probably takes one fifteen inches long. Larger saddles are also available for the taller, heavier person.

It's just as important that the saddle fit your horse, so it's a good idea to ask the tack shop owner if he will let you take the saddle to the stable to try it. If this isn't possible, consider trailering your horse

201

to the shop. In any event, the saddle must sit down on the horse's back and not sit on top of it. At the same time, it should allow clearance for the withers.

If you find the saddle attractive and it fits you and your horse, before you buy it make sure it's made of heavy leather. Feel the leather to make sure it is supple and doesn't feel like cheap cardboard. Work saddles are often plain because tooling tends to chafe after long hours in a saddle. Many people consider tooling attractive even though it will add to the price of a saddle. Because it is a cost-saving process, more and more saddles have a pattern stamped in the leather by a machine rather than being hand tooled. This embossing isn't as deep as hand tooling and obviously doesn't cost as much.

If you're not sure a particular saddle is what you want, continue to shop around comparing quality and price. A saddle is much too important for the riding comfort of you and your horse to be purchased hastily.

Saddle Pads

Because of the weight of a Western saddle, a pad or blanket must always be used under the saddle to protect the horse. Many trail riders use two or even three pads under their saddles, especially if they are going for a long ride.

Originally, horsehair pads were largely used with work saddles as well as woven woolen blankets that were exceptionally durable and absorbent. Although these pads and blankets are still used, synthetic fleece pads are currently very popular. They come in many different colors and shapes to fit round or square skirted saddles. Most have two layers, but some triple thick pads are now available.

Colorful plaid pads made of woven fabrics are commonly found. These pads will last longer if you buy the kind with a strip of leather sewn on each side where the pad comes in contact with the girth.

Bridles

Western bridles come in three basic styles, a browband, a shaped ear and a split ear. Which of these you choose makes no difference to the horse, it's simply a matter of you deciding which you think looks and fits best. Many people select a bridle to match their saddle. Just be sure it's heavy enough to hold up through a great deal of use. Look for supple leather and sturdy buckles and other hardware. If a bridle is stitched lengthwise along each side, it won't stretch as much as one that is not stitched.

The browband style of bridle is becoming very popular among people who show their horses, especially when it's decorated with fancy silver trim. Some Western bridles are plain, while others are buckstitched or have ornate tooling. The leather may be flat, round or braided, narrow or up to an inch wide. Although most are made of leather, once in a while you might see a bridle made of nylon or webbing.

Western bridles have cheekpieces similar to English bridles to which the bit is attached. The bit is fastened into place with a screw called a Chicago screw or with a narrow leather thong which is laced through the cheekpiece. Western bridles may or may not have a throatlatch.

Split reins are the most commonly found type used by Western horsemen. They consist of two separate leather straps about six feet long and three eighths to one inch wide. Split reins are long enough so that the loose ends can be used as a whip to urge on a sluggish horse.

Roping reins consist of one continuous strap which runs from one side of the bridle to the other. Many roping reins today are made of flat nylon webbing. Those that are made of leather are braided in the center for a better grip. Roping reins are used in roping as well as in gaming events and sometimes by trail riders. One great advantage of these reins is that if the rider loses his grip on them, they will not fall to the ground as split reins do. They remain on the horse's neck where they can easily be retrieved. Also, because they are one continuous rein, you can easily put equal pressure on both sides of the bit with one hand, while the other is busy with a rope.

A combination of these two styles is known as the rein and romal, a style popularized in California and most often used with Arabians and Morgans. It is actually a roping rein with a lash or whip attached to the center. This whip or romal is fastened to the rein so it can easily be removed.

BITS

Western bits come in an almost bewildering range of styles. Large tack shops display so many bits, beginning horsemen often wonder how they can ever choose the correct bit for their horse.

The first thing you can do is consult the horse's previous owner to find out what bit the horse has worn in the past. In most cases that type of bit or something very similar is the one you will want to continue using. If you find the previous owner was using a very harsh bit, you might want to try something a little less severe. Just remember that different bits are usually used for a special purpose, so be wary of unusual behavior whenever a new bit is tried.

If you look carefully at the huge variety of Western bits in a tack shop, you'll soon realize that most of them are variations of the curb and simply have a mouthpiece and two shanks. The variations you will

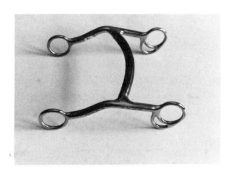

Mullen mouth Western bit.

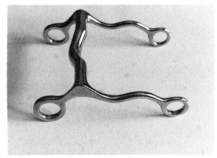

Western curb bit.

Western high port bit with roller.

Silver mounted Western curb bit with roller.

find are due to changes in the mouthpiece, especially the size of the port, or by changing the length or angle of the shanks.

The first bit usually carried by a young Western horse is called a colt breaking bit, which is also known as a Tom Thumb snaffle. This bit has a broken mouthpiece and the shanks of a curb.

Once a horse is used to this bit, a regular curb with a solid mouthpiece can be introduced. One variation of this standard curb is a grazing bit. These have swept back shanks that allow the horse to graze while the bit is in his mouth.

Some curb bits have rollers inside the arch of the mouthpiece, which just give a nervous horse something to do with his tongue. This roller can have a cover over the top and is called a hooded roller.

Curb bits with extremely high ports are called spade bits. Because they can be quite severe, they should only be used on correctly trained

Horse wearing a hackamore.

horses by skillful riders. Most spade bits have what is known as a loose jaw, which means that they are hinged where the mouthpiece meets the cheekpiece of the bit.

Another popular type of Western bit has a broken mouthpiece with long shanks. This bit works well for horses that prefer a broken mouthpiece, but need the control that a long shank provides.

BOSALS AND HACKAMORES

Sometimes with young horses a bosal is used instead of a bit in order to preserve the delicate feel of the horse's mouth. Bosals are simply braided rawhide nosebands which act on the nose and jaw of the horse rather than his mouth. A bosal is used with thick reins that can easily be felt on the horse's neck. A horse five or under may be shown with a bosal; however, after that time they must have graduated to a bit.

A mechanical hackamore is a modern version of the bosal. It has long shanks which attach to the noseband and, when pulled, tighten a chain under the chin. Mechanical hackamores cannot be used at horse shows except in gaming classes and on roping horses.

HALTERS AND LEADS

Although they are not used for riding, something every horseman must have is a strong halter and lead so his horse can easily and safely be tied up and worked around.

Halters today are most often made of nylon, leather and a kind of plastic known as polypropylene. They come in a wide variety of prices and quality; however, we strongly recommend against buying the cheap nylon or rope halters as they tend to break, usually at the most awkward time.

The double- or even triple-ply nylon halters with strong brass hardware are the most popular today and represent a good value. They don't require the care that the leather ones do and can easily be laundered if you get concerned about the dirt. Also, they come in a variety of colors that can be coordinated with whatever you have around your barn.

Something particularly to look for in nylon halters is the buckle on the side at the crown. We prefer a tongue buckle with eyelets. Cheap halters have a slide buckle, which after some use becomes difficult to fasten because the bottom edge of the nylon frays. It is extremely frustrating when you're trying to halter a horse to find you can't fasten the buckle!

Some nylon halters come with a snap at the throatlatch as well as a buckle at the crown. Many horsemen like this snap which can be unfastened instead of the buckle when putting on or removing the halter. We don't use halters with this feature because, if a horse suddenly pulls back, it's this snap that's most likely to break.

We'd also like to give you a word of caution about nylon halters. Never leave one on an unattended horse. Should a horse get caught, it is doubtful a strong nylon halter would break before the horse was seriously injured. We turn our horses out in the pasture without halters. If your horse is hard to catch and you leave a halter on him, use an inexpensive rope or leather halter that will break more easily. A nylon halter can be a real death trap.

Good leather halters are usually more expensive than nylon halters. They are most often found around such places as Thoroughbred or Saddlebred farms. The best leather halters are made in England of one to one and a quarter inch wide, triple stitched leather with solid brass buckles on each side of the crownpiece. Race horses are fitted with leather halters that are individualized with a brass name plate.

Simpler made leather halters, called turnout halters, are available too. These are fine for turning a horse out in a pasture. Inferior leather halters are now available, but should be avoided because of their tendency to break.

Leads got their name from the fact that they allowed a handler to lead a horse without worrying about the horse jerking away. In the past, leather leads were used when owners had grooms with nothing to do but stand and hold their horse.

Today, of course, all of that has changed. Leather leads that were fine for leading horses are simply not satisfactory for tying a horse, which is what most of us groomless owners need to do. This means that while you might have a leather lead for more formal occasions, you'll need a sturdy rope lead with which to tie your horse.

The leads or tie ropes we prefer are made of three-quarter-inch cotton and are about ten feet long. Cotton is strong and it won't burn your hands badly if the horse pulls away suddenly. Tie ropes should not have a chain end. The snap which is used to attach it to the halter must be sturdy. This snap will be stronger if the rope at the snap end is woven back into itself.

You'll find inferior leads that have thinner rope, are too short, have flimsy snaps or have snaps attached with clamps that soon pull out. Flat nylon leads are good for leading and can be used as ties if they don't have a chain end.

LONGEING EQUIPMENT

If you can't ride your horse very often, you still might want to exercise him once in a while on a longe line. At the very least, the equipment needed includes a sturdy halter, a longe line and a whip.

If you are going to use a halter to longe your horse, don't use a rope halter as they tend to slip around the horse's head too easily. Flat nylon

Longeing caveson.

or leather halters work fine, but of course a longe caveson made especially for this purpose is best.

There are some reasonably priced nylon longe cavesons that have a sheepskin covered noseband as well as large D-rings at the center and side of the noseband, to which the longe line can be attached. Leather cavesons are excellent for longeing, but represent a considerable investment in equipment that's not justified unless you use it often.

Longe lines should be at least twenty-four feet long and made of cotton webbing or flat nylon. It should have a strong snap and be made of relatively heavy material so it won't tangle and become knotted.

Although experienced horses don't always need to be prompted by a whip when longeing, one is necessary when working with some horses. We prefer a longe whip with a six foot stock and drop lash of equal length. This means you'll have a total reach of fourteen or fifteen feet. If you try to get by with a shorter whip, your horse will soon realize you can't reach him, making the whip all but useless.

TRAINING EQUIPMENT

While most of the following items won't be needed by the average horseman, if you ever decide to train a horse or try to correct some irritating faults, these rather specialized items can be most useful.

WHIP

The first thing that must be mentioned about a whip is that it is not a device to inflict pain. From the ground, it is a tool used to correct improper or dangerous behavior, or to act as an aid when giving a command. Remember that a horse's skin is very sensitive, so in most cases a light touch with a whip is enough to attract his attention.

For any of the purposes we just mentioned, a thirty-six to forty-five inch whip will work best. With this length whip you can reach a horse's flank when leading him, which is often necessary when you teach him to trot out while being led. When riding with any whip shorter than thirty-six inches, the rider moves his hands out of position when he uses the whip to cue his horse.

BITTING HARNESS

A bitting harness is used whenever a trainer wants a young horse to learn to respond properly to the bit before the horse is old enough to carry weight on his back. Basically, it consists of a bridle equipped with a snaffle bit, and side and overcheck reins. To this is attached a surcingle, or a strap which goes around the horse's body and a crupper, which is a loop that goes around the horse's tail.

Trainers sometimes have horses wear a bitting harness while standing in a stall or while being worked with a longe line or long lines. In addition to getting a horse used to the bit, it also teaches him to flex at the poll.

SIDE REINS

Side reins are elastic or leather straps that are attached from the bit to the saddle. They are used to teach a horse proper head carriage,

Horse being driven in side or draw reins to teach him to lower his head and flex at the poll.

210

Horse being driven in long lines. Note the protective splint boots. The horse is also wearing a bitting harness to encourage proper head carriage while it supples and improves his balance and stride.

which requires him to flex at the poll. Side reins are used with a bitting harness, or they can be attached to a saddle and used while longeing. Then too, they can be used in addition to regular reins while the horse is being ridden. Of course, they are considered training devices and can't be used in a show ring.

Long Lines

Long lines are used when a trainer wants to drive a horse from the ground without having to attach a buggy. They are used with young horses that aren't ready to be ridden or to exercise older horses that trainers don't want to carry weight every day.

Long lines are attached to a snaffle bit and should be run through the D-ring of a surcingle or the hobbled stirrups of a saddle so the reins won't become tangled. They can be made of either flat or round nylon or leather straps.

MARTINGALES

One kind of martingale is called a running martingale, which in Western riding is called a running W. It consists of a strap of leather which attaches to the girth with a loop, then it runs between the legs to the chest where it splits, each end being attached to a rein. The martingale is attached to the rein with a ring, which allows it to slip up and down. Because of this, a rein stop should be used to keep the ring from getting hooked on the bit. In English riding, a neck strap is added to keep it toward the horse's chest. Otherwise, a horse could possibly get a foot through it.

Running martingales are attached to the snaffle rein. When used in this way, the pressure of the bit is altered in such a way that the horse is encouraged to lower his head and flex at the poll. Again, this is training equipment and not allowed in pleasure classes.

A standing martingale, or tie downs as it is known in Western circles, limits the extent to which a horse can lift his head. It is attached to the girth and runs through the front legs, then fastened to the underside of the noseband. English versions have a neckstrap to keep the martingale in place, while Western versions don't. Standing martingales can be adjusted, but should never be so tight they severely restrict the horse. They are used primarily with horses that tend to toss their head.

CARING FOR TACK

While we realize that everyone enjoys riding their horse much more than cleaning tack, all leather requires a certain amount of care so it will look good and last a long time. Most "experts" will tell you to clean your tack after each time you use it. If you're like most of us, it will get done whenever you get in the right mood, which somehow isn't very often! Regardless, you should at least wipe off the obvious dirt with a damp cloth after each ride. Also, rinse the bit in water and wipe it off to keep it clean and shiny. Finally, hang the saddle pad in a well ventilated place and brush it off before you use it again.

How often you thoroughly clean your tack has to do with how often it's used as well as how long it's been since the last time it was cleaned. Because leather has a tendency to dry out, it needs attention even if you seldom use it. While we realize how easy it is to put off cleaning tack, if it is kept clean and supple it will last much longer and be more comfortable for you and your horse.

If you ride daily, you really should clean your tack every week or ten days. Just as you check for minor problems when you groom your horse, when you clean your tack you'll be more likely to notice such things as loose stitching or cracked leather. Clean tack reduces saddle sores and chafed spots which are caused by dirty or ill-fitting equipment. Lastly, all of us feel a certain amount of pride in having a well groomed horse fitted with neat, clean equipment, instead of looking and smelling as if we had just finished a 100 mile endurance ride.

Assuming you've finally decided to give your tack a good cleaning, the equipment you'll need includes a bucket of water, a sponge, soft cloths, metal polish and a hook and rack for your saddle and bridle. Tack hooks are quite handy and can be suspended from the ceiling while you work. If you don't have a saddle rack, a wooden sawhorse works quite well. If nothing else is available, the back of a chair will do.

To do a good job, you'll need to take your bridle apart and remove the girth and stirrups from your saddle. Begin with a damp sponge and saddle soap. Work the lathered saddle soap into your tack. If you are cleaning a tooled Western saddle, a soft brush like a toothbrush works well for getting into the deeply tooled places. Rub the saddle soap into a small section at a time. After lathering one section thoroughly, rinse it with a damp sponge. If you try to do too much at once, the lather will dry before you can rinse it. Once the leather is dry, you can buff it with a soft cloth to make it shine.

As we mentioned before, leather tends to dry and crack with age. Saddle soap will help keep it clean and soft, but if it gets excessively dry, you can soften it by applying neatsfoot oil. To oil the smaller pieces of leather, pour a small amount of oil in a pan and carefully dip each piece of leather. After each piece has been dipped, hang it somewhere out of the sun to dry. Remember, leather is porous and you'll probably be surprised to see how much oil a dry piece of leather can absorb, so just dip it and don't let it soak.

It's particularly advisable that new leather be oiled in this manner. It will do much to soften the leather and also help to protect it.

For the metal parts of your tack, use one of the many metal polishes on the market and follow the directions on the can. Be sure not to apply it to the mouthpiece of the bit.

To keep your girth and saddle pad clean, launder them once in a while. Between launderings, brush any places that become particularly dirty. As we said before, it's important to hang your saddle pad in a place where it can dry after each ride.

SPECIAL EQUIPMENT

BREASTPLATE

A breastplate or breast collar is used to keep a saddle from slipping back. Racing and polo breast collars are narrow straps of leather which run across the horse's chest to a D-ring on each side of the saddle. Western breast collars are also made this way, but sometimes have a ring at the center of the chest. Another strap is attached here and runs between the horse's legs and snaps to a ring on the girth.

Breastplates, although made somewhat differently, are also used to keep the saddle in place. They are attached to the girth, then run through the horse's legs where they attach by means of a large ring to a neck strap that encircles the horse's neck. This is held in place by two small straps that attach to D-rings on the saddle.

Breastplates and breast collars are especially helpful to hunters, jumpers and trailriders who go up and down a lot of hills as well as for horses that don't have high enough withers to keep the saddle in place.

CAVESONS

In addition to the regular cavesons we mentioned in the section on bridles, there are also dropped cavesons which are effectively used on

214

horses that try to open their mouths to evade the bit. Dressage riders favor them for this reason.

A dropped caveson is very similar to the normal style; however, it is worn below the bit and is buckled in the chin groove. Because it is placed so low, it is impossible for the horse to open his mouth or get his tongue over the bit.

Another type of caveson is known as a figure-eight caveson, which as its name implies is shaped like the number eight. Although this is seldom seen in everyday riding, it is occasionally used on race horses and by hunters and jumpers.

Large riding stables get good use from a hot walker such as this one which can cool down four horses at a time.

CHAPTER 9

Riding Your Horse

Now, we've finally got around to talking about what you really bought the horse for in the first place, riding! To simply climb onto a horse's back and go bouncing around merrily is actually not very difficult, but to be able to ride well, feel comfortable and move gracefully with a horse takes a great deal of practice and patience. In this chapter we don't intend to make anyone a proficient rider; we just want to give the reader enough information so he can mount a horse and get started. We'll leave it up to you to improve. Of course, lessons are always a good idea, especially for a beginner. An instructor has the advantage of having corrected in others many of the same problems you will have. He also can stand aside and objectively notice exactly what you need to do to become a better rider.

Placing the saddle on the horse's back.   *Tightening the cinch.*

SADDLING UP

The first thing you must be able to do is saddle and bridle your horse. While this may sound pretty basic to some, we actually know of people who have tried to put the saddle or bridle on backwards, so you can imagine what other difficulties they're liable to get themselves into! On the other hand, it is possible to ride bareback, but it isn't really very comfortable or secure, so you'd better learn how to saddle and bridle a horse.

Before you do anything, be sure to tie your horse securely, either in crossties or to a sturdy post or rail. Most people will put the saddle on first and then the bridle. This seems to be a good idea because once you have the bridle on, you can then untie the horse and lead him somewhere to get on.

Before you put the saddle on, give the horse a thorough brushing in the area where the saddle goes. There's going to be a lot of weight pushing down on this area so that even a small bit of dirt can cause a lot of irritation or even sores. Don't forget to brush the area between the legs where the girth goes. This is something many people neglect.

Now you're ready to put the saddle on. First, place the saddle pad on

217

the horse's back slightly forward of where you want it to go, then slide it back to the proper place. If you slide it forward, the hair will become ruffled and irritate your horse.

Smooth the pad carefully, making sure all of the wrinkles are out. Then place the saddle easily on the horse's back. There's no need to slam it down. This only disturbs the horse, making him reluctant to be saddled the next time. Girth the horse at this time only snug enough so the saddle won't fall off. Tighten it securely just before you're ready to mount. Western saddles often have a second or flank cinch. This should not be buckled very tightly. Also, there should be a connecting strap running from the cinch and the flank cinch. Otherwise, the flank cinch could slide back, causing the horse to buck.

At this point, we want to remind you that all of the saddling and bridling should be done from the left or near side of the horse. This is the side horses are used to being handled from. They can get confused if saddled from the other side.

BRIDLING

Now you're ready to put the bridle on your horse. In order to do this, you need to remove the halter from his head, but you still need to keep your horse restrained in some way. Simply unbuckle the crown buckle of the halter, remove it from his head and buckle the crownpiece around his neck. He'll then be secure enough for you to be able to bridle him. While some horses might stand patiently when being bridled without being tied in this way, it's an easy enough precaution to follow. In case something startles him, it might save you from chasing him around a pasture, parking lot or whatever. If the reins are closed, it's a good idea to put them over the horse's head before you begin bridling. Then there is no chance they could get stepped on or caught on something.

To put the bridle on, stand on the left or near side of the horse, holding the crown piece in your right hand. Now position the bridle in front of the horse's face, slightly lower than the position it will be on the horse. Place the fingers of your left hand under the mouthpiece of the bit and slide your thumb in the left side of the horse's mouth at the bars. Don't worry, he can't bite you because he has no teeth there! Usually,

This series of pictures show the steps taken in bridling a horse. First (top left) the halter is placed on the horse's neck; the bridle is held in position before the bit is inserted (right). Notice that the reins are looped over the rider's arm. The bit is placed in the horse's mouth (center left); the bridle is maneuvered over the horse's ears (right). The tightness of the throatlatch is checked (bottom).

219

this will cause the horse to open his mouth. If it doesn't work right away, apply more pressure to the bars with your thumb. Just keep at it, we've never seen a horse that hasn't eventually opened his mouth.

As soon as the horse opens his mouth, slide the bit into it by pulling up on the crownpiece. Then slip the crownpiece behind his ears. If the bridle has a browband, make sure it's positioned so that it's comfortable. Buckle the throatlatch loosely. Remember, the windpipe passes through here and you don't want to restrict the horse's breathing. If the throatlatch is properly adjusted, you should be able to slip your fingers between it and the horse's jaw.

The correct way to mount an English saddled horse. Notice that the rider's left hand is on the pommel of the saddle while her right hand steadies the stirrup.

Finally she lifts her right leg well over the saddle and the horse's croup.

She grasps the saddle with her right hand as she prepares to mount.

If the bridle has a caveson, or a nose band, fasten it tightly. It is supposed to keep the horse's mouth shut so unless it's buckled snugly, it will be all but useless.

On Western bridles, the curb chain, or strap, is usually not undone when the bridle is taken off. On English bridles that have a curb strap or chain, these are hooked and unhooked each time. Because of this, when you hook a curb chain or strap be sure it's snug and the chain isn't twisted, which can be uncomfortable, if not painful, for the horse.

Geldings and stallions sometimes grow tushes, which are somewhat like wisdom teeth, in their bars. If so, make sure the bit doesn't touch them.

MOUNTING

Now that your horse is properly saddled and bridled, you can lead him to the mounting area. Once you're there, retighten the girth, making sure it's fastened tightly.

Again, remember to stand on the left side of the horse, facing the croup. If you have an English saddle, you'll need to stand near the horse at about the withers. Put your left hand on the horse's neck, grabbing a little mane if you like. With your right hand holding the stirrup still, place your left foot in the stirrup. Now, put your right hand on the

Preparing to mount a Western-trained horse.

cantle and lightly spring into the saddle. Keep your right leg straight as you bring it across the horse's croup so it does not touch the horse. Sit down in the saddle easily. If you plop down hard, you could startle your horse and begin the ride much earlier than you planned! Now, put your right foot in the stirrup, grasp the reins correctly and you're ready to begin riding.

If you have a Western saddle, the procedure for mounting is very similar. Grasp the reins the same way in your left hand. However, you want to stand facing the front, slightly behind the stirrup. Instead of grabbing some mane, you have a big saddle horn to hang onto. Western stirrups hang stiffly, so you don't need to hold it. Just put your left foot in the stirrup and lightly spring into the saddle.

Stirrup Length

Generally, the stirrups should be adjusted so that the bottom of the stirrup comes to the rider's ankle bone. Some riders, however, prefer

Dressage saddle with stirrups run up. Notice that this saddle has long billets so that the buckles do not create extra bulk under the rider's leg.

222

either a shorter or a longer length and that is, of course, perfectly all right. Just be sure you're comfortable when sitting in the saddle with your feet in the stirrups.

RUNNING UP THE STIRRUPS

English saddles have metal stirrups which, if left hanging down when not in use, will bang into the sides of your horse. Because of this, the stirrups should be run up when they are not in use. To run them up, simply grab the outer stirrup leather and slide the iron up to the top of the inner leather. When the iron is up, run both the inner and outer leathers through it to hold it securely in place.

IN THE SADDLE

HOW TO HOLD THE REINS

If you're riding English with a simple snaffle bridle, you will hold one rein in each hand. The rein should run under your little finger, up the inside of your fist and out over your thumb. If you're using

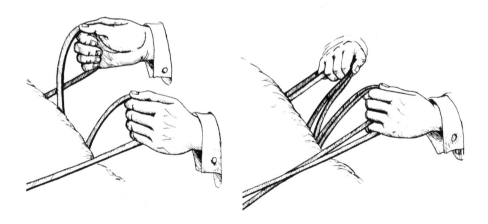

Holding the reins when riding English style. Single rein bridle (left). Double-rein bridle (right). Note that the snaffle rein is held under the little finger, while the curb runs between the little and ring fingers.

223

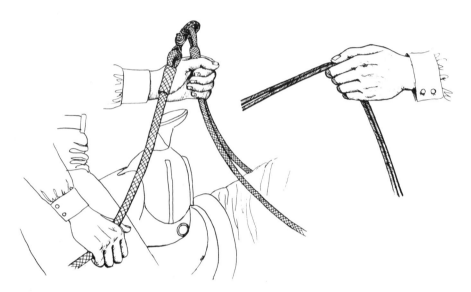

Holding the reins when riding Western style. Reins and romal (left). According-ing to American Horse Show Association rules, the hand holding the romal must be at least 16 inches away from the hand holding the reins. The hand must be around the reins (right). When using split reins, and both ends of the reins fall to one side, the rider may place one finger between the reins.

four reins, the snaffle rein should run under your little finger and through your fist, while the curb rein runs between your little finger and ring finger.

If you're riding Western, both reins will be held in one hand. The bottom of the fist should face down, while the reins enter between your thumb and forefinger.

POSITION IN THE SADDLE

Each style of riding has some variation in its position. Basically, general principles have been devised which help the rider maintain his balance and move comfortably with his horse. In giving riding lessons, one of the first things we notice is that, with the exception of

224

young people, most beginners are nervous and tense, which is their greatest obstacle to becoming a good rider. It's difficult to do anything when you find yourself in this state, particularly ride a horse. With this in mind, the first thing you need to do is try to overcome whatever fears you might have.

While there are many rules and regulations concerning just how you should sit, hold your legs, hands, and so on, the most important thing is for you to be comfortable. There are special horse show classes called equitation classes for persons under 18 years of age in which their riding ability is judged, but many of us are too old for these classes anyway. So whenever you are riding, remember simply to remain relaxed and comfortable, enjoy yourself and you'll do just fine.

Once you're in the saddle, settle in the deepest part of the seat with your shoulders back and your head erect. It's usually a good idea to look straight ahead between the horse's ears. His ears are a good

Basic dressage position.

indication of his feelings. If they are suddenly pricked forward or laid back you'll know to prepare yourself. Then too, by keeping your head up you'll straighten your back and have better posture.

The inside of your thighs and knees should fit snugly against the saddle. Your lower leg should be stretched downward so that it is directly under your body. Rest the ball of your foot in the stirrup, with your heels down and your toes straight ahead. There is an easy way to tell if your legs are in the right position. Take your feet out of the stirrups and notice where they hang naturally. When you place your feet back in them, the stirrups should be neither forward nor back. Leg position is important because you cannot be balanced when your legs are too far forward or way behind you.

Keep your elbows close to your body, not behind your back nor in front of your hips. Relax your wrists so you'll be better able to communicate with your horse. If your fingers are closed softly on the reins, you can feel your horse's mouth. You'll also be less inclined to jerk your horse rather than easily giving and taking with your hands.

THE AIDS

Now that you are sitting correctly, the next problem is to tell your horse exactly what you want him to do. To do this, you'll need to use natural aids such as your voice, hands and legs along with the artificial aids which include the whip and spur.

Generally speaking, you'll use your legs to encourage your horse to move forward, while your hands call for a halt and tell him which direction to turn. Artificial aids, such as a whip or spurs, are only used to reinforce the natural aids.

THE WALK

To ask the horse to walk, simply squeeze your legs at the girth. Although you should continue to have light contact with the horse's mouth, once you have asked the horse to walk, you'll want to ease up the contact.

Once the horse begins to walk, you should keep your body erect and your eyes straight ahead, making sure you watch where you are going. As the horse walks along, try to be aware of his movement

Walking the English horse. *Walking the Western horse.*

under you. Feel the rhythm of his stride and try to move with it. To get the horse to turn, simply move your hand or hands, depending on your style of riding, in the direction you wish him to turn. Once the horse turns that way, return your hands to their normal position.

THE HALT

To tell the horse to stop, sit deeply in the saddle and tighten your fingers on the reins. This slight pressure should cause most horses to stop, but if he continues moving, exert more pressure on the reins until he finally stops. The horse should be willing to stand quietly until you once again ask him to move.

At this point we should point out that, whenever you ride a horse, it's essential that you act firmly and forcefully with him, making him obey your commands. It's common for beginners to ride very timidly and let the horse do pretty much what he wants to do. Most older riding horses soon figure out if you are afraid to make them behave. From that point on you'll find yourself having difficulty.

If you are riding with a group of horses, most horses will want to follow along with the group, stopping, starting and turning whenever the others do. If you want your horse to learn to obey you, act forcefully from the start and keep after him until he does what you ask. Once he gets away with misbehaving he'll only be worse the next time.

THE TROT

In English riding, it is customary to "post" the trot, which means the rider rises slightly out of the saddle on every other step of the horse. Posting the trot is less tiring for both the horse and the rider. The rider escapes the jarring of the trot and the horse's back is spared the constant bouncing.

If you remember our previous discussion, the trot is a two-beat gait, which means two of the horse's legs strike the gound on each step. In the case of the trot, the right front and left rear strike together, then the left front and right rear. In order to post, all the rider has to do is sit on one beat and rise on the next. When we say rise, we don't mean that the rider stands up in the stirrups. This rising motion is done from the thighs, knees and upper calf and most of the energy comes from the motion of the horse.

To practice posting, try lifting yourself out of the saddle first at the walk. After you begin to feel comfortable at the walk, ask the horse

Trotting the English horse.

Jogging the Western horse.

228

to trot and try to continue this easy fluid motion. Remember, the horse is supposed to thrust you upward. At first, you'll feel a bit awkward, but relax, try to feel the rhythm of the beat and let the motion of the horse do the work.

A requirement of showing in English tack is that the rider post in unison with the outside front leg, or the outside diagonal as it's called. In other words, you should be in the saddle when the outside leg hits the ground and out of the saddle when that leg is in the air. To determine the position of the leg, simply glance down at the horse's shoulder. Since it must also move forward when the leg does, this will tell you the position of the leg. Whatever you do, don't lean over the horse to see what diagonal you're on. Keep straight in the saddle with your head up. Just glance down with your eyes, not your head.

Sitting the Trot

Western horses trot or "jog," as the gait is called in Western circles, smoothly and slowly enough that you can sit instead of posting. At times, for schooling purposes, it's also good to sit the trot on an English horse as it is an excellent way to develop a secure seat in the saddle.

When beginning to sit the trot, first ask the horse to trot slowly, as this will be much easier for you. Be sure to keep your back supple so it will be able to absorb the shock of the gait. Once you become comfortable at a slow trot, ask the horse to increase his pace. Eventually, you should try to sit the trot without stirrups, as this is another excellent way to improve your seat.

The Canter

The canter or "lope" as it's called in Western riding, has three beats and then a slight period of suspension. Because of this, it's a rolling, comfortable gait, a fact that is not always easy to get across to beginners who become terrified with the increased speed. Actually, any well trained horse can canter quite slowly, which along with the smooth strides makes the canter a very pleasant gait to ride.

Before you ask your horse to canter, sit deeply in the saddle and

Cantering the English horse.   *Loping the Western horse.*

take your weight out of the stirrups. If you rely on the stirrups for support, you'll find yourself being thrown out of the saddle. Now, try to relax and, from the walk, ask your horse to canter using whatever aids he is familiar with.

Once the horse is cantering, feel the distinctive rocking motion. It helps at first to keep your back quite limber. Try to move with the motion of the horse, as if you are wiping the saddle from the back to the front with your riding pants.

DISMOUNTING

To get off of the horse, place both reins in your left hand. Remove your right foot from the stirrup. Lean forward from the waist and place your right hand on the horse's neck or the pommel or horn of the saddle.

Now, swing your right leg up over the horse's croup and bring it down even with your left leg. If you're using Western tack and your legs are long enough, you can step on to the ground and remove your left foot from the stirrup. Otherwise, lean forward on the saddle and, with your right hand on the cantle of the saddle, remove your left foot from the saddle and drop to the ground.

230

PRACTICES OF A GOOD HORSEMAN

1) Be considerate of your horse. Warm him up slowly by walking first, then trotting and cantering. Also, cool him out slowly after each ride. Walk him for the last few minutes on your way home. If he's still not dry once you get home, walk him until he's dry.

2) Don't run your horse on pavement or other hard surfaces. It's very hard on his feet and legs, not to mention dangerous for the horse and rider, if the horse should slip and fall. Some of the most serious injuries to horsemen we know of occurred when a horse slipped on a roadway.

3) Allow your horse to walk up hills and rest at the top if he's winded. During rest stops, loosen his girth slightly. Offer him a drink of water if it's available, but don't let him gorge himself.

4) Don't ride your horse right after he's eaten a large quantity of grain. Allow at least an hour for him to digest his food.

5) If flies or other insects are a problem, use a repellant.

6) When you ride along the side of a road, keep all of the horses on one side. If a car or truck passes, keep the horses moving. They will be less inclined to shy if they are moving.

7) When crossing a road, don't leave one horse stranded on the other side. He will want to join the other horses and might panic and run in front of a car.

8) When riding in a ring or on a trail, keep at least one horse-length between you and the horse in front of you. Many horses resent another horse on their tail and may be tempted to kick.

9) Never run up behind another group of horses. They may become startled and may start to run or kick at the intruder.

10) When entering a riding ring, close the gate behind you and walk to the center of the ring to mount. Then you won't disturb the other horses working on the rail.

RIDING PROBLEMS

We've read many books that give complicated instructions on what to do when a horse rears or bucks or runs away. But most people quickly forget all of these rules if the occasion ever arises. Everyone's first instinct is survival. Too often this instinct causes us to panic, which only makes the situation worse. We'll list some of these rules just for the record, but probably the best advice we can give you is just hang on and try to stay calm. The horse eventually has to tire and slow down, so you can regain control. The trick is to stay on until this happens.

If a horse bucks, try to raise his head up with the reins, which should slow him down. Once he stops, check the saddle to be sure nothing is irritating him which could have caused him to buck. If you're on a Western saddle, check the flank cinch to make sure it hasn't slipped back.

Sometimes horses that aren't ridden much buck from exuberance, especially in spring. Otherwise, other than an occasional lapse, well-mannered horses shouldn't buck.

Rearing is a most dangerous habit. Well-mannered horses just don't do it. If you have a horse that rears periodically, we suggest you sell him before he falls over backwards, seriously hurting someone.

If you do find yourself on a horse that is rearing, don't panic and don't pull on the reins! This will only cause him to go back further. Keep your weight as far forward as possible, too, so you don't pull him over.

Runaway horses are best prevented, not stopped. Don't overmount yourself or anyone else on a horse that is more than you can handle. Don't get in the habit of allowing your horse to run back to the barn, either.

If you should find yourself on a runaway horse, don't scream or drop the reins. The scream will only frighten the horse. The panicky rider all too often throws away the reins and instead grasps for dear life to the saddle horn, which does nothing to help the situation.

If there is a wide enough area, try to turn the horse in a circle. If not, pull on the reins with one hand and then the other in a see-saw effect to try to get the horse to respond. Finally, just try to stay on and remember that every horse eventually must stop.

Another word of caution about runaways. If you see another horse running away, don't follow in hot pursuit. You'll only add fuel to the fire and make matters worse.

CHAPTER 10

Training Your Horse

When seeing a chapter entitled "Training Your Horse" in a horse care or riding manual, many novice horseowners say to themselves, "My horse is already trained. I don't have to worry about training him now." This statement couldn't be further from the truth. Horses are very impressionable and every time they are being handled, they are being trained, whether for good or for ill. Even though your horse may have learned only good habits up to the time you bought him, it's very easy for you to teach him just as many bad habits without even being aware of the problems you may be causing.

One good case in point concerns a young horse that a trainer we know has had for beginning work under saddle a couple of times. It so happens that this horse, like many others, requires a certain amount of discipline before he will perform well. While the trainer rides him, the horse is on his best behavior because he is aware of the certain consequences of misbehavior.

The problem is that the owner sees the horse too much as a pet and will never discipline him. Once the horse is taken home, he realizes he won't be punished and subsequently begins behaving badly. Quite unaware of what he is doing, the owner has taught the horse, or trained him if you wish, that any behavior is acceptable and that at home he will never be disciplined. The owner blamed the trainer and took the horse back for further training, but this was all for nothing because the same conditions existed once the horse was taken home again.

SHOULD YOU TRAIN YOUR OWN HORSE?

First of all, to teach a horse even the most basic skills requires a certain amount of time each day, which in itself is a big problem for many of us. Young horses just getting started under saddle need thirty minutes to an hour of time at least six days a week. An older horse doesn't have to be worked so often, but younger ones need this continual reinforcement. Professional trainers have time available to them and are thus able to turn out trained horses more quickly than someone who works with a horse infrequently.

Next, in order to train a horse to work under saddle, you'll need an enclosed area or pen of some sort. Training pens are excellent, but at the very least you'll need a fenced riding ring that has good footing. Because young horses aren't as well coordinated carrying weight as older horses, you must be particularly cautious about the footing. A spill can undermine the confidence of a horse as well as possibly cause him to be injured.

Finally, any person training a horse has to be more than just a good rider. He must be able to teach a horse proper behavior, at the same time keeping the horse cheerful and willing. This requires considerable tact on the part of the trainer, who must know when he can ask more of the horse and when to be satisfied with only a slight improvement.

Established trainers often spend years in apprenticeship learning their skills through much observation and long hours of working with horses. Because experience is such an invaluable aid in training, veteran trainers are aware of potential problems and can often prevent them from happening. For example, good trainers can not cure a horse from bucking, but many times they can keep a horse from acquiring this habit in the first place.

Although not a training pen, because of its small size and round corners this would make an ideal ring for starting young horses.

How To Choose a Professional Trainer

If you are thinking of sending your horse to a trainer for beginning work under saddle or for some advanced training, you are probably wondering how to find a good trainer and then how to choose among those that you find. First, it's always best to ask among your knowledge-able horsemen friends or at your local tack shop. The reputations of local trainers are usually well known and can be discovered quite easily. Then, if that fails, look in the ads in horse publications or even the yellow pages of the telephone book.

Next, make an appointment to visit and talk with the prospective trainer. Selecting a trainer can be just as important as selecting a horse and as such must be approached very carefully. During your visit, inquire about fees, facilities and just what the trainer thinks he can do for your horse and how long it will take.

When considering cost, by all means remember that the lowest monthly rate isn't always the least costly way of getting your horse trained. We are sorry to say that people have taken their horses to trainers with low fees only to find that their horses were hardly ever taken out of their stalls and remained as poorly trained when they got

235

them home as when they had brought them. The monthly fee is based on the knowledge, experience and reputation of the trainer as well as the facilities and the care the horse receives. A trainer can shave dollars off the monthly bill by feeding less or poor quality feed, but of course this is really no savings at all to you.

How long it takes to train a horse is very difficult to determine. Beware if you are promised a well-trained horse in thirty or even sixty days. Each horse is different in his response to training, making it nearly impossible to predict how long a particular job will take. Thirty days, a standard training period, just isn't enough time to turn out a finished horse. Most horses can be green broke in this time, but certainly not finished.

Finally, when selecting a trainer, consider what you want your horse to be trained to do. Obviously, a professional who turns out champion jumpers isn't the best qualified to train a cutting horse.

If you just want a young horse broken to ride, most any competent trainer should be able to get the job done. Don't be afraid to ask the prospective trainer for names of satisfied customers as references. If he's done a good job for others, chances are you'll be pleased, too.

HOW TO TRAIN YOUR HORSE

Basic Considerations

Most any horseman should be able to teach a young horse the basic skills we're going to discuss in this chapter. No special equipment or talent is required. Just remember to proceed slowly and ask your horse to learn nothing new until the previous lesson is well understood. Also, it's important to realize that horses are easily distracted and respond much better if there is nothing else to draw their attention. Keep onlookers to a minimum and try to work in a secluded area. In the beginning, you can accomplish a great deal in the horse's stall, which is a place where he'll feel comfortable.

Naturally, you must maintain your composure, no matter how poorly a lesson goes. Losing your patience will only make things worse by confusing your horse even further. A horse often does not respond the way we want because he has no idea of what we want

236

him to do! To be able to train a horse, we must reinforce and encourage good behavior, while we discourage poor behavior. Of course, it's even better if we can prevent the unwanted behavior. Then the training will take less time and be much easier on both you and the horse. This is one reason why you might want to stop for a moment and decide if you want to continue training your horse yourself or if it might not be better after all to send him to a professional.

EARLY LESSONS

Even though most novice horseowners buy a horse that is already at least partially trained, most horses begin training when they are young foals, so for the purposes of this chapter we're going to begin at that point.

It takes no great skill or knowledge as a trainer to begin working with a young foal. All that's required is a little patience and common sense. Newborn foals have no initial fear of people. If you begin handling them soon after birth, they will soon begin to enjoy the attention. Foals should be quietly touched and rubbed all over so they will realize that you won't hurt them. They particularly like being scratched and eventually will look forward to your attention.

When the foal is a few days old, a halter can be placed on him. Being able to halter a foal at an early age will make it much easier when the veterinarian or anyone else needs to work on him.

These first halter lessons should take place in a roomy box stall. We like to have a second person around to help restrain the foal and keep him from getting hurt or running away if he gets frightened. Begin by pushing the foal's mother against a wall with her head in a corner. Then, encourage the foal to move next to his mother with his head in the corner, too. In this way, he can't move any way but backward. If you approach gently on a diagonal from behind, it's likely the foal will just stand there while you slip a halter on him.

At that point, if the foal becomes frightened and struggles, you'll need someone to help hold him. This is done by grasping the tail close to the base with one hand and placing the other around his chest. Since the tail is sensitive, you should now let go and reach that arm around the buttocks. With this method you can restrain the foal so he can't struggle and hurt himself. Obviously this procedure can only be used on young foals. Once they get too large, it's impossible to restrain them this way. This is another reason why a foal should get used to a halter at a young age.

Once the foal is restrained, a second person can put the halter on him, making sure it's adjusted properly. Then, don't let him go until he's quiet—they rarely struggle very long. Otherwise, you will have taught him that by struggling he can get away, which is exactly what you don't want to teach him. We never leave a halter on an unattended horse, but regardless of your policy, remove the halter after ten minutes or so, using the procedure we just described if it's necessary.

Horses learn best if they're taught only one thing at a time. For that reason, we don't do much with a young foal until after he accepts the halter without being frightened. Once he relaxes a bit with the halter on, we begin scratching and rubbing him once again until he is no longer worried about our presence.

It's essential that these early lessons go well, because what the foal learns about human handling now will set the stage for how he reacts to later training. We do all of the handling of young foals in a large, safe stall, so the foal can't get away from us or hurt himself. Patience, quiet and determination are most important at this time. Another point to remember is that foals have a very short attention span. They begin fussing after only a few minutes, so keep your lessons brief. Two five-minute lessons per day is often better than one lasting ten minutes.

As soon as the foal loses his fear of you and the halter, you can begin to pick up his feet. He'll eventually need to have his feet trimmed and this can't be done with his feet planted firmly on the ground. Simply run your hand down his leg to the fetlock and gently but firmly pick the foot up. Hold the foot up for a few seconds and gently place it down again. After a few days, you should be able to lift each foot and hold it for a few seconds. If the foal resists, put him in a corner and restrain him just like you would to halter him. This is usually the safest and least frustrating way to catch and handle a wary foal. All you're trying to teach him in this lesson is that when you touch his leg in a certain manner, he should pick up his foot and that it's not going to hurt him.

When he's a few weeks old, you can start teaching the foal to lead.

To begin, snap a soft cotton rope onto the foal's halter. Since trying to pull a horse forward will only make him resist by pulling back, the rope you use must be long enough to reach behind the foal's rump so your efforts will be to urge him forward from the back.

Next, have a second person lead the foal's mother out into the corral and follow right behind with the foal. This is usually the easiest way to begin, but eventually you're going to want to take the foal somewhere he doesn't want to go and without his mother leading the way. This is when a rump rope is essential. You can use either a long lead or a separate rope. If you use a separate rope, make sure it's a soft rope at least five feet long.

Whichever rope you use, run it around the foal's rump so it rests at the back of the gaskin. If you're using a separate rope from the lead, the two ends should meet on the back at about the loin area. Grasp the ends with your right hand, which will leave your left hand free to hold the lead near the halter.

If you prefer to use a long lead, it needs to be about ten feet long. Run it from the left side of the halter to the middle of the foal's left side. Then run it over the back to the right hip, around the buttocks and back to the left side. Bring the end up to the middle of the back, so you can grasp the end and the rope where it crosses the foal's back with the right hand. The left hand can hold the lead near the halter.

In order to get the foal to move forward, apply pressure on the rump rope. The lead rope will keep the foal from tossing his head or rearing up, while the rump rope pushes him forward. The first time or two, you should be happy to move the foal only a few feet forward. Once you get him to move forward, ask him to whoa and stand still for a moment or two. Then remove the halter and lead and end the lesson. Very soon, the rump rope won't be needed, but for the first few times it can be a big help.

If you don't begin to teach the foal to lead until he is older and too big to use a rump rope on, you can use a thirty-six inch whip to urge the horse to move forward. To do this, stand at the horse's left shoulder facing forward. Hold the lead near the halter with your right hand and hold the whip in your left. Ask the horse to "walk" and then you step out. Because the horse has no idea what you want him to do, chances are that he'll just stand there. In order to get him to move, reach behind you with the whip and tap him on the flank. Invariably, he'll move forward a step or two, which at this point is enough. After a few steps forward, tell him to "whoa" and stop. If he doesn't stop when you do, repeat the word "whoa" as you jerk and quickly release the lead line once or twice. As soon as he stops, pet and praise him so he'll know he did the right thing.

Sometimes young horses are too exuberant to handle with just a cotton lead. Fillies are usually quiet, but colts are prone to playfulness, possibly even rearing. If this is the case with your horse, you should use a lead with a chain end. Run the chain over the nose or under the chin, whichever you prefer. A few jerks on the lead will then keep the colt's mind on the business at hand. Don't exert continuous pressure on the chain, just jerk when the colt misbehaves or when you want him to stop, then release it at once.

We don't ordinarily tie a foal until he's several months old, but you can start teaching him when he's only a month old. For this lesson, be sure to find a safe spot with good footing. Concrete is a poor choice as is an area where the foal can get his foot caught. Again, a stall is probably the best place.

To begin, simply tie the foal using a strong halter and lead. Be very certain the rope is not so slack he can get his foot over it. About eighteen inches to two feet will do. Use the knot we've shown in the picture below. This knot is universally used for horses, because it can easily be released if need be. Tie the knot no lower than the foal's withers.

The first several times he's tied, the foal will probably vigorously fight the rope. That's why you must use strong equipment. If he isn't able to free himself, he'll eventually calm down and you'll always have a horse that will be mannerly on a rope. Once you're sure the foal understands the rope, you can begin grooming and handling him when he's tied.

LONGEING

Longeing is a way of exercising a horse on a long line while he moves in a circle around his handler. The advantages of longeing are obvious in that it is a good way to teach a young horse some basic skills before he is old enough to carry weight on his back. Also, it provides a way to exercise a horse and teach him to wear a saddle

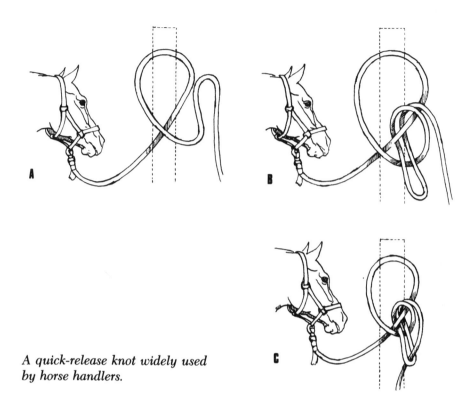

A *quick-release knot widely used by horse handlers.*

and bridle. On the other hand, we must pass along this word of caution. There are many trainers who argue that young horses should not be worked on a longe line. They say that working a horse in a tight circle is unnatural and causes undue stress on their legs. If your horse is under two, you might want to check with your veterinarian before you begin to longe your horse. In any case, it's a good idea to use splint boots to help support and protect the horse's legs.

In order to teach a horse to longe, you'll need a longe line, caveson or halter, splint boots and a whip. You'll also need to have a suitable area to work in. While few of us have the advantage of an eight-sided training pen, this does simplify the task for the handler and makes it easier for the horse. But if you don't have a training pen, the corner of a riding ring or corral works well enough. In this way, the horse will be somewhat restricted. If you're wondering why a fence is important, you'll find out soon enough that running away is the defense of young horses when they get confused. Also, many young horses tend to pull out on the longe line if they aren't confined. Another advantage of a training pen is that there is no corner for the horse to run to, which is something else they will usually try sooner or later. Nevertheless, most horses are taught without the advantage of a pen, so obviously it can be done.

The first time or two we try to longe a horse, we like to have a helper handy. First, snap the longe line to the side ring of the halter. Then, as a precautionary measure, put splint boots on the horse's front legs. These boots will help prevent the horse from injuring himself. If the horse is to be longed to the left, place the longe line in your left hand and give the whip to your helper.

The line should be folded in foot-long lengths so that it can gradually be payed out. For your own safety, never wind the line around your hand. If the horse takes a notion to run away, you can easily be jerked around or even worse be dragged quite unwillingly behind him.

Position the helper at your right side and the horse parallel to the fence. Then, move a step or two away and ask the horse to "walk." Chances are he'll try to face you, especially since he really doesn't know what you want him to do. But if your helper does a good job, the horse will soon realize what's expected of him. As soon as you say "walk," the helper should gently tap the horse on the heels with the whip. Continue this until the horse moves forward.

Using the whip to keep him moving forward, gradually move further away until you are at the center of a circle with the horse walking around you. When you want the horse to stop, say "whoa" and at the same time jerk on the line once or twice and lay the end of the whip down. With enough repetition of this procedure, the horse can be taught to stop simply by lowering the whip, but now we are a long way from that point.

As soon as the horse has stepped out and stopped several times, then turn him around and work him in the other direction, reversing the hand in which you hold the line and the position of the whip.

After a time or two, you should be able to continue the lessons yourself without a helper. As soon as the horse learns to walk and stop, you can add trot and eventually canter. In order to help the horse understand that he is to move faster in these other gaits, just flick the whip at his heels until he begins to trot or canter. Actually, the trot is the preferred gait on the longe line. Remember to work equally in both the left and right directions. If a horse is more awkward moving one way than the other, he should be worked longer that way.

Should the horse be rank or hard to control on the longe line, just continue to exert a steady pull on the line. If he really gets stirred up, let him go around a couple of times by himself until he slows down. A horse won't maintain full speed very long. If you try to pull him down, it will probably only excite him more. As soon as he begins to slow down, then ask him to trot or whoa while you jerk on the line to get his attention.

INTRODUCING THE BRIDLE

Soon after a colt is a year old, you can introduce him to the bit and bridle. For this lesson, we have found it best to choose a time when the horse is still in his stall, just before we are about to feed him.

Use a sturdy bridle without reins to which you've attached a mild snaffle bit. If you can get one, a training snaffle with dangling keys is a good mouthing bit to use on young colts. For the first few times, it's a good idea to unfasten the cheekpiece on the left side of the bridle to make it easier to slip the bit in the horse's mouth.

Once you've slipped the bit in the horse's mouth, he'll probably mouth it furiously in an attempt to get rid of it. It's just new to him and this is nothing to worry about. Then, you can go ahead and feed the horse, which should take his mind off the bit for a while.

It's been said that a colt must get used to wearing a bit just as a person gets used to wearing false teeth. While this isn't a perfect analogy, it does give some idea of the horse's feelings at this time.

The first day, leave the bit on the horse for about a half hour and then work up gradually to an hour or so. Continue this until the horse accepts and seems comfortable with the bit.

INTRODUCING THE SADDLE

Just exactly when first to saddle a young horse depends a great deal on his mental and physical development. Thoroughbreds that must race as two-year-olds begin their saddle training as late yearlings. On the other hand, most breeds mature slowly and shouldn't begin this early. We prefer to wait until a horse has at least his second birthday before we saddle him, and his third before we ride him.

Again, it's a good idea to begin the lesson in a roomy stall. Using a large cloth or saddle pad, start to "sack out" the horse by flapping and rubbing the cloth on his back. This procedure simply acquaints the horse with flapping around his body. It's a good idea to hold the colt by a lead rope with one hand while you flick the cloth on his back with the other. If tied, he might have a fit and fight the rope. Just try to keep the colt as quiet as possible. Begin by talking to him in a soothing manner as you gently rub his neck with the cloth. As soon as he stops flinching, continue to the rest of his body, gradually flicking the cloth as you go. Be sure to sack out both his left and right sides. Depending on the reaction of the colt, you might not sack him all over the first time. After all, you're not trying to scare him to death, but to accustom him to different sensations on his body.

Consider the sacking out procedure finished when you can flap the cloth or pad anywhere on the colt's body including his legs without him flinching.

Once you've reached this point, the horse can be introduced to the saddle. The first time or two, you might put just a saddle pad on his back, even giving him some grain as you do so. Then, assuming all goes well, while the colt is in his stall, very quietly place the saddle on his back. If you've gained the colt's confidence, you should have no trouble now. When you girth the horse for the first time, do so carefully. There's no need to excite him by girthing him too tightly. After all, you're not going to ride him yet, so you just need to tighten it enough to keep the saddle from slipping.

For the first day or so, just walk the horse around the stall with the saddle on his back. In order to create positive associations at this point, there is nothing wrong with giving him some grain during the lessons.

Assuming the horse is quiet and not disturbed by the strange equipment on his back, you can then lead him outside his stall for a few lessons. Begin by just walking him and then trot a few steps.

Along with these lessons, slip an arm over the horse's back and press down on the saddle to get him used to a bit more weight. Of course, in no way do you want to hurry a young horse. Continue with these lessons until you are sure the horse has no fear of the saddle.

If all goes well, begin longeing the horse with the saddle on his back. Again, begin slowly at a walk and gradually increase the pace.

Mounting the Horse

Exactly when you should begin riding a young horse also depends a great deal upon his physical and mental development. Quarter Horses are started as two-year-olds with no apparent adverse effects. To be on the safe side, we prefer to start this work in the fall of the second year with no serious training until the horse is three the following spring.

For these initial lessons, choose a time when the horse isn't too fresh, either after he has been turned out or after he's been worked on a longe line.

With a helper to hold the horse, begin by saddling him just as you ordinarily would in his stall. The first few times just lay across the saddle while the helper leads the horse around the stall. Then, once the horse gets used to having weight on his back, get off, go outside and try this procedure a few more times.

After a few days of this, you can then sit on him for the first time. At first, just have the helper lead the horse around slowly. Gradually, you can begin giving aids from the saddle, as well as from the handler on the ground. Add reins to the bridle and begin asking the horse to walk out, turn and stop.

As soon as your horse is paying attention, begin riding him in an enclosed arena without a handler on the lead. At first, only ask that he walk, turn and stop. Make these lessons brief and pleasant for him, praising your horse whenever he does well.

Only after the horse has mastered the above lessons should you proceed to the more advanced stages. Nowhere is it more true than with horses that haste makes waste. Be sure to remember that you don't want the horse to learn any improper behavior. To insure this, proceed slowly trying to avoid any situations that might upset the horse. Of course, if he becomes rebellious, he must be corrected and made to behave. This is where experienced trainers have an advantage over beginners, by knowing how much force is necessary and how to apply it.

It would sound nice to say that if you continue exactly in this way, you eventually will have a perfectly trained horse. Unfortunately, this just isn't the case. Young horses quite often become unruly and really need an experienced hand to keep them in line. Let's face it, sometimes simply reading and following instructions isn't enough: it must be reinforced by experience. If you do start to have problems, don't be embarassed. Remember that it's still not too late to go to a professional trainer. Also remember, however, that the longer a young horse gets his way, the longer it will take to retrain him.

But if the training is going along nicely, gradually ask the horse to trot and then to canter. He might give you a buck or two off the canter, but usually that's all it amounts to.

Even if you're teaching the horse under English tack, it's best if you don't post the trot for the first few lessons. The colt will have enough trouble balancing himself and posting will only make matters worse.

As soon as possible, it's a good idea to vary the colt's routine. Ask him to do figure eights, small circles and serpentines when you feel he's able. Change directions often, making him work both to the left and to the right. Some horses work better in one direction than the other. If this is the case, you should work the colt more in the direction in which he's less handy.

If you are working with a young Western horse, you'll want to teach him to neck rein. At first, of course, you'll simply have to plow rein him or turn him in the direction you want by pulling on that rein. Eventually, as you continue to turn him with that method, begin laying the opposite rein on his neck. As the horse begins to associate turning with rein pressure on his neck, he'll soon begin to turn from only the rein pressure.

Before you begin to canter a horse, make sure he is well settled at the walk and trot while working both ways in the ring. Although we prefer not to run a horse into a canter from a trot, you can do that by simply making him trot faster and faster until he begins to canter.

When teaching a horse to canter, we prefer to wait until the end of a lesson when he is somewhat tired. To get the horse to canter from a walk, gather the horse together by using slight leg pressure. Turn the horse's head slightly toward the rail and use your rail leg slightly behind the girth. If the horse doesn't react or is somewhat sluggish, use a whip to reinforce the leg aid. With patient continuation of this procedure, the horse will soon understand and you can canter him a time or two around the ring.

A WORD ABOUT LEADS

Some well balanced horses have little difficulty with the leg they lead with at the canter, while others take much more time before they become accustomed to one or the other. Much more common is the horse that favors one lead and wants to use it both ways in the ring. When we have a horse like this, we largely rely on the longe line to correct the problem. Since it is very difficult for a horse to canter on the wrong lead in a small circle, we longe him in a circle small enough so he must use the correct lead. Eventually, this should build up his muscles and better balance him so that he can comfortably canter on both leads. After he is cantering correctly on the longe line, you should then mount him and begin cantering him in small circles, which again should make it difficult for him to canter on the wrong lead. By the way, cantering in small circles is a good way to wear down a bold, aggressive horse.

STOPPING

Certainly, one of the most important words your horse needs to know is "whoa." All well trained, good mannered horses know what the word means and respond to it. The early work on the lead and longe line should have acquainted the horse with the word. Now all you have to do is teach the horse to respond under saddle. Since the first few times you ride the horse you should have a handler at the lead line, your job is easy. Frequently, ask the horse to whoa and gradually use the reins and leg aids to reinforce the command. Do this by using leg pressure and tightening slightly on the reins. If you pull on the reins, the horse will simply pull back. Done correctly, the horse should associate "whoa" with stopping in a very short time.

Since a young horse has a tender mouth, a snaffle bit will usually work best. With a snaffle, the horse feels only a slight pressure on the bit. If you don't abuse him now while he's young, you'll be able to preserve the sensitive feel of his mouth.

BACKING

Once your horse is moving forward freely and comfortably with you on his back, you can then teach him to back. First, you'll need to acquaint him with the procedure from the ground. Simply tap his chest with a training whip while asking him to back. It's fine at this point if you only get him to move a step or two in the right direction. In order to preserve his free forward movement, always ask the horse to move forward a few steps right after he has stepped back.

As soon as the horse understands what you want him to do from the ground, ask him to do the same from the saddle. First, make sure you have his attention. Then ask him to back as you squeeze your legs. The leg pressure should tell your horse that he is to move. Now, prevent him from moving forward by tightening your hands on the reins. If you keep your hands low and alternately tighten and release the reins, the horse should step back. At first, be satisfied with only a step or two. Then, as he begins to understand better and as his muscles develop, ask him to take more steps backwards.

RIDING OUTSIDE THE RING

Once you feel you are able to control your horse in an enclosed area, you then should think about riding him outside to further his education. Ring work will soon bore a young horse, while riding him outside will help keep him fresh. If you are lucky enough to have a place to ride that has hills to climb or creeks to cross, so much the better.

The first time or two you go out, make sure the horse is a bit tired. Longe him or ride him enough to take the freshness out of him. Then, when you do go out, it's best if you are accompanied by an experienced horse and rider. Also, try to choose a day that's not too windy, as that tends to make horses more energetic.

Because horses are herdish, a colt will be much calmer with another horse along. Alternately ask your horse to lead and follow. If he refuses to cross an obstacle or is afraid of something, have the older horse go first. The odds are good that the younger horse will follow right along. By all means, don't let him get away with refusing. If you have to, get off and lead him, but make sure he passes the obstacle.

After a few months of these very basic lessons, although your horse will still be very green, he should be able to walk, trot and canter fairly well. If you started him in the fall of his second year, it would be a good idea to turn him out and let him rest through the winter. Then, when he is brought in the next spring he'll be old enough and strong enough for advanced work.

RETRAINING

Most horses begin their training quite bright and agreeable. Either because of some problem with either the trainer or the horse, this agreeable nature is sometimes lost. If you acquire a horse that is totally spoiled or has dangerous habits such as kicking or rearing, get rid of him! No horse is worth the risk of a nasty accident.

On the other hand, if you find you have an otherwise agreeable horse with a bad habit or two, perhaps that habit is worth correcting. Horses that don't lead well, don't stand tied or are hard to lead can be corrected. But the older they are and the more entrenched the habit, the more persistent you'll have to be in correcting it.

HARD-TO-LEAD HORSES

We've seen horses that sort of amble along with their handlers, wandering whichever way they want to go. Also, there are horses with bad manners who get excited and dance around, sometimes landing on their handler's feet.

This habit is not difficult to correct. More than anything, these horses need discipline. First, get a lead with a chain. Run the chain through the ring on the left side where the noseband joins the cheekpiece. Then run the chain across the nose and up the right cheekpiece, fastening it to the top ring on the right side.

With the chain over the horse's nose, you should be able to handle even the most aggressive horse. First, ask him to walk. If he ignores you, jerk on the chain once to get his attention. As soon as the horse knows you mean business, he'll respond. Then, if he fails to move forward, tap him on the flank with a whip.

To get the horse to stop, say "whoa" and give the horse a chance to respond. If he doesn't, give the chain a jerk. Once the horse clearly understands what is expected of him and is on good behavior, you can try to lead him with the chain removed. Depending on the horse, you may be able to eliminate it completely.

HALTER PULLING

Some horses have the bad habit of pulling back against their lead rope while they are supposed to be standing tied. They will do this when they are frightened suddenly or simply when they don't feel like being tied anymore and want to get away. In any event, it's a dangerous habit and must be corrected.

The halter pulling probably began sometime in the past when the horse was successful in getting loose, so the first thing you need to do is get a sturdy halter and lead. If you're not sure one lead will hold him, add another just to be sure. As long as he's able to get loose, he's sure to keep trying.

Next, tie him in the usual manner with about eighteen inches of slack rope. Make sure he is tied at least as high as his withers to a very stout post. Then, get another sturdy cotton rope and tie one end with a slip knot around his girth. Run the other end through the horse's front legs, then the halter ring and tie it securely to the post.

Whenever the horse pulls back, the rope around his girth will tighten, making it uncomfortable for him. When he quits pulling, the rope will loosen, easing the pressure on his girth.

We've never known this procedure to fail, but we do know of a mare that wouldn't pull when tied with a body rope, but would when tied without it! At least the body rope kept the mare from pulling when we didn't want her to. Most horses aren't this clever, however, and using the body rope two or three times should do the trick.

LOADING

Before a horse reaches his first birthday, he should be taught to load and unload from a trailer. Before you begin this lesson, it's a good idea to hook up the trailer to your towing vehicle. Otherwise, a horse that starts thrashing about might pull the trailer backward, getting both of you in a lot of trouble. Something else we've learned is to allow plenty of time for this lesson. Once you start, you must keep trying until the horse is loaded, so you certainly don't want to be rushed.

First, put plenty of straw in the trailer, so the footing will be similar to what the colt is used to in his stall. This will give him one less thing to be fearful of. Next, lead the colt quietly to the back door of the trailer. Allow him to sniff around if he wants to. As soon as he seems to lose his initial fear, position him with his head inside the trailer, if that's possible.

Now, you want to remove as many of the options available to the colt as possible. If he walks on in the trailer, fine. That's all you wanted him to do. But if he is reluctant, as most are, there are a few ways to urge him in. Run a long line from his halter through the ring at the front of the trailer and back to you. This will keep his head straight and keep him from turning sideways. Don't pull on the rope, just keep the slack out.

Next, have a helper push on the horse's rump. Sometimes that's enough to get him to step inside. More often than not, however, it will take a bit more prodding. Take a heavy rope and loop it around the colt's rump. If you don't have a helper, tie one end to the side post of the trailer, pulling on the other end with your free hand. You'll find this a pretty big handful, however, and this is one time we really prefer to have some help. The idea of the rump rope is to push the horse forward into the trailer.

We have seen many times when horses have reared up, sat down and even fallen in their efforts not to be loaded into a trailer. Most of the time, these horses have been hurried or have not been correctly trained in the first place. We have never failed to load one of our own horses using the method we just described. But, to be honest, sometimes it has taken quite a long time getting the job done.

Along with the rump rope, or instead of it in some cases, many horsemen use a whip to get the horse to load into the trailer. While this is another possibility, it requires quite a bit of tact to keep the horse from getting overexcited. When not properly used, the whip can cause a horse to pull or react violently by kicking or rearing. When a whip is being used, it should be used on the horse's heels. The idea is not to beat the horse, even though you might feel like it, but to worry him enough to step inside the trailer.

Remember, once you've begun the process of loading your horse, you have to stay with it until you get the job done. If you don't, you'll have taught the horse exactly what you didn't want him to know; that he doesn't have to do what you want him to do. Once you have him inside, praise him and give him some feed. Tie him and give him a few minutes to settle down before you unload him. If you repeat the lesson a few times during the next few days, you should have a horse that's always easy to load.

During the second or third lesson, it's a good idea to take the colt on a five- or ten-minute ride in the trailer to get him used to the movement. Be sure to start and stop carefully and to corner slowly. When it's time to unload, untie the colt before you open the back door. Horses sometimes want to scramble out quickly. If he's still tied when he begins backing, he might panic when he discovers he's tied.

If the horse doesn't want to back out, snap two ropes to his halter and run one on each side to the back of the trailer. Keeping the ropes low, alternately pull on the left, then the right rope. This way the horse won't be able to rear or turn his head around.

LOADING OR TRAILERING PROBLEMS

In this day and age, it's essential that even a pleasure horse load, unload and ride quietly in a trailer. If he doesn't, many enjoyable horse activities will be closed to you. Loading problems either result from a horse being rushed, improperly trained or frightened by a bad experience around a trailer.

In any event, you can usually correct the problem with time and lots of patience. We've seen people use grain, whips and ropes, as we just described, all with varying degrees of success. Generally speaking, enticing a horse into a trailer with grain isn't an answer to the problem. We do reward a young horse with grain once he's in the trailer; however, holding grain in front of a horse that won't load is another matter. The horse must learn to load whenever we ask him to, whether or not he is hungry!

Carefully follow the instructions we've given in loading. If your horse becomes too much to handle, consider turning him over to a professional trainer.

REFLECTIONS ON TRAINING

1) Establish the horse's confidence in you.
2) Keep the work periods short.
3) Teach one thing at a time—don't ask the horse to master a new idea until he has mastered the old.
4) Treat a horse according to his mental level.
5) Have patience.
6) Never put a horse away unless he has successfully completed an assigned task or until you have succeeded in getting him to do what you want.
7) Be consistent in your aids.
8) When introducing something new, try to avoid conflict, establishing pleasant associations instead.
9) Horses have an excellent memory. Because they are creatures of habit, we can get them to obey.
10) Latent learning does seem to occur in horses. By this we mean a certain amount of time might be necessary to absorb and assimilate the lesson. This consolidation period, or latent learning as it is called, can occur while a horse is stalled.
11) Progress is seldom uphill all the way. There are peaks and valleys, so don't be too easily discouraged if a horse has a bad day—his next might be the best yet.

CHAPTER 11

Showing Your Horse

Many thousands of horsemen keep their horses through the long dreary winter with one major goal in mind, the summer horse shows! As they muck out stalls and chip ice out of frozen water buckets, they dream of warmer days, long blue ribbons and gleaming trophies. Of course, their prize winning horses, especially in the Northern states, probably resemble hairy goats more than horses, but remember we're talking about dreams.

Although at this time you might not be thinking about showing, sooner or later most horseowners decide they'd like to see how their horse would do in competition. While the amount of money people spend on show horses can be staggering, the roar of a cheering crowd, along with the great feeling of accomplishment all somehow combine to make it worthwhile.

If you think you might be getting the horse show bug, first ask yourself what you really know about showing. If you're taking riding lessons, the instructor can give you a pretty good idea of what to expect. He or she should also know whether or not you are ready to compete.

As we'll discuss a little later, there are many different levels of shows, from those held locally to national championship competition. While in some things it's good to go for the top, in this case it's probably best to think small in the beginning. While dreams of glory are nice, the chance of an amateur newcomer winning at a big show is nearly fantasy.

If you have decided to show your horse, the first thing to do is attend as many shows as you can as a spectator. Observe what the riders are wearing and how they groom their horses as well as what goes on in the ring. There is much more to a horse show than the classes and, if you are observant, you're sure to learn a lot. We have found it helpful to watch the horses as they warm up for their classes. Look particularly for the exhibitors who are winning. We guarantee you'll learn enough so that you'll feel your time was well spent. It will give you an idea of what the judge is looking for and how you would fit into the various classes.

At the same time you are learning and preparing yourself, you must try to objectively evaluate your horse. Quite often a first horse is bought as a pleasure horse. When the owner decides to show, his horse just doesn't measure up. If this is the case, it could be you'll have to either change horses or be content not to be a winner most of the time. While showing in itself can be rewarding, since it is competitive, winning also can be nice.

HOW HORSE SHOWS ARE ORGANIZED

The governing body for most horse shows is the American Horse Shows Association or the AHSA as it is usually called. The AHSA is then divided into several different divisions which include Hunters, Jumpers, Arabian, Morgan and American Saddlebred. Quarter Horses are shown under the rules of the American Quarter Horse Association or AQHA.

Shows approved by the American Horse Shows Association are rated A, B or C. The rating is determined by both the classes offered and the prize money awarded. If a particular show has different divisions, say for Saddle Horses, Hunters and Jumpers, it can be rated differently in each division. While some very large shows have many divisions, others may have only one. Also, many shows are devoted to just one breed, such as all-Arabian or all-Morgan shows.

In addition to competing in these approved shows, horses which have been properly nominated compete for Horse of the Year awards. To win this title, they accumulate points throughout the year at various approved shows.

STATE HORSE SHOW ASSOCIATIONS

Some states have their own horse show associations which are smaller versions of the AHSA. These associations sponsor shows at the state level. Points are awarded to nominated horses, with year-end awards given to winners in the various divisions.

BREED ASSOCIATIONS

In addition to registering member horses, most breed organizations sponsor shows. These shows are limited to one particular breed. The competition is usually stiff, as the breed's best horses compete.

Some breeds have additional honors which are awarded to top horses. These coveted titles include the Arabian Legion of Merit and the Quarter Horse Register of Merit.

LOCAL SHOWS

Many small shows are organized and sponsored by local horse clubs. The classes they offer usually reflect the interest of the club's members. These local shows abide by either AHSA or AQHA rules. They are often informal affairs and as such are an excellent place for a beginner to start. Also, small local shows are an excellent way of introducing a young horse to the excitement of a show.

Sometimes, boarding stables organize "fun days" for their stable residents. Some of the classes included might be musical chairs, tandem bareback and catalog races. Shows such as these offer a not yet too proficient youngster a chance to win his very first ribbon, a memorable ac-

This scene is typical of small horse shows where the horses are readied for the ring at any handy location.

complishment to be sure. They also can provide a setting in which a nervous, older rider can compete in a more relaxed manner.

It's much better to sharpen your skills at this level and perhaps taste success, than to set your heights too high and compete on a level above your ability. Smaller shows have the advantage of low entry fees, camaraderie and a less formal atmosphere.

HORSE SHOW CLASSES

As we mentioned before, there are many different classes to choose from. Because of this, you must pick those which best fit you and your horse's abilities. To enter more than three or four classes a day will surely take the winning edge off your horse and leave you looking for a soft spot to lay your weary head.

In some shows, the first classes serve as preliminary rounds for the championship class. Then, the winning horse in the preliminary classes must show back in the championship or forfeit the winnings. Hunters and jumpers, on the other hand, accumulate points with the championship awarded to the horse with the greatest total points. The horse that is runner-up to the champion is awarded the reserve championship.

Performance Classes

Among the most popular and exciting horse show events to compete in are the many different performance classes. There are performance classes of an almost endless variety with each breed having some special classes which their horses perform uniquely well. Performance classes range from the more sedate English and Western Pleasure classes where the horses are judged largely on their ability to provide their rider with an enjoyable riding experience, to the tremendously exciting, fast paced classes such as the Saddlebred Gaited classes where their horses are judged on their brillance and showmanship. Other classes range all the way from the trail classes where horses exhibit their ability to cope quietly and willingly with a variety of obstacles they might confront on a trail ride, to driving classes where the drivers wear formal attire and drive exquisitely turned-out buggies.

To get a better idea of the various performance classes available, you should attend some shows in your area, both open competition and breed specific. After you become familiar with the various classes, you may find one in which you wish to compete.

Then, if you become interested in showing in one of the performance classes, it is essential you select a horse uniquely fitted to performing well in the class. First understand the requirements of horses in the class you are interested in and select a horse already trained for that class or have someone help you choose one that shows the abilities to perform well in such a class after the extensive training that is often required.

Cutting Horse Contests

One of the fastest growing equestrian events are "Cutting Horse" contests where the horses must exhibit the ability to cut a calf from a herd and then try to keep that calf from returning to the herd. The horses are judged on how well they perform this task and awarded points on the basis of how well they do.

Cutting horse contests seem to attract riders from all aspects of society from the very wealthy and famous to real "cowboys" and today, the larger contests have awards of many thousands of dollars. At the same time, the breeding of good cutting horses has also become a big business. Generally cutting horse contests are not for the novice rider or horse, but it is exciting to watch and something you may wish to participate in sometime in the future.

DRESSAGE AND HORSE TRIALS OR COMBINED TRAINING EVENTS

Another activity rapidly growing in popularity among horseowners is competing in dressage contests or "dressage tests" as they are formally referred to and also what are known as Combined Training, Horse Trials, or at the highest levels such as the Olympics, "Three-Day-Events."

Only a few years ago, these contests were largely known to the general public only as Olympic events and involved only a relatively small number of horseowners and riders. In recent years however, many more people have become interested in these events and the number of shows and training clinics has been increasing tremendously.

While the advanced levels of dressage and horse trial events require the highest level of skill and ability on the part of both the horse and rider and this only comes after many arduous hours of training, there are different levels of tests which include both beginning horses and riders.

The purpose of dressage is to achieve the highest level of training for both the horse and the rider. In fact, dressage is a French word which means training. The dressage test judges the performance of the horse on the basis of its obedience to the rider, its suppleness and its willingness to respond to the commands of its rider. In a dressage test, the participants are given a specific riding pattern to perform which involves a variety of activities of varying levels of complexity depending of the level being tested.

An important aspect of dressage tests and horse trials that many horseowners find attractive is the fact that the horses compete at different levels depending on their ability and experience and the events are specifically established to measure the expected ability of the horse and rider at each level. The riders compete not so much against each other, but against a standard of excellence that increases in difficulty as they progress through the various levels.

"Horse Trials" or "Combined Training" events include dressage as one aspect of the competition, but also include jumping, either in a closed stadium or on a cross country course, or sometimes both. Again, as with the dressage test, the horses compete and are judged at different levels, depending on their experience and ability.

The jumping event in a stadium course requires the horses to compete in a timed event over a wide variety of obstacles and fences, with penalties for faults where the horses fail to cleanly clear all of the obstacles. The variety of obstacles is largely dependent on the organization sponsoring the event, however they might include fences or hedges of all kinds.

The cross country event in a horse trial is the ultimate test of a horse's training. The real purpose of dressage training is to make the horse more responsive under extreme circumstances such as are found in the cross country event. The horses are required to jump over a demanding course consisting of a wide variety of fixed obstacles, usually including a water based obstacle which requires the horse to jump into or out of a pool of water. Depending on the level of the horse, the course may be 1.5 miles long or more.

As we mentioned earlier, these events are among the fastest growing equestrian competitions. The participants in dressage or horse trial events say they prefer them to traditional horse shows because the contest is based more on the ability of the horse and rider and not the subjective whim of a horse show judge. For those of you with a real dedication to precision riding and are willing to put in long hours of training for you and your horse, these events are some of the purest forms of competition to be found. They are certainly worth observing to see if they may be of interest to you.

HALTER OR IN-HAND CLASSES

In addition to performance competition, most shows have classes in which the horses are judged on their conformation, or the way they look. These are more than beauty contests, however, as horses are judged on their correctness, way of going and overall balance. Horses which are shown at halter must be carefully groomed according to the requirements of the breed.

The various breed classes are so different that one could scarcely recognize a Quarter Horse halter class after seeing one in which Saddle Horses are shown. In the case of Quarter Horses, the entries walk into the ring being led by a handler, then stand squarely on all four feet before the judge. Saddle Horses, on the other hand, are briskly trotted into the ring with a whip bearer running alongside to keep the horse trotting. The horse is encouraged to display his natural animation as he stretches or "parks" in front of the judge.

Halter classes are divided so that the entries are grouped according to age and sex. In this way, the weanling fillies compete in one class, the weanling colts in another, then the yearling fillies and so on. Horses four years old and older are usually grouped together, divided only by sex.

FUTURITY

It's a long time to wait between the conception of a foal to his birth nearly a year later. In the time they are waiting, many horsemen try to speculate on how the foal will turn out. Undoubtedly, this is how futurities began.

Since many horsemen are gamblers, futurities are a way for them to bet on their future horses. In futurities, the horse breeder pays money into a fund prior to the birth of a foal. This money, or nominating fee, is held for a predetermined period of time, then distributed to the owners of the horses that win in a certain show in the respective categories.

Among many others, there are futurities for running horses, halter horses, cutting horses and English and Western pleasure horses. In halter futurities, the purse is often divided. In these cases, a portion of the prize money is paid to the yearling winners, two-year-old winners and, finally, the three-year-old winners.

The largest purse in horse racing is the All-American Futurity for Quarter Horses. This hotly contested prize of more than a million dollars is partially paid for by optimistic Quarter Horse breeders who paid the substantial fee with the hope that the foal his mare will drop in the spring will be the one to win.

WHY SHOW?

It seems to be a part of human nature to show other people that which you are proud of. Just as parents love to present their scrubbed and fashionably dressed children to relatives and friends, horseowners love to display their carefully groomed horses to an admiring public. Shows, it seems, are one way to confirm or not confirm the results of your shrewd buying, breeding or training.

While obviously the object of showing is to win, that isn't the only reward of showing. At horse shows you'll enjoy the camaraderie and fellowship of others who share the same love of horses. Even if you are out of the ribbons, if you watch the winners and keep an open mind, you're sure to learn and eventually improve your position. Not only will you improve your horsemanship, you'll learn to remain poised in front of spectators, regardless of how poorly your horse performs.

Although we wish you better luck, you might even learn to be a good loser! But even if this happens, don't be discouraged. Very few horsemen start out with blue ribbons. Just like the rest of us, they have to work at winning—which, with enough patience, you're sure to do.

If you've decided your horse is good enough to show, you'll need to work on his skills as well as your own. Decide in which category you want to compete and then train accordingly. Before you start, read either the AHSA or AQHA rules by which your class is to be judged. You'll never do well until you understand the basis by which the class is being judged.

Once you've decided in which area to compete, you'll have to choose the exact class. If you are showing at a small show, there might be only one or two classes in each category. The larger the show, the more you'll have to choose from. For example, if you've decided to show your horse Western Pleasure, some of the possible groupings include: Junior Exhibitors, Junior Horses, Mares, Geldings, Stallions, Ladies, Gentlemen, Novice Riders, Novice Horses, as well as classes limited to amateurs or professionals and those open to anyone. These divisions allow the horses and riders to compete at their own level. Without them, an inexperienced twelve-year-old could find himself or herself competing against an experienced professional—somewhat of an unfair situation.

PREPARING FOR A SHOW

Now that you've decided that you and your horse are ready for a show, it's time to think about what you'll need. We'll assume you've decided on a small show for your first outing. In this case you won't have to worry about pre-entering before the show. To find where the shows are to be held, go to your local tack shop or check the bulletin board at a local boarding stable. At any of these places you're sure to find some show bills during the show season, which varies in different parts of the country. Show bills are often mimeographed sheets which list the date, place and time of a show, as well as the classes offered, prize money and entry fees. They also have the name and phone number of the person to call in case you have any questions.

From the show bills, decide which shows have the classes in which you are interested. Once you decide on a show, check the show bill to find out what health papers are required. If none are listed, call the show secretary to find out what the requirements are. You might need either health papers or a Coggins test or both. Your veterinarian can issue health papers on short notice, but a Coggins test requires that a blood sample be sent to a laboratory for examination. This will take two weeks, so you'll have to think ahead.

Something else to plan ahead for is your farrier's next trip. It's best to have your horse shod a week or two before the show. Then you'll still have time to have any corrections made if they are necessary.

We'll also assume that you've been working your horse in preparation for the show. Getting a horse to the point where he will show at his best, but is not sour, is quite an art. You want your horse to peak at the time he is being shown. There is no magic formula one can follow to achieve this goal. Between shows, some trainers work their experienced horses enough to keep them in good physical condition. During these work sessions, the horse is not asked to perform at his maximum level.

Saddlebred trainers use all kinds of ingenious devices to keep their horses showing brilliantly. They rattle tin cans, shake rags and shoot off fire extinguishers to keep the horse alert. But if you have a pleasure

A pony being readied for a Roadster class.

horse, you certainly won't want to use any devices such as these. As a matter of fact, a quiet leisurely trail ride can refresh a pleasure horse that is starting to get sour or bored in the ring. We have one old gelding that knows his role in the show ring so well that he is just about as sharp after a several month layoff as he is after being ridden every day. As a matter of fact, he's a good example of a horse that just needs to be kept in condition between shows.

While you are sharpening up your horse before your first show, if your horse has never been shown, it might be a good idea to play a radio loudly both in the work ring and the stable to get him used to some confusion. Although the noise is not quite the same as a crowd, it will introduce him to some new sounds. You'd be surprised at how frightened a young horse can get if he's only used to being ridden alone.

We like to show yearlings and two-year-olds in a few halter classes before they begin their saddle training. Then they'll be a little calmer when they are old enough to compete in performance events.

The first few times you go to a show, you're sure to forget some essential item. We've had friends who have forgotten girths and stirrups as well as other less essential paraphernalia. To our horror, we once arrived at a show without a saddle suit in which to show!

So take a word of advice and make a list. On it, write down all of the items both you and your horse will need. Include grooming tools, tack and your personal attire. If you're going to a small show, you might want to include a few items for your personal comfort. Folding chairs, insect repellent and a cooler with a lunch and soft drinks will make the time between classes more enjoyable. Remember, too, to bring a show bill or premium list. At small shows, where horses aren't stalled, we tape the show bill to the inside of the tack compartment of our trailer. Then we know at a glance when our classes are to be called.

THE LARGE SHOW

Large shows usually have printed premium lists. These are booklets that list the essential information about the show. Premium lists are mailed to those exhibitors who have attended the show in the past as well as members of horse clubs who might be potential exhibitors.

Show dates are usually advertised in horse magazines. If you find a show listed you would like to attend, write the show secretary, whose name and address will be given as well as the date and location of the show. Try to get a premium list at least a couple of months before the show. Some large stables plan the show season months before it begins. While most shows allow entries right up to the day of the show, they also have an entry closing date of about 30 days before the show. Entries are accepted after this date, but the fees are higher, in some cases doubled! Also, the longer you wait, the fewer stalls are available. If you don't enter until a day or two before, some shows won't have enough stalls available for all the horses showing. In fact, at some shows the horses are expected to stand tied to the trailer. In such cases, try to arrive early enough so that you can park in the shade!

Now that you have a list of equipment, we advise you to assemble everything the night before the show. Unexpected delays so often crop up, you don't want to be rushed in getting to the show.

What To Take to a Show

While the number of items below might seem overwhelming, if you're going to a two or three day show, you'll need just about everything on the list.

Grooming Equipment:

Shampoo
Brushes
Rub rags
Sponge
Hoof dressing

Coat Conditioner
Water hose
Hoof pick
Braiding equipment

Stable Supplies:

Insect repellent
Fan (in hot weather)
Feed tub
Water bucket
Feed

Liniment
Antiseptic wound ointment
Saddle soap
Manure fork
Manure basket

Tack—to be placed in tack trunk:

Cooler
Sheet, blanket or
    fly scrim
Leg wraps
Halter and lead

Saddle
Bridle
Breastcollar
Whip
Longe line

Wearing Apparel:

Riding habit
Boots
Spurs
Hat

Gloves
Raincoat
Jacket
Stable boots

Some Extras:

Folding chairs
Book (to read between classes)

Snacks
Camera

Important Papers:

Horse's registration papers
    or copy

Health papers
Premium list

AT THE SHOW

Most experienced exhibitors like to arrive at the show grounds well before their classes. If you arrive the night before the show, you will have time to work your horse in the show-ring. Also, your horse will get a good night's sleep before the big day.

When you arrive at the show-grounds, first check in at the show office. Here you will confirm your arrival and verify the classes you've entered. At the show office you will be given a packet containing a show schedule as well as your number. Except for equitation classes, the number belongs to the horse. If you are showing more than one horse, write the name of the horse on the back of the number so you're not embarrassed by entering the ring with the wrong number on your back.

If health papers are required, you might need to show them. If the show office doesn't have the stall assignments, you'll have to go to the barn office. Once you've received this information and know exactly where your stalls are, you can unload your horse. We always check the stall first, however, to make sure it's all right. The stall rental fee should include the first night's bedding. We spread out the bedding, then unload the horse. Once the horse is safe in his stall, you can bring in your gear. If you have paid an additional fee for a tack stall, place your equipment in it. Otherwise, it should be in front of your stall, against the wall. Of course you don't want to block the aisleway, so make sure your things are orderly. Most shows don't allow untended dogs, so if you bring yours, you'll have to supervise him and otherwise keep him leashed.

Conditions being what they are, be sure to lock your tack trunk while you're away. Think how disappointed you'd be to return to your stall to find some expensive equipment missing.

Now all you have to do is tend your horse and get a good night's sleep. Check again to make sure you know when your class will be called.

In a full day's showing, three sessions will be held. These will be in the morning, afternoon and evening. The program cannot state the exact time each class will start, but it will list the time each of the sessions start. In an average performance class which does not require individual workouts, we allow twenty to thirty minutes per class. So if your class is the third class in the afternoon session that begins at 1:00 p.m., the class should start sometime between 2:00 and 2:30. You can count on equitation classes, large stake classes, trail classes or hunter and jumper classes taking more time than this.

Of course you don't want to arrive just in the nick of time! On the morning of the show, feed and water your horse as usual. An hour or so later, you can work your horse for a bit to settle him down. Usually the main ring is only available for workouts early in the morning, between sessions, and again after the show is over for the day. Makeup or work rings are usually available. They'll often have a jump or two set up if you choose to use it.

We figure that we should be saddling our horse when the second class before ours is being judged. Then, we warm up the horse while the class before ours is being shown. Some horses require more work and some less before a class, so this is only an example.

Usually the barn manager has an announcer call the classes for the exhibitors in the barn. First and second calls will be announced. Typically, the first time the announcer might say, "First call for class 33, Western Pleasure Stallions." At this time you should be getting ready. The second call goes out as the preceding class enters the ring. At some shows, you are requested to enter the makeup ring now and check in. The next step, of course, is the big one. Before you move to the main ring, make sure your number is on correctly and is plainly visible. Girls with long hair should have it done up neatly with their number placed in such a way the judge can plainly see it.

As the preceding class is lining up, your class will move toward the in gate. Then your class will be assembled and ready to enter the ring, so the show will move along smoothly and without delay. AHSA rules allow the gate to be held for up to two minutes for tardy exhibitors. After that, the gate is closed—so don't be late!

Remember that you are being judged from the moment you enter the ring. The horses enter the ring in a counter-clockwise direction. Make sure you are completely ready, then enter leaving at least one and better two horse-lengths between you and the preceding horse. Not only is it dangerous to get too close, but there is no way you can make a favorable impression on the judge if he can't see you.

From the time you enter the ring, don't be distracted. Concentrate on the job at hand. Experienced showmen are able to keep one eye on the judge and one on the horse. For now, just try to view them alternately.

The judge will position himself so he can easily view the class. Of course, judges do turn around, so you must show all the way around. As you approach the judge, try to position yourself so your horse can be seen. No one ever won a blue ribbon plastered against the rail with two rows of horses between himself and the judge. With experience, all of this will become much easier for you. Whatever you do, don't be so intent on being seen that you cut-off other riders. Not only is this rude, it can be quite dangerous!

After working at all the gaits in one direction, the horses will repeat them in a clockwise direction, then will line up in the center of the ring, or where the ringmaster indicates. Here, the horses may be asked to back, if class specifications require. The judge will move from one end of the line up to the other. In some stake classes the horses may be stripped, or have their saddles removed so the judge can better observe their conformation.

You should keep your horse showing and looking sharp right up to the time the judge turns his card in. Many placings are reversed when a judge makes a last second change. So whatever happens, don't undo your good work by a lapse now.

Sometimes, before naming the winners, the announcer will ask that the horses move to one end of the ring. Then, beginning with first place, the winners will be announced. As each number and name is called, the winner advances to the center ring and accepts his award, usually from the class sponsor. After all the winners have been called out, the first place horse may take a victory lap for the pleasure of the crowd.

If you have been fortunate enough to win, congratulations! If not, remember when you show, you only pay for one person's opinion; although it is usually an expert one, an opinion nevertheless. Many times we've been well pleased with our horse's performance, but have come home empty-handed. At other times, we've been lucky enough to take home ribbons despite a mistake or two.

Although you might not place exactly where you think you should each time, in the long run it will average out. In a large class there is an element of luck involved. Whether your horse makes his mistakes in front of the judge or behind his back has much to do with the outcome.

An important element of showing, however, is your assessment of

First Place ribbon being presented to the winner of the Arabian Western Plea-sure class. (Photo courtesy of Jim Taasaas, Showtime Stables, Inc., Prospect, Kentucky.)

how you and your horse have done. If you are pleased with your per-formance, you'll be elated; otherwise, you should at least come home realizing where you need to improve. Win or lose, you'll probably start looking up the next show date—then you'll know you are really hooked!

Show Personnel

Show Manager: He or she is in charge of the show. Although respon-sible for the show, most of the work is delegated.

Show Committee: Works with the show manager to organize the show. The committee decides the date and place of the show as well as the classes, premium and judges.

270

A ribbon is presented to the winner of a driving class. (Photo courtesy of Jim Taasaas, Showtime Stables, Inc., Prospect, Kentucky.)

Show Secretary: The secretary sends out the premium lists, receives entries through the mail and at the show.

Barn Manager: Assigns stall and arranges for bedding. Manages the barn or stable office. Usually large charts are available so that the exhibitors can find the stalls assigned to them.

Show Office Personnel: During the show, the show office is the control center. All incoming exhibitors check in here. The show office keeps track of the class winners to determine if the horses are eligible for the stake classes.

AHSA or AQHA Steward: The steward's job is to represent the association under which the show is run. He is available to judges, exhibitors, and management should any questions arise. The steward, however, has no authority regarding the management or judging of a show.

Ringmaster: The ringmaster assists the judge and exhibitors in the ring. He gives exhibitors directions during the class should they be nec-

271

essary. In case of an accident, the ringmaster lends a hand.

Judge: An AHSA or AQHA show is required to select a judge from a list provided by the governing association. Judges are approved after a long apprenticeship, during which time they must prove their knowledge, discretion and ability. During a show, the judge's word is final.

AWARDS

In each class, a first place or blue ribbon is awarded. Other places also may be given depending on the show. At large shows, these can go down to eleventh place. Sometimes a trophy is also given to the winner of a class.

Money is awarded to the winners according to a predetermined schedule. If the prize money for a class is $100, it could be divided $30, first place; $25, second place; $20, third place; $15, fourth place; and $10, fifth place. Money is not awarded to winners of youth or amateur classes, however.

In some shows, the first several horses placing in each class must show back in the championship class or forfeit their winnings. This is because the preliminary classes are considered qualifying classes for the championship. The class winners show for the championships, which are the last classes to be held. Champion and Reserve Champions are chosen. Trophies usually are awarded for these placings. Championships are highly coveted, as they mean the horse has not only won his class, but defeated all of the horses in the same division.

CHAPTER 12

Breeding Your Horse

You've waited eleven long months and the magic moment when your mare will bring her foal into the world has arrived. According to your careful calculations, it was due two days ago and each night and morning you've crept breathlessly out to the barn only to find your mare calmly munching her hay.

And then one morning, when you've just about given up hope, you matter-of-factly stroll out to the barn and find what has to be the most wonderful foal anyone has ever produced! He's spindly and awkward and shy, but at that moment when all of your hard work and planning has finally shown results, he is a dream come true.

To selectively breed a mare and stallion and see their foal come into the world and grow into a top quality horse is one of the most rewarding feelings any horseman could have. It's the result of patience, hard work, careful planning and your best judgment on how to produce a better horse. Secretariat didn't just happen to be one of the greatest

273

Mare and young foal at pasture.

race horses of all times. He was the product of many generations of selectively breeding horses so that each new generation is one step closer to being the ultimate race horse.

From a business point of view, raising horses for a profit is best done by large breeders who have the knowledge, facilities and financial backing necessary for such an operation. It isn't easy for a small breeder to make a profit by raising horses, especially when you think about all of the risks they are facing. If you are just interested in making money, there are many other more promising businesses to get into!

The question of money aside, however, almost nothing is more satisfying to a horseman than to see a foal come into the world and grow into a special kind of horse. While most people keep horses for riding, many others keep them only for breeding. Regardless of profit, they are happy raising good, usable horses.

We wouldn't be entirely honest if we didn't warn you of some of the problems involved in running a small breeding operation. First, it is not likely that you will be able to maintain a stallion. From the beginning, you will have a big investment in a breeding fee, transportation and the cost of caring for your mare while she is away being bred. Just getting your mare in foal can be a problem. We know of several people who paid hundreds of dollars in mare care and veterinarian bills while their mares were at a breeding farm. Since the mares came home not in foal, the money was just lost. If you raise horses, you will have such losses once in a while.

You are going to need more elaborate facilities if you raise foals than if you just keep a riding horse. At the least, you will need a roomy, dry box stall where your mare can foal comfortably and a small paddock where she and the foal can exercise. Finally, if you expect to sell your foals, it is more difficult for a small breeder who doesn't have the money for expensive promotion and advertising. With most breeds, the foals of well-known horses from large farms bring more money than other horses of equal or even better quality from small breeders.

If we haven't completely discouraged you by now, there are also some advantages to being a small breeder that we'd like to tell you about. Even though you will have to pay a breeding fee, there is an advantage in being able to select from the many stallions at public stud and choose the one that would be best for your mare. By breeding to a stallion from a large breeding farm, you can take advantage of their advertising and promotion without any of the expense.

Since you're only going to keep a mare or two, you can be sure they are top quality. While we are trying to be a little more positive at this point, this is another pitfall you should be warned about. We've seen too many breeders begin with mares of poor quality. They find themselves producing foals they can't possibly sell or don't even know what to do with. It's much better to keep your numbers small and of top quality than to produce many horses that you can't really be proud of. This leads us to what we feel is the real advantage of being a small breeder and that is being able to enjoy your horses and to look with pride at what you have been able to produce.

In this chapter we want to give the novice breeder some practical suggestions on what's involved in raising a foal. We hope to present enough information so that you can intelligently breed your mare, care for her properly, oversee the foaling process and raise a healthy, sturdy foal.

275

SELECTING BREEDING HORSES

First, we need to discuss the mare and the stallion that you're planning to breed. There are some additional things to look for in a breeding horse that aren't required for a riding horse. To begin with, make sure that the mare or stallion you intend to breed is really a good horse. Remember, what you are going to do is at least in part reproduce what you already have. If your mare has some serious faults, think about whether her good points merit taking a chance on passing these faults on in her foals. If they are so serious that they affect her serviceability, then she shouldn't be bred. There are enough top quality horses around that we don't have to continue producing mediocre or poor ones. While we realize that it is hard to admit that your mare is anything less than the best, do try to look her over critically before you breed her. Remember that while it's easy to sell a good horse, if you produce a poor one, in addition to losing money you will be faced eventually with the problem of what to do with a horse you're unable to get rid of.

Something else you must think about in a breeding horse is its pedigree. Each horse is the result of mating a mare and a stallion and the foal that results inherits a gene for each characteristic from each of its parents. Half are shown in what he looks like and half are not shown, but could show up in his foals. Thus, what a horse can produce is as much the result of what his ancestors are like as what he himself is like. You should study the pedigree of any horse you intend breeding or breeding to and look for consistently good horses. Don't be impressed by one or two outstanding horses far back in the pedigree. You must find consistently good horses. If the pedigree shows the characteristics you think a good horse should have, then it's likely the horse will produce foals with those characteristics. Secretariat was the result of many generations of mating horses that were able to run fast and their good points all came together in this one outstanding horse. If you looked at the horses in Secretariat's pedigree, you would find the height, the powerful hindquarters, the desire and all of the other qualities that made him able to run fast.

Finally, the most important thing to look for in breeding horses, is their breeding record. Obviously, the best way to do this is by looking at the offspring he or she has already produced. Since mares can produce only one foal per year, you of course won't have many to observe. Stallions, however, can sire many foals each year and you are able to see what they are getting. What you should look for is consistently good foals. If a stallion gets one outstanding foal and ten mediocre ones, then the odds are ten to one that yours will be mediocre. Of course, the quality of the mares bred to him will make a difference, but don't rationalize on this point and select a poor stallion simply because he's close or cheap or you're a friend of his owner. You'll wait eleven long months to see the results of a lot of hard work and it is foolish to wait this long only to end up with a poor foal.

The study of genetics is extremely complex and, sadly enough, there isn't a great deal of solid information to be presented specifically on the subject of horse breeding. Until recently, raising horses hasn't been important enough financially to warrant as much research as breeding other animals such as cattle and hogs. Genetics, however, is the basis for breeding and there are a few basic concepts every serious breeder should know about.

Just exactly what determines how a horse will look are called genes. They can be described as a kind of code that translates into all of the characteristics that make up a horse, from disposition, to size, to color. When the sperm from the stallion fertilizes the egg in the mare, each provides a set of genes for all the characteristics of a horse. For each of these characteristics, either a gene from the mare or a gene from the stallion will be expressed. The gene that is not expressed is still carried in the genetic structure of the horse and could easily show up in the next generation. This is why it is very important to study the pedigree of a prospective breeding horse. It is possible for an undesirable gene to be carried for several generations without being expressed, until it shows up in your foal.

One reason a gene from one parent will show up rather than one from the other is that one gene can show dominance over another gene that is recessive. Simply stated, a dominant gene will always be expressed if it is inherited by a foal, regardless of what gene is inherited from the other parent. A recessive gene will be expressed only if a similar recessive gene is also inherited from the other parent.

To illustrate this, we'll use the rather straightforward example of color. In horses, the gene for the color black is dominant and the gene for the color chestnut is recessive. Thus, if a black gene is inherited from one parent and a chestnut gene from the other, the resulting foal will be black. This doesn't mean, however, that a black horse mated to a chestnut horse will produce only black foals.

Using (B) for the dominant black gene and (c) for the recessive chestnut gene, if we take a black stallion which inherited a black gene (B) from one parent and a chestnut gene (c) from the other he will be black—but remember he also carries the chestnut gene (c) and it could show up in his offspring. Now let's look at what happens if he is mated to a chestnut mare. If she is chestnut, she must have inherited chestnut genes (cc) from each of her parents. Chestnut is recessive and would only be expressed if both genes are chestnut. If a black gene (B) is inherited from the stallion, since the black gene is dominant and only a chestnut gene (c) can be inherited from the mare, the foal will be black. If a chestnut gene (c) is inherited from the stallion, however, the foal will have received two chestnut genes (cc) and will therefore be chestnut.

The problem any breeder must face with genetics is that there are no characteristics, even color, inherited in such a straightforward manner. The good points that we want in our horses result from many genes and other factors that affect these genes. For example, a good disposition depends upon qualities such as intelligence, willingness, calmness, affection or even physical characteristics such as eyesight and hearing. The number of combinations of genes that influence disposition is overwhelming.

Going back to the color example, what would happen if a horse inherited black genes from both his parents (BB)? Since black is dominant, he could only produce black horses. If the genetic structure of a horse is such that the genes he inherits from both parents are the same, it is said to be homozygous. If the genes are not the same, it is said to be heterozygous. It is easy to see that a horse genetically homozygous for dominant genes for good characteristics can only produce these good characteristics. Such a horse is called prepotent and would be extremely valuable for breeding. The only way to determine the degree of prepotency is by examining the pedigree and the foals already produced to see what genes have been expressed. Some breeders will mate very closely related horses (brother and sister or parent and offspring) simply to test for undesirable recessives. Horses that are intensely inbred are usually more homozygous because the genetic pool they draw from is small. Their offspring are usually very similar.

NICKING

Nicking is a term often used by horse breeders. When two families of horses consistently produce good foals when mated together, it is said there is a good nick between the families. Again, Secretariat was the result of what had proven to be a good nick. His sire, Bold Ruler, had been getting horses that were very fast at short distances, but did not have the stamina for longer races. His dam was Something Royal by Princequillo which had been producing tough durable horses that were effective for long distances. This combination produced Secretariat who fortunately combined the best of both families.

REPRODUCTION

THE STALLION'S REPRODUCTIVE ORGANS

A stallion's reproductive organs are designed to produce sperm and introduce it into the mare's reproductive system at the appropriate time. A stallion has two testicles, each of which produce sperm and the hormone testosterone. This hormone is responsible for the masculine appearance and behavior of a stallion as well as regulating and maintaining the reproductive tract. A horse that is gelded has his testicles removed. The tremendous difference in the appearance and behavior of stallions and geldings illustrates the powerful influence of this hormone.

Stallions are often sexually mature as yearlings, so many farms separate the colts from the fillies at weaning. They should not service mares, however, until they are at least two—and then only on a limited basis. At four, they may breed up to fifty mares during the breeding season. Stallions are usually fertile into their twenties, but of course breed fewer mares as they grow older.

A stallion that has only one testicle descended is called a cryptorchid. Such horses are able to breed mares and have all of the characteristics of a stallion. A cryptorchid should not be allowed to breed, however, as the trait is inherited and could be passed on to a foal. The problem is that cryptorchids often have a very disagreeable nature and castration requires major surgery resulting in an expensive gelding.

THE MARE'S REPRODUCTIVE ORGANS

The mare's reproductive organs consist of an ovary on the left and right side, an oviduct or fallopian tube that connects the ovaries to the horn of the uterus, a uterus, cervix and vagina.

The ovary produces the egg or ovum which is enclosed in a sac called a follicle. Each ovary contains hundreds of follicles and throughout the sexually active life of the mare she will continually produce hormones that cause the follicle or sac to rupture and discharge an egg.

After the egg is discharged, it travels through the oviduct to the uterus where the unborn foal develops. The uterus has a soft, spongy lining with many tiny blood vessels into which a fertilized egg develops. The cervix is closed tightly during gestation and when the mare is not in heat. Only when she is in heat and ready to be bred does it open to allow semen to enter.

HEAT CYCLES

A mare's heat period comes about every 21 days and lasts approximately five days. During her heat period, or estrus as it is sometimes called, a mare is likely to be a little irritable. She will "show" to a stallion by urinating frequently in small quantities, by relaxing and contracting her vulva (this is called winking) and by swishing her tail up and to the side.

Most unbred mares will have heat periods during the entire year, but in the spring they'll be much more intense. Each mare is different, so it's a good idea to learn the peculiarities of your own. For example, some mares are in heat a day or two longer in spring, while others are shy and never show very obviously.

Twenty-four to forty-eight hours before her heat period ends, a mare will ovulate, or release an egg to be fertilized. It is during this time that she must be bred so that the egg can be fertilized. Many breeding farms have an experienced person palpate or try to feel the egg through the rectal wall. If the egg has been released, the mare is ready to be bred. Timing is very important as sperm cells live only about twenty-four hours and it takes five hours for the sperm to travel from the uterus to the oviduct where fertilization occurs. Also, the egg is viable for only four to six hours.

Breeding a mare every other day beginning with the second day of her heat period is the commonly accepted practice. Some breeding farms will rely entirely on manual palpation and breed only about the time the mare ovulates. This is most often practiced if the stallion is in heavy use, as it limits the number of times he must serve the mare.

CONCEPTION RATES

While the conception rate for horses is generally poor, it's best among mares from age three to thirteen, that are in good health and neither too fat nor too thin. A mare shouldn't be bred for the first time before she's three years old. Although it's possible to get a younger mare in foal, this is an extremely poor practice and condemned by most horsemen. Some mares produce foals until into their late teens, but as they get older it becomes more difficult for them to conceive and to foal.

Obviously, a barren mare is worthless as far as producing foals is concerned, although she may still be a fine riding horse. Some mares are permanently barren because of a physical problem or improper development of their reproductive organs. Others are barren temporarily due to any of a large number of problems such as infection, the season of the year or a hormonal imbalance. Because of this, an aged mare that currently isn't in foal is a poor choice as a brood mare.

BREEDING AFTER FOALING

About nine days after foaling, most mares come back in heat. Many experienced horsemen routinely breed their mares at this time. If you would like an earlier foal, breeding your mare on her foal heat will move the birth date of her next foal up a month. Of course, if the mare had trouble foaling, she shouldn't be rebred this early. Unless there is a special reason to do so, the next heat, which will be about thirty days after foaling, is a much more sensible time to re-breed. This gives the mare's reproductive organs more time to recover and, if she settles, the foals will be born about a year apart.

BREEDING

There are several different breeding methods currently being practiced. These include hand breeding, artificial insemination, pasture breeding and corral breeding.

Hand breeding, or breeding while the mare and stallion are held by handlers is most commonly used. First, the external genitals of both the mare and the stallion are washed thoroughly to help prevent infection. A mare that has been determined to be in heat by rectal palpation or by teasing is led to a breeding chute. She is held by an experienced handler and may be further restrained by breeding hobbles or a twitch. The stallion, also held by an experienced handler, is allowed to approach the mare from the side. A mare ready to be bred will show interest in the stallion by squatting, urinating and by raising her tail up and flipping it to the side. If the mare is ready to be bred, she usually won't need to be restrained, but some stallion owners insist on it to avoid injury to their horse. The actual breeding takes only a few minutes, after which the mare is walked for ten to fifteen minutes to prevent her from straining and urinating.

Artificial insemination is being used by horsemen much more frequently today, but it still has a major drawback in that horse semen can't be successfully stored by freezing, and the conception rate can be lower than with natural breeding. Artificial breeding is very useful when several mares that are in heat at the same time must be serviced by the same stallion. The procedure requires that a stallion ejaculate into an artificial vagina, after which the semen is deposited in the vagina of several mares. Sanitation is of the utmost importance, since the semen is deposited directly into the mare's vagina and could easily cause an infection if it has become contaminated. It's likely that artificial insemination will become more popular among horsemen since there is less chance of injury to either the stallion or the

282

mare. Most breed registries have strict regulations for artificial breeding, so be sure to check first with your registry.

Pasture breeding is nature's way of reproducing horses and has the best conception rate, but it's seldom used today. With pasture breeding, a selected band of up to forty mares is turned out with a stallion. It's then hoped that he will cover the mares at the appropriate time. This saves the time of the handler, but the risk of injury to the horses is greater.

PREGNANCY

On large breeding farms, it is customary to tease a mare twenty-one days after she has been bred to see if she's actually pregnant. At that time, if the mare shows no signs of being in heat, the odds are that she's in foal. A mare should be teased for at least six days, beginning eighteen days after she's been bred. Assuming that she doesn't show any interest in the stallion, at about forty days after breeding she can be rectally palpated by a competent veterinarian. Rectal palpation requires reaching through the mare's rectum and feeling for the developing embryo. If a mare is actually in foal, by this time the embryo is about two inches long and big enough to feel.

Once you're sure your mare is in foal, don't make any drastic change in her care. Pregnant mares need the same good care you should give any horse. It is particularly important that a pregnant mare gets high quality feed rich in protein and have ready access to minerals. For the first seven months, it's not a good idea to increase her feed. Fat mares have more trouble delivering foals and being overweight is just as bad for horses as it is for people.

In order to have a good abdominal muscle tone, be sure your mare gets enough exercise while she's pregnant. It's not a good idea at all to keep her locked up in a stall. If she is trained to be ridden or driven, you can exercise her in this way. Be careful and don't run her to the point of exhaustion or do anything that might make her strain or fall. As time goes on, she'll become a little awkward and you'll probably want to stop riding her at least a couple of weeks before the foal is due.

During the last four months, the unborn foal will grow rapidly. You might want to give your mare a little more feed at this time, but again don't give her so much that she gets fat. Usually she'll exercise less and be able to get along quite well on what you've been feeding her. Many horsemen give their mares a food supplement that is rich in vitamins and minerals. There are several special products for pregnant mares you should be able to buy at any feed store.

At birth, a fully developed foal will weigh from eighty to one hundred pounds, depending on the size of his parents. While still in the mare, his skeletal structure and vital organs are formed. If this development is stunted because the mare isn't getting the proper feed, it will be very difficult to make it up later.

FOALING

Mares have done quite well for a long time having foals out in the wild without any help from man. This is perhaps the most important thing to remember as your mare approaches the time of foaling. On the other hand, it is possible that something out of the ordinary might happen, so it is a good idea to stay near.

The average duration of pregnancy or gestation for a mare is 340 days, but this can vary a couple of weeks either way without hurting the foal. If it's earlier than two weeks, the foal could be weak and have trouble getting out of the sac. Later than two weeks might mean complications, so if it goes this long, call your veterinarian for his advice.

Begin making preparations several weeks before you expect the foal. There are some signs to watch for that will show you how things are progressing. A mare will usually follow the same sequence, so if you write down the changes as they happen during her first pregnancy, you'll have a good idea during any following pregnancies of the exact time of foaling.

About six weeks before foaling, your mare will begin to "make a bag." This means simply that her udder will get larger. About a week before foaling, her teats will fill out completely. Some first-time mares are a little slow to make a bag, so this is not always an exact indication. A few days before foaling, the muscles around the tailhead relax and produce a sunken effect. A day or two before foaling, a kind of waxy bead may appear on the nipple. Some mares never wax and some wax several times, although in most cases it is a final sign. Make note of when it happens with your mare, so the next time she's in foal it will be more meaningful.

Your mare should be moved to the place where you want her to foal several weeks before you expect it to happen so she'll have a little time to get used to her surroundings. The ideal place is a roomy box stall, but you'll obviously have to make do with what you have. Try to find a place as clean, dry and draft-free as possible. Be sure it's at least large enough for her to lie down and stretch out in.

Before you move her in, clean and disinfect the stall as thoroughly as you can. Then add a lot of bedding, preferably straw. Make sure there are no sharp objects around, as the mare and foal might thrash around a lot and could be injured quite easily.

Just before foaling, your mare won't be inclined to exercise much, but it's always nice if she has a small paddock where she can get fresh air and sunshine. If it's possible, your mare will do better at this time if she's separated from the other horses. Probably the cleanest place to foal is a pasture, but it's not a good idea since it makes her very hard to keep track of in case she does run into trouble and, of course, you can never be sure of the weather.

As the time of foaling grows closer, make sure someone is available in case your mare runs into trouble. You don't want anyone bothering her all of the time, but you do need someone on hand just in case. The foal should be delivered rather quickly once labor begins. If the foal is not visible within 20 to 30 minutes, or if the foal is not presented correctly, call your veterinarian immediately. When the foaling process begins, your mare will need to be left alone. In the wild she would leave the rest of the herd and go off by herself. Many times, if people are around, a mare will delay foaling until she is left alone. Some breeding farms have a small window looking into their foaling stalls, while others even have closed circuit television so they can watch for any trouble without being noticed by the mare.

There are some things you'll want to have on hand when the mare is ready to foal. You'll definitely need a bottle of iodine to treat the foal's navel after the birth. This is very important as it must be treated immediately to prevent infection. Again, we want to remind you to have the stall thoroughly disinfected before the foaling. Infection is one of the biggest problems for young foals and you should do everything possible to prevent it. Especially in cold weather, you'll want a towel to dry the foal and prevent him from getting a chill. You might want a blanket to cover your mare just as you would after any strenuous activity. A small syringe is necessary to give the foal an enema if he becomes impacted. A tail wrap is useful in keeping the mare's tail from getting soiled and out of the way. Of course, this isn't necessary, but it does make cleaning her tail afterward a lot easier.

Once the foaling actually begins, your mare will get restless. She will urinate frequently and empty her bowels. She will lie down and get up repeatedly. She may bite at her flanks and due to the strain break out in a sweat. A large amount of fluid contained in the fetal membrane is released as the actual foaling begins. Soon after this, the forefeet with the hoofs down will become visible. In a normal delivery, the forefeet are presented first with the head tucked between them. Then the shoulders, body and outstretched hindlegs appear. If the foal is presented in any other way, call your veterinarian immediately. During the actual delivery a mare will usually lie down. This

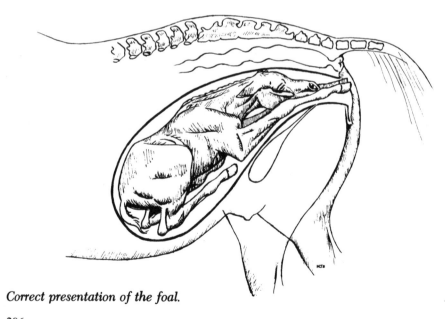

Correct presentation of the foal.

isn't always the case, so don't panic if your mare is standing. It's not uncommon for a mare to stand up while the foal is only partially delivered.

After the foal is born and in some cases even before his hindlegs are delivered, he will begin thrashing about to free himself from the sac that surrounds him. If the foal is weak, which is sometimes the case if it's premature, it might need help in breaking out of the sac. He can't start breathing until the sac is broken, so don't hesitate to step in and help if it looks as if he's having trouble. Once he's out of the sac, he'll soon try to stand on his still-wobbly legs. The umbilical cord is usually broken when the mare stand up. You should never immediately cut the umbilical. The best policy is probably not to fool with it at all. The blood must drain down the cord back to the foal, and if you would cut it with a sharp knife, you could cause both the mare and foal to hemorrhage.

It is very important that you treat the navel as soon as possible by thoroughly daubing iodine on the stump. This is an open wound and an ideal spot for infection to start. You must treat it right away! It doesn't do any good to daub iodine on it the next day. The damage has already been done and you could find yourself with a very sick foal.

Once the foal is on his feet, he'll begin nudging his mother in search of food. For some foals this can be very frustrating as they nudge everywhere except the udder. An experienced, patient mare will stand still until the foal finds the source of his dinner. Watch any first time mares to make sure they let the foal nurse. If your mare doesn't hold still for the foal, put a halter on her and back her into a corner until the foal finds her udder. Many times the mare is hesitant because her udder is sore, but once the foal nurses and the milk starts flowing she is relieved.

The first milk the foal receives is different from milk that's produced later. It is called colostrum and contains antibodies that help protect the newborn foal. Colostrum is also high in protein and vitamin A. It serves as a natural laxative and helps remove the fecal matter that has collected in the foal's digestive tract.

The matter in the foal's digestive tract is called meconium. It is blackish in color and must be eliminated or the foal could become fatally impacted. A healthy foal will begin straining to eliminate this substance soon after birth. Many large breeding farms routinely give enemas to all their newborn foals to be sure the meconium is eliminated. If you notice your foal straining excessively, you'll need to give him an enema. A small ear syringe filled with warm water works quite well. Signs of straining could be noticed for several days after birth, so watch for any indications such as tail switching or excessive nervousness. Then step in and give your foal an enema.

The other extreme from impaction is scouring or diarrhoea and this can be a real problem for some foals. Almost all foals scour when their mother first comes in heat nine days after foaling. If your foal scours, reduce the concentrate feed ration of the mare. Persistent scouring will seriously weaken a foal, so if this doesn't help you should call your veterinarian.

Once the foal is delivered, your mare will probably rest for a moment and then rise to her feet. She'll nicker to the foal and start to lick him dry. The licking dries and stimulates the foal and acquaints the mare with her foal's special scent.

Shortly after the foal is born, the mare will deliver the fetal membranes. This should be completed an hour or two after the delivery. Don't worry if your mare experiences contractions and lies down again after the foal has been delivered. She does this to expel the afterbirth and it's perfectly normal.

After the delivery of the foal, the membranes can be tied to the mare's tail until they are completely expelled. Tied up like this, they won't drag on the ground where they could accidentally be pulled and torn by the mare or her newborn foal. If the membranes have not been delivered within four hours, call your veterinarian immediately. A retained placenta can cause serious problems. This is why it's important to inspect the placenta after it has been delivered. Any tears or evidence of a missing portion should be reported to your veterinarian as this is an extremely serious matter.

Once the afterbirth has been completely expelled, inspect it and then get rid of it immediately. Probably the easiest and safest thing to do is bury it in lime. If you don't get rid of it soon, it can become a breeding ground for infection and will attract stray animals.

After the foal has been attended to, you can offer your mare a few sips of water. Make sure it's not ice cold and don't let her drink all she wants at once. She'll undoubtedly be hungry, so you should give her a moderate amount of grain. A laxative feed such as bran is particularly good at this time. For a few days after foaling, a few handfuls of bran added to your mare's ration will help regulate her bowels. Before you leave the mare and foal so they can get better acquainted, remove any dirty bedding and replace it with fresh. Also, if the weather is cold you might want to cover your mare with a blanket.

Only for the first few days of his life will a foal live entirely on his mother's milk. Within a week after birth, he'll be trying to eat hay and grain. You should try to encourage this by first feeding him a few handfuls at a time and later by adding a creep feeder. A creep feeder is simply a device that allows the foal to eat and keeps his mother or other horses out. A very simple one is just a normal feeder that has slats narrow enough to keep the mare out. You can buy simple creep feeders that are nailed on the wall and taken down once the foal is weaned. More elaborate creep feeders can be used in a pasture, but they are practical only if you have a lot of foals.

Make sure your foal has full access to the feeder and is provided a nutritionally balanced ration. If you must have the feeder outside, provide a cover so the feed doesn't get wet every time it rains. If your foal doesn't eat all of the grain in one day, replace what's left with fresh at the next feeding.

If the weather is nice, you can turn your mare and foal out in the pasture. Wait at least twelve hours and don't put them out if the weather is cold and damp or if there was any trouble with the foaling. Otherwise, your mare will enjoy the sunshine and fresh grass. Exercise helps the mare's reproductive system return to normal and strengthens the foal. There is less evidence of impaction in foals that are allowed to exercise.

The new mother will be extremely protective of her baby. Try to keep her away from any stressful situations such as noisy barns or too many visitors. Don't turn them out with any other horses for at least a week or two after foaling, but if you have to, be careful the foal isn't hurt.

Nutritionally, the most important part of a horse's life is from birth to one year. If he's deprived of the necessary vitamins and minerals during this time, it's almost impossible for him to make it up. Growth is so rapid that a foal that weighs 100 pounds at birth may weigh 600 pounds on his first birthday. He must get the right food during this time if he is ever to reach his full potential.

Also, a young foal needs a carefully planned health program. Inevitably they get infested with worms that if not treated can cause severe debilitation or even death. Routine health care after foaling should first include tetanus and antibiotic injections that will protect him from a variety of problems.

With the right amount of good food, exercise and sunshine your foal will grow quickly and remain healthy. Assuming that he is getting along all right, you can safely wean him when he's between four to six months of age. You don't want to wean him any earlier than this unless special circumstances arise, such as a poorly milking mare. Weaning after six months only wears the mare down unnecessarily and provides more stress on the foal at weaning time.

The simplest method of weaning is to put your foal in a stall and move his mother out of sight. The foal will be upset for a few days, but eventually he'll settle down. In any event, don't get soft-hearted and put them back together too soon or you'll have to go through the same agony again. If possible, it's a good idea to wean two foals together so they can keep each other company.

A day or two before weaning, cut the mare's feed so she will begin to produce less milk. Allow her the freedom of the pasture during this time as the exercise will help prevent undue soreness in her udder. For a day or two after weaning, her bag will be very large and sore. Without stimulation from the foal, it will soon decrease in size and return to normal. If the foal is put back with his mother too soon, she will probably let him nurse and this could cause her to produce milk again.

Index